PERSPECTIVES ON CHINESE CINEMA

distributed
by
INDIANA
UNIVERSITY PRESS

PERSPECTIVES ON

CHINESE

CINEMA

EDITED BY CHRIS BERRY

BFI PUBLISHING

First published in 1991 by the
British Film Institute
21 Stephen Street
London W1P 1PL

British Library Cataloguing in Publication Data
Perspectives on Chinese cinema.
    1. China. Cinema films
    I. Berry, Chris
    791.430951

    ISBN 0–85170–271–6
    ISBN 0–85170–272–4 pbk

Cover design by Andrew Barron
Front cover still from *Yellow Earth*

Typeset in 10 on 11½ pt Sabon by
Fakenham Photosetting Limited,
Fakenham, Norfolk
and printed in Great Britain by
The Trinity Press, Worcester

Contents

Acknowledgments

Leo Ou-Fan Lee's 'The Tradition of Modern Chinese Cinema: Some Preliminary Explorations and Hypotheses', Catherine Yi-Yu Cho Woo's 'The Chinese Montage: From Poetry and Painting to the Silver Screen', Chris Berry's 'Sexual Difference and the Viewing Subject in *Li Shuang-shuang* and *The In-Laws*', Paul Clark's 'Two Hundred Flowers on China's Screens', and Marie-Claire Quiquemelle's 'The Wan Brothers and Sixty Years of Animated Films in China' all previously appeared in the first edition of *Perspectives on Chinese Cinema*, published in 1985 as no. 39 in the Cornell East Asia Papers series. Esther C. M. Yau's '*Yellow Earth*: Western Analysis of a non-Western Text' first appeared in *Film Quarterly*, XLI:2 (Winter 1987–8). '*Red Sorghum*: Mixing Memory and Desire' first appeared in a slightly different version under the title 'Mixing Memory and Desire: *Red Sorghum*, a Chinese Version of Masculinity and Femininity' in *Public Culture* 2:1 (Fall 1989). Tony Rayns' 'Breakthroughs and Setbacks: The Origins of the New Chinese Cinema' was first published in a slightly different version in *Filmviews* 135 (1987). Chris Berry's 'Market Forces – China's Fifth Generation Faces the Bottom Line' first appeared in *Continuum* 2:1 (1988–9). 'Problematising Cross-cultural Analysis: The Case of Women in the Recent Chinese Cinema' by E. Ann Kaplan was first published in *Wide Angle* 11:2, and Jenny Kwok Wah Lau's 'A Cultural Interpretation of the Popular Cinema of China and Hong Kong' was first published in *Wide Angle* 11:3.

Introduction

The idea of a second, expanded edition of *Perspectives on Chinese Cinema* was conceived well before the Tiananmen Massacre. At that time I saw it as marking, indeed celebrating, the emergence both of Chinese cinema on the international film scene and of Chinese film studies within academia. Now that I am writing this introduction on the eve of the first anniversary of the massacre, all that seems sadly ironic. It is still unclear what effects the current political freeze is having on film production. Nevertheless, it clearly isn't improving the already difficult circumstances of film-makers in China, or making access to materials any easier for scholars.

However, in these troubling times it is all the more important not to lose sight of just how much has been achieved in the last few years. In 1985, when Cornell East Asia Papers published the first edition of this book, Chinese cinema was barely on the horizon. Few people outside China had seen many Chinese films, and even fewer claimed to understand or like them. Within months all that changed when *Yellow Earth* appeared at the Hong Kong Film Festival. The birth of a new wave was proclaimed. In its wake came a series of films by young, so-called 'Fifth Generation' directors.

The Fifth Generation drew the attention of the international film world eastwards to encompass not only mainland China, but also the young film-makers of Taiwan and the thriving popular cinema of Hong Kong. In 1988, Chinese cinema's place at the cutting edge of international cinema was affirmed when *Red Sorghum* won the Golden Bear at the Berlin festival, soon followed in 1989 by the Venice Golden Lion for *City of Sadness*. Looking back from this vantage point, I wonder whether Leo Ou-Fan Lee might not nominate these years as a third 'golden age' in his periodisation, originally written in 1982?

Paralleling this remarkable transformation, Chinese cinema studies have also become an established feature of the academic film scene since the first edition of this book. In 1985, scholars of Chinese cinema working outside Chinese societies could have met comfortably in the average living room, and indeed on one or two occasions most of us did. In January 1990, however, the University of California held an international conference devoted solely to Chinese cinema, and attended by participants from all over the world. In publishing the first edition of *Perspectives*, we hoped to draw attention to a neglected area of study and encourage more work on it. There is clearly no longer any need to repeat that call: more and more scholars are writing on Chinese cinema every year.

1

As a result of this activity, a terrain is certainly emerging more clearly, with certain points of intersection and focus. The articles in this volume are intended to represent some of the best writing that has worked to build that terrain. In choosing them, I have been struck by the way they intersect with each other. When the first edition was put together, it seemed that each of us was working more or less in a little world of our own. Now, however, articles bounce ideas off each other, take each other as starting points for further work and utilise each other as context and backdrop. For that very reason I have refused any temptation to break down the pieces collected here into neat sections under headings like 'history' or 'national identity'. The overall picture is still fragmentary and incomplete, but the multivalent interaction across all the articles may help us map out where we are and determine targets for future research.

The process of mapping is indeed one of the driving forces behind a number of pieces in this anthology. Leo Ou-Fan Lee, Paul Clark, Marie-Claire Quiquemelle and Chiao Hsiung-Ping are all engaged in that tradition of film history. They are all concerned in their different ways to identify broad themes, key moments and major players, and to integrate these and other elements into a broad picture. Both the textual and institutional tendencies in film historiography are represented in these writings. Marie-Claire Quiquemelle and Paul Clark are highly institutional in their approach, Clark concentrating on the political dimensions of film-making in China and Quiquemelle concerned to identify the economic, technological and organisational foundations of the various developments in animation that she identifies. Leo Ou-Fan Lee and Chiao Hsiung-Ping tend more to the textual approach, identifying and examining aesthetic trends in the overall Chinese film tradition and in the Hong Kong and Taiwanese cinemas respectively. All four articles are concerned with demarcation and periodisation. Lee's article is unabashedly evaluative, carrying over the 'humanistic' tradition of May Fourth literature to identify 'golden ages' in the Chinese cinema. For Clark, the effort is also to identify particularly significant periods, which he correlates to small windows of relaxed political control after 1949. Chiao and Quiquemelle are also engaged in the periodisation of the particular cinemas they deal with.

Work such as this is essential to the development of the field. Without it, it is impossible to place more focused studies such as those which make up the rest of the book in any context, or to begin to identify their broader significance. However, there is and will be an inevitable dialectical relation between these types of work. Broader history provides scholars with crucial junctures and texts on which to perform closer analysis, which in turn may lead to revision of initial broad schemas in the future.

Among the more specific phenomena making up the Chinese cinema, it is unsurprisingly the Fifth Generation that has attracted most attention in recent years. Four of the new articles included in this volume deal with it. My own article on the economic and political problems facing the Fifth

Generation and Tony Rayns' analysis of its origins both focus on the institutional context determining the Fifth Generation. Esther Yau and Yuejin Wang's articles look at two specific (and particularly successful) Fifth Generation films in attempts to identify both their significance and their significations.

Interestingly, both Yau and Wang find sexual difference an especially useful way into the films they analyse, and this focus has been one of the most important common points characterising much recent work on the Chinese cinema. In this anthology, my own article on *Li Shuangshuang* and *The In-Laws* and E. Ann Kaplan's piece on Chinese women's cinema also take this angle. It seems that these efforts to analyse the deployment of gender and sexuality in the potential relationships which films can be said to construct with their spectators look to deeper ideological patterns in Chinese cinematic discourse. Kaplan is specifically concerned with the patterns emerging around women directors and women spectators, but Yau, Wang and myself all take up gender as broader political metaphor, linking male- and female-typed characteristics such as aggressivity, obedience and so forth to traditions including Confucianism, Daoism and Maoism.

This ideological impetus ties work on gender and sexuality into other articles concerned with broader patterns of Chinese culture. Catherine Yi-Yu Cho Woo is concerned to identify signifiers from traditional poetry and painting that make their way into the cinema, and Leo Ou-Fan Lee's article concentrates on the connections between cinematic and literary traditions. Jenny Kwok Wah Lau, on the other hand, contrasts mainland Chinese and Hong Kong cinemas in terms of deeper cultural difference, basing her work in both Western and Chinese cultural theorists.

In writing about gender, national identity, the community, the individual and the various other issues that are drawn from within the Chinese cinema by these articles, the writers have made a series of connections with Western film and cultural studies. As E. Ann Kaplan points out forcefully in her article, all writing on the cinema is not detached or objective but rather a dialogue, and this is especially so in the case of writing that is in some way or other cross-cultural. By writing about the representation of women in China, crises of masculinity, the relationships between communal ideologies and feudal hierarchies, and by comparing Western, mainland Chinese, Hong Kong and Taiwanese cinemas, the authors of the articles in this collection have made the Chinese cinemas participate in broader debates that cut across individual national cultures.

Reflecting on this burgeoning variety of work, I have two concerns for the future. First, considerable progress has clearly been made in the past few years, but the work that has been done also points to unfilled gaps and new directions. For example, although Paul Clark has provided us with an excellent basic institutional history of post-1949 mainland

3

cinema, we still lack reliable English-language histories of the Chinese cinema before 1949, the Taiwanese cinema and the Hong Kong cinema.* Marie-Claire Quiquemelle has given us an excellent outline of the animation cinema, but individual genres of feature film, documentaries and newsreels remain largely uncharted. Although a good number of close analyses of individual Fifth Generation films has been generated in the last few years, similar work on the Taiwanese New Wave, Hong Kong popular cinema and older mainland films is still largely lacking.

I am sure I speak for all the contributors to this book in hoping that this new work can be accomplished and that existing work can be broadened and developed further. However, there are many obstacles to the realisation of these hopes. If in the past there was a shortage of scholars working on Chinese cinema, now the problem is often one of access. There are plenty of people who would like to write about the films of the 30s and 40s or the Hong Kong martial arts film industry, but getting access to materials is a considerable problem. Commercial film companies in China, as in the rest of the world, put little value on the preservation of no longer current films or documentation. No copies survive of the great majority of pre-1949 Chinese films.

What makes the situation far worse is the failure to gather what remains from the past and what is being produced now, or the difficulties in accessing those collections that do exist. Hong Kong has no real film archive. Mainland China does, but getting access to it is notoriously difficult. If the rest of the world is finally willing to acknowledge the tremendous achievement of Chinese cinema, then now is the time for the various Chinese regimes themselves to recognise this cultural heritage. This involves further archival activity, and, equally important, the opening of those archives to the ever-growing ranks of scholars eager to work on their contents.

However, and this brings me to my second concern for the future, if access to materials is such a problem, I feel there must be a reason for this. It is no accident that both Leo Ou-Fan Lee and Paul Clark find the most productive periods of Chinese film-making at times when centralised control is most relaxed. Much the same has been true of writings about the Chinese cinema, particularly the recent explosion of work represented in this book. It seems that establishment authorities in China, whether in the mainland, Taiwan or Hong Kong, are often as suspicious of independent-minded scholars as they are of independent-minded film-makers, and that they identify continued political tenure with the freezing of debate and change.

In English we say 'It's academic' when we mean 'It doesn't matter', and many people insist on seeing the arts as 'mere entertainment'. However, it is almost impossible to imagine any discursive production, be it film or

* Paul Clark, *Chinese Cinema: Culture and Politics since 1949* (Cambridge: Cambridge University Press, 1987).

4

academic writing, regarded so lightly in Chinese culture. Rather, all cultural production is assumed to be not merely reflective but an active participant in social praxis.

At the moment, the authorities in the mainland seem to be making a concerted effort to freeze change. However, although the Fifth Generation film-makers are often thwarted, Taiwan's political and cinematic culture is opening up, as indicated most notably by Hou Hsiao-Hsien's *City of Sadness*, which is set against political events whose existence was suppressed for some forty years. To the very limited extent that film criticism outside China can help to maintain diversity and debate, I hope that this collection marks not only the achievements of the past few years, but also a determination that those achievements should continue.

Chris Berry
Melbourne, 1990

Note on romanisation and translation

In preparing this book, I have attempted to standardise romanisation and translation, to avoid confusion for readers. All Chinese names and words have been rendered according to the pinyin system of romanisation. Exceptions occur in the case of Taiwanese or Hong Kong figures whose names will be better known to readers in other forms. In these and other similar circumstances, the more common form has been retained and the pinyin form entered in parentheses afterwards.

In regard to translation, I have used the standard export English title of films, where it is known to me. However, because films are often known by other titles, the pinyin form of the original title appears in the filmography appended to each article. Where Chinese terms and phrases have been translated in the main body of the text, a pinyin form of the original Chinese appears in parentheses immediately following. The same holds for titles of books, articles, publishing houses and so forth cited in the notes. Each pinyin rendering occurs only once in each article, the first time it appears.

The translation of certain Chinese terms into English remains a contentious issue. Unless authors have specified otherwise, I have used the English version current on the mainland for such terms. For example, the events of 1966 to 1976 are rendered as 'cultural revolution', not as Cultural Revolution, with the exception of Esther Yau's article where the author specified a preference for the latter version.

Finally, because many characters are homonyms, pinyin is often inadequate for research purposes. I have therefore gathered all the pinyin renderings that occur, with the exception of the appendices, and reproduced them together with the Chinese character form in a glossary (Appendix 3). The simplified form of characters used on the mainland has been chosen for this glossary.

CB

The Tradition of Modern Chinese Cinema
Some Preliminary Explorations and Hypotheses

LEO OU-FAN LEE

As a literary historian I am not qualified to discuss the development of modern Chinese cinema on its own terms.[1] Rather, my interest lies in seeking the relationship between film and literature and between historical trends and artistic forms of expression. It is my central contention that the modern Chinese film grew into a mature art form by virtue of its closer interaction with modern Chinese literature, specifically spoken drama (*huaju*). Accordingly, in so far as we can speak of a 'tradition' of modern Chinese cinema, its artistic roots are to be found in the New Literature, with which it shared some common 'obsessions'. In my research on the history of modern Chinese literature, I have discovered that in each historical period there tended to be a corresponding literary genre which was dominant. To put it somewhat schematically, I would suggest that in the early May Fourth period (1917–27), the dominant genre was the short story; in the next decade (1927–37), the novel; in the period of the Sino-Japanese war (1937–45), the spoken drama; and in the post-war years (1945–9), it was definitely the film. In this rough scheme, the period of 1945–9 also stands, in my mind at least, as the 'golden age' of modern Chinese cinema: the level of artistic excellence it attained has remained unsurpassed down to the present day.

Since much research is required for this neglected area, my bold claims can only be regarded as tentative hypotheses which should be subject to further testing against more evidence and revision by other scholars who are currently studying the subject more extensively.[2] However, in this preliminary essay I would nevertheless like to argue my case, if only to provoke further debate and draw more scholarly attention. My thesis is that the interaction between literature and film, which began in the early 30s and culminated in the late 40s, produced a generic tradition of social realism which in turn yields an aesthetic legacy of film style. Any sensible approach to the study and analysis of contemporary Chinese cinema must be grounded in the knowledge of this tradition. An obvious layman in film aesthetics, I can only pose a number of speculations on the formalistic implications such a tradition entails.

The development of modern Chinese cinema did not converge with that of literature until the early 1930s. The Literary Revolution, which had occurred in 1917 as part of the overall intellectual movement for New Culture (referred to by most historians as the May Fourth Movement), had apparently little effect on the burgeoning film industry which in the 1920s remained a commercial enterprise for urban popular entertainment. In 1926, Tian Han, one of the pioneers of modern spoken drama, organised a 'drama and film society' called 'Southern China' (*Nanguo*). In his inaugural manifesto, Tian Han praised the cinema as one of the three 'major achievements of mankind' (the other two being, for a self-styled romantic, wine and music). Film, being the youngest of the three, was also the most 'spellbinding' for him because it was capable of 'creating dreams in broad daylight'.[3] Despite this personal interest in film, however, Tian Han's efforts in this period were nevertheless focused on drama.

In 1931, the first Chinese 'talkie' was released, thus bringing the film medium even closer to spoken drama. The major thrust of drama into film took place in 1932 when a number of leftwing dramatists and writers, working with the underground Chinese Communist Party, decided to join the Mingxing (Star) film company.[4] It was a move comparable in significance to the transformation a decade earlier of the commercial magazine *The Short Story Monthly* (*Xiaoshuo Yuebao*) from a journal of leisure and entertainment to a serious forum for New Literature. It was with the serious films produced mainly at Mingxing that the tradition of 'socially conscious' cinema was first established. Aside from Tian Han, the other major movers at Mingxing were two prominent playwrights, Xia Yan and Yang Hansheng. Xia Yan wrote his first film script, *Wild Torrents*, a detailed shot-by-shot scenario for the silent film, in 1933 and also adapted Mao Dun's famous story *Spring Silkworms* into film. Yang also began writing screenplays at the same time.[5]

One need not agree entirely with the assessment of the official Chinese film historian, Cheng Jihua, that since 1931 the Chinese Communist Party, through its front organisations such as the League of Leftwing Dramatists, had 'led' the movement in modern Chinese cinema.[6] The Party, then underground, was too weak organisationally to provide the kind of leadership which later was to dictate the contents of art and literature. It can be argued that the leftism which engulfed most writers in the 1930s was basically a social stance of discontent. In both fiction and film one finds an overriding obsession with the ills of contemporary society. The basic artistic mode in which this obsession was expressed may be termed 'social realism' (or 'critical realism', to be differentiated from the later, more ideological mode of 'socialist realism').

While it definitely has political connotations, the vision of reality evolved in each work remains anchored in the subjective perception of the individual writer or film-maker – a conscience-stricken individual profoundly dissatisfied with the environment in which he (or she) lived and yet unable to offer tangible solutions to its problems. Thus the basic ethos of 'social realism' is criticism and 'dark exposure' motivated by a humanistic concern for the plight of the Chinese people. And because of this 'hard-core, rock-bottom' humanism, the film's didactic messages are often couched in sentimental and naively idealistic terms.[7] If the despair with present conditions compels hope, as the logic of social exposure dictates, then the object of hope is also vaguely defined. More often than not, the political message merely calls for an end to the present suffering without, however, pointing to any definite future. Part of the reason for this amorphousness of political purpose can be attributed to government censorship, with which the leftist writer and film-maker had to play a perpetual game of camouflage in order to hide his real intentions.[8] But surely the lack of a well-organised and consistent revolutionary programme, coupled with a residual individualism inherited from the May Fourth era, also led to this artistic effort of realistic portraiture: social realism is, in short, a committed art burdened with ethical and emotional weight but not necessarily with doctrinaire propaganda. This in my view characterises the best of modern Chinese films made in the 1930s and 1940s.

The number of first-rate social realistic films made in the 30s is, on the basis of my preliminary research, not comparable to that of the golden age of the late 40s.[9] The film industry of the 30s was still fragmented by different interests and produced both socially conscious films and films of entertainment and escapism. To this extent, the 30s era also witnessed a broader spectrum of film-making. (A few films which presumably catered to popular tastes were also capable of turning out a few artistically striking images or segments.) Thus I would like to argue that, although the social realistic mode was established at this time, it was not until the late 40s that it became a dominant mode.

The participation of leftwing writers in the film industry in the early 30s, though significant, was still limited. As the war with Japan soon enveloped the population, most writers rechannelled their creative energies into various forms of drama, which was deemed a better medium for patriotic propaganda. In wartime Chungking (Chongqing), the impoverished material conditions of film companies (mostly government-owned) were such that they were unable to purchase enough blank film footage for shooting. Thus many film performers, now 'unemployed' in their own profession, were drawn into the numerous theatrical troupes in the service of the nation, thereby contributing to further cross-fertilisation between the two media, and to drama reaching an apogee of popularity.[10] Some of the most productive playwrights – Cao Yu, Xia Yan, Yang Hansheng, Chen Baichen, Tian Han – and the most popular players – Zhao Dan, Bai Yang, Shi Hui, Liu Qiong – of this period eventually returned to the film world after the war was over. Moreover, in Japanese-occupied Shanghai, another pool of dramatic talent – the director Zuo

Lin, and writers like Ke Ling, Eileen Chang (Zhang Ailing), Yao Ke – also made the transition from drama to film.[11] Consequently, with the end of the war in 1945, the coastal cities, especially Shanghai, regained their important place as centres of film-making. As the Shanghai natives resurfaced and the dramatic personnel from the hinterland returned after disbanding their theatrical troupes, a surge of creativity thus resulted in the golden age of films' prosperity.

Yet this resurgence of artistic vitality occurred in the most trying circumstances of post-war chaos. The general popular desire for peace and security was not fulfilled. Instead, civil war between the Nationalists and the Communists broke out into the open. The cities ran rampant with flagrant corruption and inflation. Thus the direct clash between ideals and reality begot a group of outstanding films of social exposure which reflected this chaotic situation. The high-handed, irregular practices of the so-called 'confiscation tycoons' from Chungking, who made personal fortunes in the name of the nationalist government by confiscating property owned by former collaborators with the Japanese, were bitterly criticised in *Diary of Returning Home*, directed by Yuan Jun (Zhang Junxiang) and based on his own experience. The sense of disillusionment felt by the young intellectuals who returned after eight years of patriotic service during the war was powerfully conveyed in Shi Dongshan's film, *Eight Thousand Li of Cloud and Moon*. The story focuses on a young couple who join a theatrical troupe and work actively for war propaganda only to be caught upon their return in utter chaos. Another long film (in two parts), *A Spring River Flows East*, written and directed by two other veterans from the 30s, Cai Chusheng and Zheng Junli, tells a similar story by portraying the degeneration of a young intellectual by the Chungking and Shanghai nouveau riche in contrast to his virtuous and long-suffering wife. As Shi Dongshan summed up his own feelings, which are also representative of the whole generation who had emerged after eight long years of tribulations: 'The eight years of war were hard for us, but we can find reason and justification for this hardship. It is more difficult for us to understand why in the months after victory we felt so defeated.'[12]

This sense of spiritual defeat was translated into bitter satire or anguished protest. For instance, *The Make-Believe Couple*, one of the most popular films of the period, contains the surface plot of how a poor barber, camouflaged as a rich dandy, courts an equally poor woman pretending to be wealthy. The comedy of errors thus veils a devastating critique of the vanity, greed and hypocrisy of the Shanghai commercial world while at the same time revealing its Westernised materialism and decadence. Another renowned film, *Night Lodging*, was adapted by Ke Ling and Zuo Lin from Gorky's play *The Lower Depths*, but the setting is changed into the 'lower depths' of Shanghai slums. The suffering of the urban poor is depicted with a ruthless realism which inevitably begs the political question: wherein lies social justice? In *This Life of Mine*, adapted from Lao She's novelette and featuring Shi Hui in a superb performance as a minor policeman, the entire social history of modern China is mirrored in the life of this 'small man' whose family has suffered through all the political vicissitudes from the Republican Revolution through warlordism to the Sino-Japanese war. At the end of the film, the old man's son becomes a Communist and joins the guerrilla movement.[13]

Whether in satirising the rich or in pitying the poor, in glorifying the oppressed or in castigating the oppressors, celebrating the virtues of decency and honesty or exposing the vices of vanity or hypocrisy, the films of this period were all infused with an overpowering humanism which was intended not only to move the audience but also to compel them to draw ethical and political lessons: what was to be done? The basic themes of the 30s were carried forward with a new, pressing urgency.

Most of the film-makers were leftists of long standing. They managed to utilise the more progressive studios, such as the Lianhua-Kunlun film company (as they had done with Mingxing in the 30s), and played a similar game with the government censors (sometimes even resorting to bribery). Some of the best films were made this way perhaps because the leftist artists took up the challenge: the darker the socio-political reality, the more fervent their creativity and dedication to their art. The most renowned film of this period, *Crows and Sparrows*, was made literally on the eve of the Communist victory and was not finished until several months after the Communist takeover. The process of its production itself makes a fascinating story:

> This scenario was born in the winter of 1948 when six film-making friends ... gathered together and decided they should chronicle the declining days of the KMT as a gift to the steadily advancing Communist armies. Chen Baichen transformed their collaborative efforts into a screenplay while a script, minus all the scenes and dialogue critical of the Kuomintang rule and stressing the film as a light comedy, was handed to the censors. The censors, however, soon discovered that what was being filmed was not the script they had approved. They prohibited further shooting on the grounds that it was 'inciting unrest' and 'destroying confidence in the government'. In late April 1949, a special court ordered that footage already shot be confiscated for inspection. Aware that a Communist victory was now imminent, Kunlun workers saved the sets while Chen constantly updated his script to reflect changing political realities. To prevent the script's seizure in the event of a studio search, it was placed in a straw-filled burlap bag and hidden in the studio's ceiling.[14]

When the film was finally completed in 1949 and released in early 1950, it received all the accolades and in 1956 was named the best Chinese film for the period 1949–55. Jay Leyda rated it 'a milestone in

Chinese film history, worthy to be shown alongside the best of international cinema produced in the post-war years'.[15] In fact, Chinese films of 1945–9 may be compared to post-war Italian neo-realist films in several respects: in terms of style and mood, of social realistic content, as well as the rather primitive and unsettled conditions in which they were made. The artistic integrity the Chinese films attained is all the more remarkable in view of what later happened to these film artists: most of them were castigated as 'rightists' during the 'cultural revolution' and (for instance in the case of Zhao Dan) met with tragic deaths. Thus films like *Crows and Sparrows* lend credence to my thesis (or hypothesis) that in China artistic creativity prospered on the eve of the revolution: the metaphor 'longest night before dawn', used by so many writers and artists, gives a vivid testimony to the kind of anguished mentality that lies at the core of committed art. It is 'revolutionary' only in the sense that through its exposé ethos it lays bare the darkness before the revolution, rather than glorifies propagandistically the revolutionary victory itself. For all their 'revolutionary' sympathies, the leftist film-makers in the late 40s were by no means united in their support of communism. Most of them had but vague ideas of its Marxist tenets or even its Maoist ideology. Their independence of spirit and their critical conscience were given full release precisely because in the last years of the Kuomintang (Guomindang) rule they had to confront the chaos and darkness of a disintegrating society.

This 'on the eve' mentality and mood has given films of this period a distinct imprint in sharp contrast to the revolutionary panegyrics produced since the late 1950s.

2

What stylistic implications can we derive from this tradition of committed social realistic cinema and its close ties with literature? Not having viewed enough films, I can only venture some preliminary speculations in lieu of detailed analysis.

In view of film's links with literature, let us begin with the film script. The two-volume anthology of *Selected Film Scripts Since the May Fourth Era* (*Wusi yilai dianying juben xuan*) published in 1962 contains only sixteen works from 1931 to 1949, of which three are synopses from the actual films of scripts which are lost. Such a slim collection (which remains the only authoritative work on the early period) bespeaks perhaps the conditions under which early film scripts were produced. What turned out to be significant films may have been based on rather haphazard scenarios which were constantly revised in the process of film production. Interestingly, the scripts for the silent films included in this anthology are more elaborate: most of them contain not only scene-by-scene but also shot-by-shot directions. The scripts for the sound films, on the other hand, read more like written narratives (sometimes divided into many brief sections) which serve at best as an outline for the final working scripts (in which presumably camera angles and shot divisions are clearly spelled out). They are like a short story or novelette, written with the intention of evoking through linguistic means the visual equivalents of the film in the reader's mind. In such scripts, descriptive verbiage tends to be rich on plot and characterisation but rather sparing in what may be construed as montage sequences. For instance, in the screenplay for *Eight Thousand Li of Cloud and Moon*, we find such lines of scenic sketch:

'Various shots of disaster in Jiangxi.'
'Scene of Shanghai after victory: floods of traffic in the big avenues, throngs of passengers, noisier than ever.'
'Jeeps of all sizes carrying American soldiers flit by. Several pedicabs ride by one after another, with American soldiers sitting in them holding Chinese or Western women: some flitting by while kissing their women, others shouting and singing.'
'Peach blossoms in full bloom, and a pair of birds chirruping on the branches.'
'A pair of Mandarin ducks with necks intertwined on the water.'[16]

Some of these sketches are vivid, but mostly they are no more than descriptive clichés. As written literature they are certainly flawed prose, but intended as film scripts they become a sort of 'shorthand' code for the director to transform them into visual images. The 'reader' is put in an intriguing position, having to imagine what they would really be like in the finished film or, alternatively, to treat the film script as a special kind of literary narrative in which certain elements (such as dialogue) are more pronounced and others more 'abridged' (such as scenic description). But even more intriguing, in retrospect, is the fact that some writers, especially in the early period, came from the ranks of fiction and drama: they simply were not equipped to write in the 'language' of the film. With the exception of Xia Yan, Tian Han and a few others who did manage to create both 'literary scenarios' and detailed shooting scripts, most writers were content to leave the technical side to the film director. Not knowing the practical limits of the new medium, they sometimes tended to indulge in too many scenes and scenic changes which a written narrative can easily afford but which may be difficult to realise in film, given the actual conditions of film-making in China. Thus this overt literariness led a few veteran directors to complain in the late 1950s (during the Hundred Flowers period) about the excessive length of some Chinese film scripts, even compared to those of Russian classics, and to stress the need to explore the unique artistic properties of film as different from narrative literature.[17] On the other hand, with the accretion of film scripts as written literature, a new convention has been established: a writer can now conceive of a literary work in the form of a screenplay, whether or not a film may eventually be made of it; in other words, film scripts have become a new literary genre, somewhere between fiction and drama.[18]

12

The 'narrativity' of modern Chinese film scripts may be seen as the clear result of the influence of modern Chinese fiction on film. But even more relevant than fiction is the example of the spoken drama in both its literary and performing aspects. It is well known that not only some of the most notable dramatists wrote film scripts but also some of the best films were originally stage plays. This close relationship leads to the 'play-like' qualities which are especially noticeable in the serious films.

With few exceptions, most films tend to be set indoors (e.g. a boarding house in *Crows and Sparrows*); the scenes are derived from dramatic acts; the reliance on dialogue is clearly a carry-over from the theatre. Above all, they are noted for the quality of *acting*, which renders the characters in the films truly memorable: Shi Hui's characterisation of the Peking (Beijing) policeman in *This Life of Mine*, Bai Yang's performance as Xianglin's wife in the film version of Lu Xun's famous story *New Year's Sacrifice*, Liu Qiong's masterful portrayal of the Ming loyalist Wen Tianxiang in *The Soul of the Nation*, based on the play *Song of Righteousness* (*Zhengqi ge*), and Zhao Dan's many characterisations of realistic figures in the films of the 40s and historical heroes in later films – these performances are now considered 'classics' in a cinematic and dramatic tradition blessed with great actors and actresses, most of whom were active in both media. Through the sheer force of their acting, they more than make up for whatever weaknesses may exist in the technical realm of film-making. Given the films' social realistic orientation, it is also through performance that they were able to bring the contemporary audience into a heightened psychological identification with the personalities in the films and into the emotional parameters of their enacted experience; they performed indeed the trick of opening up the enclosed reality within the film frames into the broad social reality which they and their audience shared in common. Thus I would like to argue that the source of the films' impact is more 'dramatic' than purely visual.

This does not mean that modern Chinese cinema is utterly devoid of visual interest. The first half hour of Jin Shan's film *Sungari River* contains such striking visual vitality (almost Eisensteinian) that Leyda considered the passage 'among the high points of international film history'.[19] One might also cite another good example: the opening sequence of *This Life of Mine*, a flashback set in an intricate and fast-moving sight-and-sound mix – a summary in montage of half a century of modern Chinese history followed by long tracking shots of the protagonist leaning against a lamp-pole, which convey both a subjective point of view and the mood of the overall environment. However, these segments are exceptional gems of cinematic flourish which are not sustained throughout the rest of the films in which they occur. The general visual style of most 40s films I have seen is subdued: instead of trick camera-work and flashy editing, they tend to rely on static long and medium shots. The close-ups are used relatively sparingly (as compared to the films of Ingmar Bergman, for instance) and mostly to accentuate a high

13

point in the characters' interaction and an emotional peak. Rapid zooms and pans are seldom used. Dissolves, wipes, fade-ins and fade-outs are generally employed to conform to the changes of time and scene (dissolves for brief time changes and fades for longer lapses).[20]

These 'normal ways' of compositional technique have been called by Western film critics a form of 'spatial realism' and a hallmark of Italian neo-realism.[21] Whatever metaphysical implications may have been derived by André Bazin and others from this 'deep-focus', 'long-take' mode of film-making,[22] the Chinese usage is, to my eyes, a direct transposition from the convention of spoken drama and serves as its cinematic equivalent. What is emphasised is the overall view, established by the 'master-shot' which becomes a frame of reference – like the dramatic set of each act or the whole play – governing the action of the players as well as the camera movement. The rhythm of this type of film is slow, rather than frenzied, and perhaps parallels the rhythm of ordinary life – Chinese-style. (Even the relatively quicker tempo in the slapstick sequences of satirical comedies like *The Make-Believe Couple* is slow by comparison with the rather smooth speed of Hollywood films such as Howard Hawks' *His Girl Friday*.) The emotional impact of this relaxed style is accumulative and developed slowly over considerable length. The contemporary audience gradually becomes immersed in the film's story and action, thus changing a spectator's objective aloofness into the intimate sharing of a common experience. Especially when the experience depicted in the film is of such magnitude as the eight-year-long war of resistance against the Japanese. One can well imagine the Chinese reception of *A Spring River Flows East*, which in its length (two parts, over four hours) is an appropriate match for the prolonged war and tells a tortured story of partings and reunions during the course of the war. Despite the film's obvious sentimental clichés, an audience consisting mostly of Chinese at a recent showing of the film at Berkeley, California wept intermittently during the film and profusely at the end, whereas a few American members of the audience walked out. For the audience of the late 1940s, the film must have unleashed even closer identifications – the reliving of a most traumatic collective experience. It is also in this sense that the 'realism' of the film style becomes transformed into the realism of lived experience.

I am suggesting, therefore, that the general 'form' of the 40s film is also appropriate to its content. Unlike modern European films of a more recent vintage (Bergman, Fellini, Antonioni, Fassbinder et al.) in which the film-maker (the so-called 'auteur' director) projects a uniquely subjective vision on to an audience who may or may not be susceptible to it, Chinese films of the 1940s 'collaborated' with the audience in the sharing of a lifelike world which is captured by the film-maker despite having to resort to contrivance (the indoor stage-like sets are not exactly conducive to a cinéma-vérité style). Yet this communal aesthetic serves to draw the audience in, instead of intruding upon it. It is, in short, the most effective way of communicating the films' didactic message. The experience of film-watching becomes not merely a way of emotional catharsis but also a form of social and political commitment.

3

If we compare this tradition of modern Chinese cinema with the revolutionary films made in the 1960s and 1970s (some of the films made during the early 1950s still inherited the 40s tradition), the differences are striking. The basic mode of the revolutionary films, following Mao's Yan'an injunctions, is celebrative, extolling the 'brightness' of the new society and its heroes as they invariably win victory after a valiant struggle with the enemy – be it the Japanese, the KMT, or American imperialism. The emphasis is focused on struggle – the clash of two forces or two 'lines' resulting in the triumph of the good over the evil. The acting is accentuated with heroic, prominent gestures, in accordance with the famous credo (during the 'cultural revolution') of the so-called 'Three Prominences', attributed to Jiang Qing.[23] The idea is to bring to the audience positive heroes and exemplary ways of life, as prescribed in the theory of 'socialist realism'. But the ironic fact is that, especially in the films of revolutionary operas, this mode of presentation serves to distance the audience from the world portrayed in the film. (Very interestingly, a large number of films have their stories taking place in the Republican period, yet their portrayal is grossly unreal when seen side by side with the social-realistic films made in the 40s.) We can speak of two different worlds: the ideal world in the film fabricated with more advanced technique than can be found in the pre-revolutionary films – a world full of dynamism and energy, broad smiles and resolute gestures – and the rather passive world of the ordinary people in the audience who are probably compelled, whether they are willing or not, to go to these films. At best, the films could be entertaining in spite of their political messages. (I still consider *Taking Tiger Mountain by Strategy* the most entertaining of all revolutionary opera films.) At worst, they become flat formulas devoid of human interest.

Of course, there have been some interesting exceptions. Aside from the historical sagas (*The Opium War*, or *The First Sino-Japanese War*), which appeal by virtue of their lavish productions and relative attention to historical details, the exceptional ones I have seen almost invariably recall films of the 40s. For example, *Early Spring*, a film whose lingering sentimentality caught in a leisurely pace succeeds in recapturing the romantic mood of a bygone era, the May Fourth period. The film is pieced together with a series of lyrical tableaux (taken by a static camera, in medium or long shots). To take another example, *Dr Norman Bethune*, another film with a slow rhythm which nevertheless builds up its emotional appeal by focusing on the humanism of Bethune (marvellously played by the American actor Gerry Tannenbaum): the hardships he shares with the New Fourth Army soldiers become part of a 'maturing'

15

'A bygone era': *Early Spring*

experience with which the audience could identify on the human level. A recent film, *The Legend of Tianyun Mountain*, becomes intensely moving again due to its lyricism captured by a slow tempo. In its unassuming style the film levels a devastating critique against the radicalism of political campaigns – from the Anti-Rightist Movement to the 'cultural revolution' – which exacted tragic tolls from ordinary human beings. Not surprisingly, most of these films were made by veteran directors from the earlier tradition.

Since the fall of the 'gang of four' in 1976 and the unleashing of the new policy of the Four Modernisations, the Chinese film industry has also exhibited some interesting changes. The 'cultural revolution' models have been discarded; the range of subjects and treatments broadened. In its reaction against the recent past, the new film of the 'modernisation' era seems also to rebel against the earlier tradition of film-making. Gone are the 'normal ways' of spatial realism and the slow relaxed tempo. Instead, one finds a splurge of fancy techniques: fast zooms, close-ups, split screens, fast cutting, superimposed images – as if the Chinese film-makers were determined to catch up with the technical progress of the West and to show the outside world that the Chinese are capable of performing all the advanced 'tricks' with the camera. (This 'foreign-consciousness' is carried to absurdity by a few films made specifically with a foreign audience in mind, for instance *Savage Land*, 1981, based on Cao Yu's play.) A much heralded recent film, *Regret for the Past*, made from a Lu Xun story to commemorate the centenary of his birth, proves to be an utter disappointment because, among other factors, the camera zooms with dizzying speed. Its 'modern' technique (a conscious choice supposedly by a veteran director who wished to go against his own past style) becomes an incongruous ploy for a 'classic' May Fourth story. By contrast, another film based on Lu Xun's work, *The True Story of Ah Q*, is more successful owing to the brilliance of acting and script adaptation (by Chen Baichen, who also scripted *Crows and Sparrows*).

I am not suggesting, of course, that Chinese cinema should go back to its old glorious tradition. On the other hand, it seems that the current Chinese film from the People's Republic of China is faced with a crisis. The obsession with sheer mechanical technique is a reflection of the 'modernisation' drive – yet in my view a very 'vulgar' way to modernise. As portrayed in a 1981 comedy, *The In-Laws*, the prototypical modernisation film has a lighter tone and faster rhythm. Albeit containing less posturing, the mood remains celebrative. But the most striking characteristic is the freshness of cinematic image: colours are bright; costumes are new, clean and gaudy; even the tractor on the farm – surely the centrepiece of the film and an obvious symbol of modernisation – is spotless. Does this represent the ideal of modernisation? What lies behind the surface glitter created by beautiful sets and fancy shots? What saddens me is not so much the tendency to incorporate new technique for its own sake, as the neglect of deeper content. As a literary historian interested in Chinese films, I am inclined toward a phenomenological view of film as an art form which contains within it the cultural resonances of its era.

What will become of future Chinese cinema depends very much on the overall cultural development. As in literature, there are already at least two legacies: the humanist social-realistic tradition of the 1940s, and the revolutionary propagandistic tradition of the 'cultural revolution'. Could there be new and original directions in the future? One might indulge in a few possibilities: in view of the popularity of written reportage, could there be a comparable documentary genre which investigates the human complicities during the 'cultural revolution'? Or a more concentrated psychological film, for which the 40s tradition did not provide any ready precedent? Or even some explorations into the gothic elements, as had been done somewhat primitively in a few films of the 1930s and 1940s (for example *Number Thirteen Haunted Residence*)? If the average films made in Taiwan, surely a more modernised society than China, serve as any indication, the artistic quality of modern Chinese cinema will not necessarily improve with the country's economic and technological advances.[24] Other factors than the material conditions of film-making are involved. What is of crucial importance remains the creative dimensions of the individual film-makers themselves. As artist-intellectuals they must be committed not only to the evolving culture and society of China in modern times but also to their own visions of it – and must have the courage and artistic integrity to realise their visions in films. This, to me, is the most enduring 'spiritual' legacy of the tradition of modern Chinese cinema.

Notes

1. The present paper is a revised and expanded version of a talk given at UCLA on 18 April 1982. I am grateful to Mr Chris Berry, who urged me to put these ideas in writing. I am emboldened to undertake this task because there has not been much interpretive treatment of modern Chinese film in English. In Chinese, the writings of Lin Niantong, a Hong Kong film scholar, bear close scrutiny (some were published in the journal *Bafang*, vols. 1 & 4). Jay Leyda's book, *Dianying: An Account of Films and the Film Audience in China* (Cambridge: MIT Press, 1972) remains the only monographic study of the subject in English. While I share and admire many of Leyda's insights, my framework and conclusions are not necessarily the same as his. The book unfortunately is marred by errors due to Leyda's unfamiliarity with the Chinese language.

2. In particular, Steven Horowitz, who has compiled (together with Yuan-tsung Chen) a catalogue of Chinese films up to 1949 for the Chinese Cultural Foundation, San Francisco; and Paul Pickowicz, who has recently done research in China on the films of the 40s and their social environment. I am grateful to both of them, and to Professor William Tay, for the many scintillating conversations we have had on the modern Chinese film and for several bibliographical leads.

3. Cheng Jihua et al., *Zhongguo dianying fazhan shi* (*History of the Development of Chinese Cinema*. Beijing: Zhongguo dianying chubanshe, 1963), vol. 1, p. 112. For all its ideological biases, this two-volume work remains the most comprehensive survey of the subject.

4. Ibid., pp. 200–1.

5. Ibid., pp. 203–13. Xia Yan's scripts for *Wild Torrent* and *Spring Silkworms* can be found in *Wusi yilai dianying juben xuanji* (*Selected Film Scripts since the May Fourth Era*. Beijing: Zhongguo dianying chubanshe, 1962), vol. 1, pp. 1–48.

6. Cheng Jihua, op. cit., vol. 1, ch. 3.

7. The phrase was first coined by Professor C. T. Hsia, whose classic essay 'Obsession with China' (included in the revised edition of his *A History of Modern Chinese Fiction*) provides the guiding framework for my discussion here.

8. This is the central political theme of Leyda's book which, like all the Chinese leftists, tends to exaggerate the viciousness of the KMT censors. That some of the best products in literature and art were produced in the 30s and 40s in spite of government censorship is a phenomenon worth pondering.

9. The best films made in the 30s are *Crossroads* (*Shizi jietou*, 1937), *Street Angel* (*Malu tianshi*, 1937), and *Song of the Fishermen* (*Yuguang ge*, 1934), which 'left an extraordinary impression on the audience at Moscow's first International Film Festival' (Leyda, op. cit., p. 93).

10. I am grateful to Mr Chen Baichen, who provided me with this information during an interview in Chicago, on 2 November 1982.

11. For a scholarly discussion of literature in Japanese-controlled Shanghai and Peking, see Edward M. Gunn, *Unwelcome Muse* (New York: Columbia University Press, 1980), especially chapter 3.

12. Cheng Jihua, op. cit., vol. 2, pp. 213–14. Part of my discussion was written for the *Cambridge History of China* (vol. 13), in a chapter titled 'The Road to Revolution'.

13. The Chinese Linguistic Project at Princeton University has a collection of a dozen or so films of this period, including those discussed here. I was privileged to see them at Princeton.

14. Steven Horowitz, programme brochure for 'Electric Shadows: A Festival of Chinese Cinema, 1937–1979', San Francisco International Film Festival (27 March–2 April, 1981), p. 13.

15. Leyda, op. cit., p. 174.
16. *Wusi yilai dianying juben xuanji*, vol. 2, pp. 23, 42–3.
17. See, for instance, Zhang Junxiang, '*Dianying juben weishenme hui tai chang?*' ('Why have film scripts become so long?'), in Cai Chusheng et al., *Lun dianying juben chuangzuo de tezheng* (*On the Special Characteristics of Film-Script Writing*. Beijing: Zhongguo dianying chubanshe, 1959), pp. 72–8. The volume also contains articles by Cai Chusheng, Shi Dongshan and others. See also Shi Dongshan's earlier work, *Dianying yishu zai biaoxian xingshi shang de jige tedian* (*Some Characteristics in the Representational Form of Film Art*. Beijing, Yishu chubanshe, 1954), which spells out in detail such issues as the differences between fiction, drama and film, film rhythm and the uses of montage. The standard Western works on literature and film I have consulted include George Bluestone, *Novels into Film* (Berkeley: University of California Press, 1961), and Robert Richardson, *Literature and Film* (Bloomington: Indiana University Press, 1969 and 1973).
18. The most controversial examples in the last few years were: *In the Files of Society* (*Zai shehui dang'an li*) by the young writer Wang Jing, and *Bitter Love* (*Kulian*) by Bai Hua; both became cause célèbres, the former filmed in Taiwan and the latter receiving two film versions (China and Taiwan). The journal *Dianying chuangzuo* (*Film Writing*) is specially devoted to film scripts whether or not they are made into films.
19. Leyda, op. cit., p. 160.
20. Ouyang Yuqian, the leading dramatist and a high-ranking official in the film world of the 1950s, has argued against not only film scripts with too many scene changes, but also irregular uses of fade-ins and fade-outs, which he compares to the curtain in stage acts. See his *Xie dianying juben de jige wenti* (*Some Problems of Film Script Writing*. Beijing: Zhongguo dianying chubanshe, 1959).
21. Stephen Heath, 'Narrative Space', in his *Questions of Cinema* (Bloomington: Indiana University Press, 1981), pp. 41–3.
22. Ibid., p. 43. See also André Bazin, *What is Cinema?* (Berkeley: University of California Press, 1967).
23. That is: of characters, give prominence to positive ones; of them, give prominence to heroes; among heroes, give prominence to the central hero.
24. To be fair, there have been a few interesting films made in Taiwan and Hong Kong, especially by the director King Hu (Hu Jinquan) who won a prize at the Cannes festival (special effects) for his film *A Touch of Zen* (*Xianü*) and brought other recent works to different festivals. But Hu's style is inspired more by traditional Chinese painting than by the social realistic tradition, with which he is of course familiar. The political prescriptions in Taiwan have forced the younger directors to explore 'unrealistic' subjects: ghost stories, historical episodes, as well as *kung-fu* movies. However, a new trend initiated by young directors from Hong Kong (most of whom trained in Britain and America and gained experience in television) may merit attention.

Filmography

NB: s = scenarist, d = director.

Wild Torrents (*Kuangliu*), s: Xia Yan, d: Cheng Bugao (Shanghai: Mingxing Studio, 1933).

Spring Silkworms (*Chuncan*), s: Xia Yan, d: Cheng Bugao (Shanghai: Mingxing Studio, 1933).

Diary of Returning Home (*Huanxiang Riji*), s/d: Yuan Jun [Zhang Junxiang] (Shanghai: Central Film Enterprise Ltd., First Studio, 1947).

Eight Thousand Li of Cloud and Moon (*Baqian Li Lu Yun he Yue*), s/d: Shi Dongshan (Shanghai: Kunlun Studio: 1947).

The Spring River Flows East (*Yijiang Chunshui Xiang Dong Liu*), s/d: Cai Chusheng and Zheng Junli (Shanghai: Kunlun and Lianhua Studios, 1947).

The Make-Believe Couple (*Jiafeng Xuhuang*), s: Sang Hu, d: Zuo Lin (Shanghai: Wenhua Studio, 1947).

Night Lodging (*Yedian*), s: Ke Ling, d: Zuo Lin (Shanghai: Wenhua Studio, 1947).

Along the Sungari River (*Songhua Jiang Shang*), s/d: Jin Shan (Changchun Studio, 1947).

Number Thirteen Haunted Residence (*Shisanhao Xiongzhai*) (Shanghai: Yihua Studio, 1948).

Soul of the Nation (*Guo Hun*), s: Wu Zuguang, d: Bu Wancang (Shanghai: Yonghua Studio, 1948).

Crows and Sparrows (*Wuya yu Maque*), s: Shen Fu, d: Zheng Junli (Shanghai: Kunlun Studio, 1949).

This Life of Mine (*Wo Zhe Yi Beizi*), s: Yang Liuqing, d: Shi Hui (Shanghai: Wenhua Studio, 1950).

New Year's Sacrifice (*Zhufu*), s: Xia Yan, from a short story by Lu Xun, d: Sang Hu (Beijing Studio, 1956).

The Opium War (*Lin Zexu*), s: Ye Yuan, d: Zheng Junli, Cen Fan (Shanghai: Haiyan Studio, 1959).

The First Sino-Japanese War (*Jiawu Fengyun*), s: Xi Nong, Ye Nan, Chen Ying, Li Xiongfei, Du Li, d: Lin Nong (Changchun Studio, 1962).

Early Spring (*Zaochun Eryue*), s/d: Xie Tieli (Beijing Studio, 1963).

Dr Norman Bethune (*Bai Qiu'en Daifu*), s: Zhang Junxiang, Zhao Ta, d: Zhang Junxiang (Shanghai and Beijing: Haiyan and August First Studios, 1964).

Taking Tiger Mountain By Strategy (*Zhiqu Weihu Shan*), s: Beijing Opera Troupe, d: Xie Tieli (Beijing Studio, 1968).

The Legend of Tianyun Mountain (*Tianyunshan Chuanqi*), s: Lu Yanzhou, d: Xie Jin (Shanghai Studio, 1980).

Regret for the Past (*Shang Shi*), s: Zhang Yaojun, Zhang Lei, d: Shui Hua (Beijing Studio, 1981).

The In-Laws (*Xi Ying Men*), s: Xin Xianling, d: Zhao Huanzhang (Shanghai Studio, 1981).

Savage Land (*Yuanye*), s: Ling Zi, Ji Si, d: Ling Zi (Hong Kong: Nanhai Film Company, 1981).

The True Story of Ah Q (*Ah Q Zhengzhuan*), s: Chen Baichen, d: Ling Fan (Beijing Studio, 1982).

The Chinese Montage
From Poetry and Painting to the Silver Screen

CATHERINE YI-YU CHO WOO

> Withered vines
>> Aged tree
>>> Evening crows
>
> Small bridge
>> Flowing water
>>> Village huts
>
> Ancient road
>> West winds
>>> Lean horse
>
> Evening sun slants west
>> A heart-torn man at the edge of heaven[1]

('Sky Pure Sand' [*Tian Jing Sha*]
by Ma Zhiyuan, ca. 1260–ca. 1324)

At first glance the cinema seems incompatible with traditional Chinese art. The cinema is a Western art, created in tune with the values of Western culture. As Bazin has pointed out in 'The Ontology of the Image', it is the apogee of the drive towards realism that has dominated the Western arts since the discovery of perspective, reproducing reality in both space and time.[2] The Chinese arts have no such drive. There is no adherence to realism, and no tradition of perspective in painting. Furthermore, Chinese painting has a tradition of using the void; large, empty spaces that could never be created in cinema.

However, despite these contradictions, Chinese directors are succeeding in the difficult task of blending the aesthetic values of Chinese visual arts with the imported Western technology of movie-making. They have learned rapidly to adapt the ability of the camera lens to expose an immediate, concrete reality to the traditional techniques of Chinese poets and painters, which have been used so successfully (often in collaboration with each other) to suggest a greater reality. ('In the strenuous enterprise of dealing with the transcendental, in expressing the well-nigh inexpressible, the collaboration between poetry and painting offers their joint best.'[3]) In this way the Chinese cinema has become an exciting, new

21

artistic medium that preserves and extends Chinese cultural patterns.

The soul of Chinese painting and poetry, and now the Chinese cinema, offers the vision of the unity of the human and natural worlds. And the technical composition of poetry and painting reveals this authentic Taoist outlook that sees man at one with all parts of nature. This sympathetic relationship is evident in the epigraph poem that heads this piece, in which the bleak weariness of a distant traveller is reflected by the late chill of age in the natural setting – withered vines, a skinny steed, cawing crows, setting sun. Human subject and natural object have reached the same stage of life and yearn for rest, for a home. This at-one-ness of man and nature is, of course, similar to the pathetic fallacy of Western Romantic poetry. In this lyric (ci), the sentimental unity of the human and natural worlds is expressed by the abrupt sequence of images – vines, trees, crows, bridge, water, house, wood, wind, horse, sun, traveller – that create a poetic wholeness of life. It is precisely by this technique of a lyrical montage of simple images filmed with a static camera that Chinese movie directors are now endeavouring to express, visually, the emotional totality of their narratives. These montages occur with such frequency and consistency of form throughout Chinese movies that they constitute, if you will, a sub-type of what Metz has termed 'the bracket syntagm', so peculiarly Chinese that they may be referred to as 'Chinese montages'.[4]

The interaction between the separate images in these Chinese montages, interweaving human and natural images, is startlingly effective on the Chinese screen, though the Western viewer will sometimes need to have the symbolic value of the natural images interpreted for him. To take an early example, there is an admirable montage of single images in A Spring River Flows East (1947). The camera first focuses on the wedding picture of a young couple, Zhongliang (Tao Jin) and Sufen (Bai Yang), on a dresser, cuts to two embroidered pillows at the top of the double bed, and then to the side of the bed where two pairs of shoes rest neatly side by side. The next image is of a leafless branch of spring blossom, followed by that of a leafy branch laden with fruit. The final shot is of a hand embroidering 'Precious Little Baby' (xiao baobao) on a bib. The fruition of life over time in the human family and in nature is tenderly communicated, with lyrical succinctness, through this sequence of static shots. Often, in Chinese poetic literature, a series of natural images similarly swiftly conveys the cycle of the seasons from spring to winter:

> The wild flowers give off their pure perfume;
> The trees with beautiful foliage offer luxuriant shade.
> The wind blows high while hoarfrost appears;
> The pebbles come out when water sinks.[5]

('The Old Drunkard's Arbor' [Zui Weng Ting Ji], by Ouyang Xiu)

22

Another excellent example of the Chinese montage can be found in *The New Doctor* (1975). Many features of the pre-1966 Chinese cinema disappeared during the 'cultural revolution' decade, but the Chinese montage thrived, employing particularly emphatic natural images to sum up the emotional highpoints in the narrative. Here, Hong Yu, the young doctor, has just saved a small baby's life. The camera cuts from a close-up of Hong Yu's gaze to a portrait of Chairman Mao, then to the sun rising over mountain peaks; a close-up of a flower; high cirrus clouds; sunlight in the mountains; and finally to a close-up of the baby's happy, smiling face.

Even now, after the fall of the 'gang of four' and the move by Chinese film-makers to utilise new techniques and styles of film-making, the Chinese montage is still going strong, and still reminiscent of the same man-nature relationship found in traditional painting as well as poetry. For instance, in *Moon Reflected on Second Spring* (1979), when the young Ah Bing is dismissed from the Taoist temple, the first shot shows the tiny figure of the protagonist in front of the towering monastery building; the second image on the screen is of a single wild goose against a vast expanse of sky; the third, of Ah Bing gazing, presumably at the goose; the fourth of a single sailboat with tall pampas grass on the shore in the foreground; the fifth of another boat on a lake; and the final frame again shows the solitary figure of Ah Bing walking on a path alongside a lake. Clearly, this series of images conveys the sad loneliness of Ah Bing's inner world by visually comparing him to the single boats and to the solitary wild goose (a traditional Chinese symbol), which usually, like Ah Bing, would be with his fellows. Similar images abound in Chinese poetry, as seen in the last two lines of 'To See Meng Hao-ren off to Yangzhou' (*Huanghelou Song Meng Haoran Zhi Guang Ling*) by Li Bo (701–762 A.D.):

> Lone sail
> Distant shade
> Lost in the green horizon
> Only Yangzi
> Flowing into the sky[6]

And 'Thinking of My Brothers and Sisters on a Moonlit Night' (*Yue Ye Yi She Di*) by Du Fu (712–760 A.D.) has lines like these:

> Frontier drums beating alarm the travellers;
> At the border the solitary cry of a wild goose.
> From today the dewdrops will be white with frost;
> In my native town the moon is shedding a special brightness.
> Homeless, I know not whether they are alive or dead;
> No mail is ever received, or is like to be,
> Since there is still no prospect of the war ending.[7]

A reassuring note in this instance of comparative natural imagery in the montage technique is that though separated from his community, Ah Bing has his counterparts in the natural world. He is alone, but not a total outcast since his plight is not unique.

Beyond the Chinese montage, the influence of Chinese poetry and painting is manifested in the symbolic values and composition of many shots. On the symbolic level, the instances of the Chinese montage I have given above are all fairly readily understood by the Western, as well as the Chinese, viewer. This is not always so. A scene in Huang Zumo's *Romance on Lushan Mountain* (1980) is designed to reveal with delicate natural symbolism the unseen, unspoken passion of human lovers. In the first shot, the camera shows two young people in love talking together in an idyllic landscape; in the second, a pond where fish are swimming freely. (Note that this cutaway shot functions in a way similar to the Chinese montage, though on a smaller scale, and that it is also formally related; a single, simple, natural image.) Whereas a Western viewer may have expected to see the passionate embraces of this Chinese Romeo and Juliet, a Chinese viewer subtly experiences the free, loving intimacy of the lovers through the image of the swimming fish. This symbolic meaning is familiar to the reader of Chinese – for example, 'like a fish in water – free and happy' (*Ru Yu De Shui*) is a very common Chinese expression. Also, as fish are reputed to swim in pairs, so a pair of fish is emblematic of the joy of union, especially of a sexual nature.[8] Thus the interwoven images of human and natural events not only reveal an implicit unity but also elicit a deeper, common yet personal emotion in the Chinese reader or viewer.

The symbolic conventions of Chinese poetry and painting also persist in the cinema's use of colours and various images of trees, flowers, plants and weather. Since these have established cultural values, a Chinese director is thus able to cue his audience for an appropriate emotional response. For example, in *A Spring River Flows East*, a few years after the main protagonist Zhongliang has left his wife in Shanghai to look after their child and his mother, thunder and heavy rainstorms erupt. This harsh weather suggests to the Chinese viewer that hard times are coming, and in fact Zhongliang, forgetful of wife and mother, is seen drinking and dancing in Chongqing with a girl whom he later marries.

Another excellent example of a director's use of these conventional symbols occurs in *Moon Reflected on Second Spring*. After Ah Bing, separated from a young street entertainer (his music teacher's daughter and his lover), comes to the Monastery of Moon Reflected on Second Spring, the screen presents the viewer with a Chinese montage composed of several symbolic images: a full moon; the name of the monastery in calligraphy; a reflection of the full moon in a pond; in daylight, the red blossoms of a bush (presumably in the monastery garden); branches of plum blossom; and again, the full moon over the monastery. This montage is framed by the image of the full moon, a symbol of yearning for love and reunion, as shown in this poem:

24

The moon, grown full now over the sea,
Brightening the whole of heaven,
Brings to separated hearts
The long thoughtfulness of night ...
It is no darker though I blow out my candle.
It is no warmer though I put on my coat.
So I leave my message with the moon
And turn to my bed, hoping for dreams.

('Looking at the Moon and Thinking of One Far Away'
[*Wang Yue Huai Yuan*] by Zhang Jiuling, 673–740 A.D.)[9]

Other symbols here suggest romance (the moon's reflection), parting (willow), courage and promise of spring and winter's bitter ordeal (plum blossom), and happiness (red flowers). The joyous quality of red is evident in this poem:

Last night wedding-chamber red candles glow
Early morning the bride faces your parents
After preparing; softly she asks
'Are my eyebrows painted in fashion?'

('On the Eve of Government Examinations
to Secretary Zhang' [*Jin Shi Shang Zhang Shui Bu*]
by Zhu Qingyu, graduated 825 A.D.)[10]

Earlier in *Moon Reflected on Second Spring*, the street entertainer, Jin Mei, has red yarn in her hair, but at her father's funeral she wears unbleached jute over her hair, a white belt and white shoes. For the Chinese, red is the colour for all happy events (New Year, childbirth, birthdays, weddings) but white is the colour for mourning, not for purity or innocence as in the West. Thus without some guidance, the Western viewer may well miss a significant clue provided in a Chinese movie using traditional symbols.

Similarly, a Chinese director automatically adopts the sentimental conventions familiar to Chinese poets and painters. For example, in *A Spring River Flows East*, Zhongliang's mother is shown sewing for her son before his departure for Chongqing. This endearing image seems almost a replica of the painting by Zhang Zhaohe, who quotes the Tang dynasty (618–905 A.D.) poem on his work: 'Thread in the hand of loving mother clothes for the wayward son' (*You Zi Yin*, Meng Jiao, 751–814 A.D.).[11] Nor do Chinese movies hesitate to show the tear-marked faces of men as pain or grief rises from their hearts. Again, the convention of poetry gives such licence:

All listeners there sobbed and wept
Who among them sobbed the most tears?
The official whose blue robe is now all drenched!

('Song of the Pi-pa' [*Pipa Xing*] by Bo Juyi, 772–846 A.D.)[12]

25

Figures in a landscape: Ma Yuan, 'A scholar and his servant on a terrace'

Moving from the symbolic to the compositional, the single image of Ah Bing in front of the Taoist monastery in *Moon Reflected on Second Spring* (referred to above) recalls so many traditional Chinese landscapes where the tiny figure of a lone man seems overwhelmed by the majesty of the surrounding mountain scenery.[13] To Western eyes, this lone figure looks forlorn and helpless, yet the Chinese viewer knows that though small, he has a part, a small part, to play in the natural scheme of things. This view of humanity's role even carries over into the urban setting of a Chinese movie, *The Lin Family Shop* (1959), where Lin's apprentice, after learning how great a sum of money is needed to get his master released from jail, walks out into the street and stands, an insignificant man, crushed by the massive buildings around him. Although his helplessness seems emphasised by the camera's focus, this little man does in fact 'move mountains', for he succeeds in raising the money necessary to rescue Lin. The traditional configuration, transferred from painting to movie screen, from landscape to city street, retains its vital man-nature relationship and its compositional features.

Among other compositional conventions of Chinese painting, even that of making the most important figure or object the largest has persisted in Chinese movies, although somewhat modified by the inevitable realism of the cinema. For example in *The Lin Family Shop*, the figure of Lin, the shop-owner, is taller though more distant than that of his assistant. This difference in height does not, however, shock the Westerner's sense of perspective as does the 'illogical' sizing of figures in traditional Chinese paintings.[14] The need to vary the height or size of human subjects or natural objects in paintings derives from the Chinese sense of hierarchy whereby one (*zhu*) must dominate over the others (*bin*). For example, in a landscape one mountain clearly towers above the others of varying sizes. This phenomenon also, of course, accords with the Chinese principle of asymmetry in artistic composition, as evidenced not only in painting but also in landscape, and which has also carried over to the Chinese cinema.

But there is an even more obvious and apparently deliberate use of landscape in some modern Chinese films. Certainly, in selecting views of the countryside as settings for the action of so much of their films, Chinese directors seem inspired by their memories of landscape compo-

Assymetry: Ma Lin, 'Listening to the wind in the pines'

27

sitions. Perhaps, too, a character is seen as though posed to imitate the painting of a figure gazing into the void.[15] However, the influence of painting with its accompanying poem is especially clear in *A Spring River Flows East*. The directors, Cai Chusheng and Zheng Junli, were no doubt on a limited budget since much of this film was shot indoors, but for the atmospheric credit titles they chose to use beautiful landscape views as backgrounds. And the title of their film, included in two lines from a Song Dynasty poem by Li Yu – 'How much sorrow do you have? The way a spring river eastward flows' (*Wen Jun Neng You Ji Duo Chou, Qia Si Yi Jiang Chun Shui Xiang Dong Liu*)[16] – superimposed on a view of the Yangzi River, at once recalls the traditional convention of painting and calligraphy.

By remaining faithful to the implicit values of their traditional aesthetics, modern Chinese movie directors are thus successfully combining the worlds of imagination and reality, or the artist's vision and the camera's lens. Contrary to the current trend in the Western cinema, especially horror movies, in which the viewer's imagination is rarely invited to participate in the visual drama made crudely explicit, the Chinese film depends on the active imaginative collaboration of its viewers to come alive. Chinese painting and poetry have extended their rich conventions to the movie screen, to help in the creation of a truly Chinese cinema.

Notes

1. Except where noted, all translations of poetry are by the author.
2. André Bazin, 'The Ontology of the Image', *What is Cinema?*, vol. 1, trans. Hugh Gray (Berkeley: University of California Press, 1967), pp. 1–15.
3. Catherine Yi-yu Cho Woo, 'Chinese Poetry and Painting – Some Observations on the Interrelationship', *Monumenta Serica*, vol. XXXIV, 1979–80.
4. Christian Metz, *Film Language: A Semiotics of the Cinema*, trans. Michael Taylor (New York: Oxford University Press, 1974), pp. 126–7.
5. By Ch'u Chai, in *A Treasury of Chinese Literature*, trans. and ed. Winberg (New York: Appleton-Century, 1965), p. 47.
6. *Tang shi san bai shou xiang xi* (Taipei: Zhonghua shuju, 1971), p. 294.
7. S. S. Liu (trans.), *One Hundred and One Chinese Poems* (Hong Kong: Hong Kong University Press, 1967), p. 39.
8. C. A. S. Williams, *Outlines of Chinese Symbolism and Art Motives* (New York: Dover, 1976), p. 185.
9. Witter Brynner (trans.), *The Jade Mountain – A Chinese Anthology* (Garden City, NY: Doubleday, 1964), p. 6.
10. *Tang shi san bai shou xiang xi*, p. 308.
11. Lubor Hajek, Adolf Hoffmeister and Eva Rychterova, *Contemporary Chinese Painting* (London: Spring Books, 1961), p. 179.
12. Wai-lim Yip (trans.) *Chinese Poetry* (Berkeley: University of California Press, 1976), p. 401.

13. See James Cahill, *Chinese Painting* (Switzerland: SKIRA): Guo Xi, *Early Spring*, dated 1072, p. 36.
14. Ibid.: Ma Lin, *Listening to the Wind in the Pines*, dated 1246, p. 64. In this instance, the scholar is shown as a far more important figure than his servant boy, though the latter is foregrounded.
15. Ibid.: Ma Yuan, *A Scholar and his Servant on a Terrace*, ca. 1190–1230, p. 83.
16. Li Houzhu, *Shi Xin Shang* (Taipei: Tushu Gongsi, 1971), p. 39.

Filmography

NB: s = scenarist, d = director.

A Spring River Flows East (Yijiang chunshui xiang dong liu), s/d: Cai Chusheng and Zheng Junli (Shanghai: Kunlun and Lianhua Studios, 1947).

The Lin Family Shop (Linjia Puzi), s: Xia Yan, d: Shui Hua (Beijing Studio, 1959).

The New Doctor (Hongyu), s: Yang Xiao, Cui Wei, d: Cui Wei (Beijing Studio, 1975).

Romance on Lushan Mountain (Lushan lian), s: Bi Bicheng, d: Huang Zumo (Shanghai Studio, 1980).

Moon Reflected on Second Spring (Erchuan Yingyue), s: E Yunwen, Liu Baoyi, Rong Lei, d: Yan Jizhou (August First Studio, 1979).

Sexual Difference and the Viewing Subject in *Li Shuangshuang* and *The In-laws*

CHRIS BERRY

I was initially attracted to a comparison of *Li Shuangshuang* (1962) and *The In-Laws* (1981) by their foregrounding of young married women in conflict with their families. However, I have come to consider these two films comparable on a broader basis because they share a whole array of common characteristics. Both are 'rural-theme' films made at the Shanghai studios. Both won many prizes in the Golden Rooster and the Hundred Flowers awards, the latter chosen by the vote of subscribers to the mass circulation magazine *Popular Film*. *Li Shuangshuang* prompted the publication of a special volume by the China Film Press,[1] and a series of pieces about *The In-Laws* appeared in a special section of the 1982 *China Film Yearbook*.[2] Both were apparently very popular at the box office, and I am told that with ticket sales in excess of 560 million by the end of 1982, *The In-Laws* is the most popular Chinese film ever made.[3]

Although the nature of an audience's relationship with a film is a highly debatable area, the popularity indicated above would seem to suggest that these films constituted something generally acceptable and recognisable to their broad audiences, including the authorities, in China. Since both films are also fairly representative of other contemporary cinematic output in the People's Republic, both in their representation of women and in their cinematic style, this suggests that my remarks on sexual difference and the viewing subject may have some broader significance, not only in terms of sexual ideology but also in terms of the Chinese cinema itself.

Turning now to the films themselves, I would like to take a lead from Christian Metz's analysis of cinematic *langue*, and separate out two levels of the filmic texts which I shall refer to as 'the cinematic' and 'the representational.'[4] The representational level consists of those elements that might be considered to refer directly to a reality (real or imagined) outside the cinema, such as characters, settings, costume and so on. The cinematic level consists of those elements specific to the cinema: camera angles, editing strategies, and so on. It is on the representational level alone that I am interested in examining sexual difference in the first part of this essay.

On this level, there is a marked difference between *Li Shuangshuang* and *The In-Laws* in their representation of women that is immediately striking, and all the more relevant because they are only the most thoroughgoing examples of what I believe to be a general change. Both films construct their narrative around family strife and its resolution. In both cases aggressive young wives are represented in conflict with their families. In the case of *Li Shuangshuang*, this is the title character with her husband Xiwang and his kinsmen in the village. In *The In-Laws*, it is the eldest daughter-in-law Qiangying with a whole extended family living in the same compound, including her husband, who, not insignificantly, is also a Party cadre. In each film a positive resolution restoring harmony to the families is achieved, and this resolution is in line with the policies expressed by Party officials in each film. However, the alignment of these various forces (the family, the young wife, the Party) is different from film to film. In the case of *Li Shuangshuang*, the Party officials side with her against her husband's feudal opposition to women's participation in labour and his nepotistic practices. But in *The In-Laws*, the Party opposes Qiangying's selfish concern with her husband and children over her other relatives, in particular her mother-in-law and grandfather-in-law, whom she does not wish to care for in their old age.

Apart from a change in the representation of the main concerns of the Party in its dealings with the rural family, I believe this realignment is also significant as an ideological change concerning the representation of women. In both films, there is no narrative reason why the gender of the characters could not have been reversed without in any way changing any other element of the films, including the representation of Party policy. There is no apparent reason why Li Shuangshuang's husband could not have been the progressive element, or Qiangying's husband the selfish one in *The In-Laws*. In other words, there is no reason to dismiss the factor of gender as coincidental, as not significant in its own right.

Indeed, in *Li Shuangshuang*, the character's support of the Great Leap is coincident with an assertion of her independence as a woman. She signs her poster with her own name, not simply as 'Xiwang's wife', and her desire to work outside the home is constructed in opposition to her husband's belief that he should not help out with the domestic labour just because she has taken it upon herself to work outside the home. On the other hand, in *The In-Laws* Qiangying's selfishness is constructed in contrast to her husband's spinelessness: towards the end of the film, grandfather tells him outright that the problem with Qiangying is partly his fault too, because he never kept her under control. Finally, whereas in *Li Shuangshuang* the Party supports what it recognises as her desire for a measure of independence, in *The In-Laws* Qiangying's desire for independence is constructed as selfishness, and the Party is seen supporting a family which, if not exactly feudal, is definitely patriarchal. When the time comes for the family to be divided, it is the Party official who takes the mediating position of Qiangying's dead father-in-law.

These contrasting representations bring out in exemplary clarity the changes that the representation of women has undergone in the cinema

31

of the People's Republic of China, for they are only the most extreme instances of a general change. Before 1976, the year of the downfall of the 'gang of four', it was unknown for women to take the role of lead villain. At most, they might appear as the reluctantly supportive wives of male villains. Now, however, selfish and uncaring aggressive women are almost commonplace. Audiences might have been delighted with *Li Shuangshuang*, but in my experience they positively cheer when Qiangying's husband finally turns round and slaps her in the face (tight close-up). If this change is claimed by some to be more realistic, then it must be remembered that realism is a convention, and if Qiangying can now be considered a realistic representation, as many of the Chinese articles cited above attest, this speaks for itself.

However, although the representational levels of these films undoubtedly lend themselves readily to interpretation in terms of Western discourses on gender ('the battles of the sexes', 'women's liberation', 'male chauvinism', and so forth), this does not mean that this is all there is to say about the issue. Firstly, none of the numerous Chinese articles cited above figures the films in terms of these discourses, or discourses on gender corresponding to them. The 'problem of women' simply doesn't appear. Rather, *Li Shuangshuang* is referred to the increased production needs of the Great Leap, and *The In-Laws* to inter-generational dispute. I will return to this intriguing absence towards the end of this essay.

Secondly, although examinations of the representational such as the above are useful in themselves, to be complete they must be complemented by analysis that takes into account the cinematic level I mentioned earlier. The cinematic is never a neutral 'window' onto the representational. Rather it interacts with it in various ways to produce meaning, whether through framing, angle, editing or whatever. Western film studies have in fact alerted us to the particular importance of the cinematic as a level on which represented sexual difference is organised for the viewing subject, and so in these circumstances investigation of this second level seems particularly important. Therefore, at the risk of gross reduction, I should like briefly to outline some of the recent developments in the context of which I wish to situate my examination of this second level.

Recent studies of the cinematic level in the West have concerned themselves mostly with the figuration and analysis of the classic American filmic text. They have noted the camera's status as a mechanism confined to the construction of the subject-place. This latter generally corresponds to the place of the camera, towards which the represented is organised to produce meaning.[5] As a development in Western culture, the origins of this subject-place so fundamental to the cinema may be traced back to Quattrocento painting.[6] This also has further ideological parallels in the very psychoanalytic discourse of the subject from which the current terminology is drawn. On the more specific level of filmic texts themselves, recent studies have also looked for purely cinematic conventions, such as Metz's inventory of large syntagmatic categories, i.e. types of shot structures.[7] In turn, this concern with conventional structures has become intertwined with the general interest in cinema as a Western technology that I have just outlined in work on the classic American cinema, most notably by Laura Mulvey and Raymond Bellour.[8] It is at this point that sexual difference enters the picture in the conventional interactions of the cinematic level with the representational level. In various places, but most noticeably in his analysis of the opening shots of *Marnie*, Bellour has analysed the consistent association of the camera/subject-place with the place of certain figures in the classic Hollywood text via shot-reverse shot, point-of-view shot and so on, so that these figures then act as relays for the viewing subject, and around which the text tends to be cinematically organised. These relays are typically the figures who guide us through the major part of the narrative, and so our understanding of and perspective on the events of the narrative correspond more closely to theirs than to that of any other figure. They are also typically male, and the object of their gaze is typically female. In this way a whole avenue of fictive subject-object play may be constructed for the pleasure of the viewing subject, and most frequently the final securing of the female figure in a stable object relation to the male subject is constructed as a central problem structuring the narrative of the film. In this Western paradigm, then, the place of male figures, the subject-place and the place in reference to which the text is ordered are all mapped on top of one another so that maleness, subjectivity and centred ordering are all hooked into each other to constitute one phallocentric viewing subject.

Turning back to Chinese film, the subject-place itself must be present here too, for it is inherent in the camera mechanism. However, it remains to be seen whether or not the same cinematic conventions are constructed in the same relations to the representational as in the Bellourian paradigm of Hollywood cinema. Is the subject-place consistently correspondent to the leading male figure, for example? Since the Chinese cinema of the early 60s seems especially close to classic American cinema in many of its cinematic conventions and structures, *Li Shuangshuang* seems a good place to begin this investigation. Furthermore, the narrative of *Li Shuangshuang*, in which the husband has to undergo various adjustments in order not to lose his wife, might lend itself quite plausibly to a male subject/female object play in the Bellourian mode.

However, this is not what happens. The film does not establish the place of the viewing subject in a stable association with the place of any single figure in the text. Although subjective camera and so forth may be used, in some scenes it is associated most heavily with Xiwang, in some with Li Shuangshuang herself, in some with a third figure. If the association of the camera with the place of figures does occur, but not in such a manner as to consistently call upon the close association of the viewing subject with the place of any one figure in the husband-wife oppositional pair, what then is the relation of the viewing subject to the figures in the text here, and how is sexual difference organised?

I would now like to refer to one of the most pronounced uses of shot-reverse shot in the film. This is a scene in which Li Shuangshuang's forwardness has again prompted Xiwang's anger, and after which he finally walks out on her.[9] If the cinematic level is examined without regard to its interaction with the representational, the scene appears to conform to Hollywood practices, progressing from establishing shot to shot-reverse shot exchange and out again. The first shot (198) is an over-the-shoulder shot of Xiwang peeking out of the window, waiting for Shuangshuang to return. The film then cuts to an interior long shot as Shuangshuang enters screen-left to find Xiwang screen-right packing up to leave (199). These two shots function to let us know that Xiwang is staging his departure for Shuangshuang's benefit.

Were this scene to conform to some of the expectations aroused by the classic American cinema, we might speculate that this shot (199) would be followed by, say, a point-of-view shot of Xiwang. This would place the viewing subject with Shuangshuang, signifying the role reversal that Xiwang has instituted, threatening to leave before Shuangshuang herself does, so that she may perceive his fear that she is stepping out of the

198

199

Li Shuangshuang   200

201

34

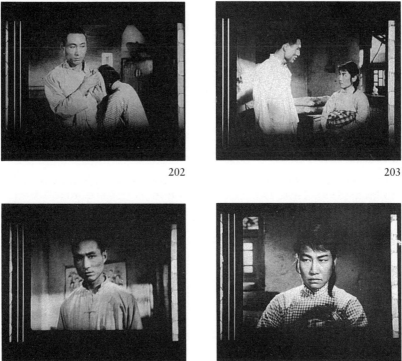

202

203

204

205

subject-object relation in her assertiveness and that he is about to lose her. Nothing of the sort occurs. Instead, in the next two shots (200, 201), the camera maintains a position from which two-shots may be constructed (shots with both figures within the same frame). Xiwang is at this time marching about the room, complaining. I would suggest that this strategy signifies the fragility of their bond at this juncture, in that, although they are maintained in the same frame, there is a constant threat that Xiwang will breach the frame. This effect is underlined by the ever greater angles of cut from shot to shot here.

Xiwang finally stops marching about in the fifth shot, also a two-shot (202), when Shuangshuang desperately agrees to listen to his conditions for staying on and throws herself on him to prevent him from leaving. As far as the viewing subject is concerned, this action also stops Xiwang from breaking the frame. This is a crucial shot in my argument here, because the camera is so placed that the viewing subject may see what Shuangshuang may not. This is the expression on Xiwang's face, full of satisfaction that his ploy has apparently worked. Like the first shot (198), this can only be read as putting the viewing subject on Shuangshuang's side, but without putting them in her place. In other words, the viewing subject is positioned in regard to figures by being constructed in a place

35

206

207

208

209

shared by no figure on the representational level.

During this fifth shot and the next one, also a two-shot and a relatively long take (203), the couple remains stable in the frame as Xiwang lists his conditions. This seems appropriate to what is a period of apparent rapprochement, in terms of the rationale I have offered for shots 199 to 201.

However, as Xiwang finishes his conditions, all of which place restrictions on Shuangshuang's activities, the long take cuts to a point-of-view shot from Shuangshuang's place, showing Xiwang now towering above her (204), and then to a reverse shot of her (205). This is a classic subject-object construct. However, when the reverse shot (205) shows the viewing subject Shuangshuang's anger, Xiwang's phallocentric assertion is made to carry a connotation very different from that of a normative paradigm. It stands rather as transgression, and is followed by further shots in the shot-reverse shot structure in which Shuangshuang turns the tables on him and throws his bedding at him, rejecting him (206–208). Here the editing maintains the shot-reverse shot structure with each figure in separate frames, and this functions here to signify to the viewing subject the collapse of harmony. The extremely negative connotation of this structure and the represented situation are confirmed by Shuangshuang's collapse into tears, her back to Xiwang and the camera, and isolated in the frame (209).

What I am suggesting, then, is that in this example the Western phallo-centrism detailed by Bellour is constructed in Chinese filmic discourse not as a primary mode for the viewing subject to be protected and asserted, but as a place of transgression and failure to be avoided. This is not to say, I wish to stress, that different roles for male and female figures are not constructed within the text, or that activities are not subject to the sanction of Party officials who are almost always male, but this is con-fined mostly to the representational level. What it does suggest, however, is that in the case of the Chinese cinema, the position of the viewing subject is not necessarily hooked up to questions of maleness in the same way as in the West. If this is to be demonstrated, it is necessary to find examples from other films.

The film I intend to turn to for this purpose is *The In-Laws*. At first sight the two films appear to have as little in common as far as their cinematic style is concerned as they do in terms of sexual difference on the representational level. *The In-Laws* is faster-paced, and, whereas *Li Shuangshuang* is dominated by two-shots with occasional descents into pronounced shot-reverse shot, as in the example discussed above, *The In-Laws* is much less prone to two-shots, tending more to mobile camera, fast cutting and unconventional angles, as well as to quite a lot of shot-reverse shot.

Despite these apparent differences, I want to argue that the same conventions tending to divorce the place of the viewing subject from the figures in the text are operating here also. I would like to draw attention to two shots, which if you have seen the film, I am sure you will remem-ber, since they draw attention to themselves by virtue of their unusual-ness. These are two 360° pans, one occurring mid-way through the film when the family is on the verge of breaking up, the other at the end of the film when they are reunited. In both cases, all the family members are seated around a table and the shot pans, or attempts to pan, full circle right-to-left from a centred point apparently somewhere on the table.

Just as Li Shuangshuang and Xiwang were tenuously maintained in the same two-shot at the beginning of the example quoted above, so the first 360° pan attempts to hold the family group in *The In-Laws* together in the same unbroken circular shot. The difficulties of doing this are signi-fied by the jerky, uneven pace of the pan as it tries to keep up with the increasingly tense interjections of various figures. And, as in the *Li Shuangshuang* example, the shot structure collapses into rapid shot-reverse shot as the discussion breaks into open and angry accusations, and the family group collapses into warring individuals and factions both literally and cinematically in the shot-reverse shot structure itself.

In contrast, the final shots of the film use the same conventions in a positive manner when the family is seated round the table again, and all difficulties have been resolved. The camera pans smoothly round the

37

table. And then, when the pan is completed, the film cuts to a bird's-eye view of the family symmetrically arranged in a circle, looking up at the camera. Finally, they are reunited in the one frame.

In these two examples from *Li Shuangshuang* and *The In-Laws*, I have examined the relation between the camera place and the place of the figures in the text to suggest a conventional association of the camera place with textual figures only to signify moments of transgression, failure, and collapse of harmony. This is contrasted to the positive connotations attached to the containment of the members of the group or couple units in the same shot, and preferably in the same frame. Now, it is necessary to complete this second section of my essay by asking where this leaves the Chinese viewing subject, since, unlike in the classic American cinema, he/she is not being called upon to participate through a triumphant phallocentrically constructed figure. I would suggest that if there is no represented figure in the text corresponding to the place toward which the Chinese filmic text is organised, then the viewer is given to understand that the place of the viewing subject in the Chinese cinema is a privileged place of perception. This third place might possibly be termed the place of a 'transcendent' or 'objective' subject, although such a term might only tend to reify the filmic construct itself. Furthermore, this place of the Chinese subject is constructed in contrast to a negative alternative, namely those shot structures that put the viewing subject in the place of a figure in the text. I would suggest that this negative alternative may be interpreted as working to communicate to the viewing subject that although he/she may associate with a figure in the text by way of a mirror relation, the place of these figures on the representational level, and presumably the corresponding places of the viewer in the life outside the cinema, are not to be confused with the abstract place of order to which the viewing subject is given privileged access in the cinema.

This Chinese convention, then, constitutes part of an anti-individualistic aesthetic, contrary to the Western paradigm, and clearly worthy of further investigation. For example, I would like to consider how this Chinese viewing subject relates to the narrative characteristics of Chinese film. It is my impression that these latter include a concern with the group and its maintenance in a play of separation and reunion, rather than the subject-object play Bellour and others have pointed to in the classic American cinema.

I would like to conclude this particular essay by returning to an earlier issue raised here, and suggesting that understanding this aesthetic may also go some way to enabling us to understand the absence of a discourse centring on gender in the Chinese discussions of these films, and similar to that which constitutes the first part of this essay. Looking again at the example from *Li Shuangshuang*, it can be seen that the viewing subject in the third place is not gender-identified, and that the place of the viewing subject only becomes gender-identified when associated with one of the figures in the scene. Since this only happens at negative points in the text, points of transgression, failure and collapse, we should not be too surprised if a discourse of sexual difference concerned with the individual interests of one gender versus the other is absent from discussion of the films as a discourse of individual interests, for in this example it is to the very negative assertion of individual interests that sexual difference is attached.

Notes

1. *Li Shuangshuang: From Short Story to Film* (*Li Shuangshuang: cong juben dao dianying*. Beijing: China Film Press [Zhongguo dianying chubanshe], 1963).
2. *1982 China Film Yearbook* (*Zhongguo dianying nianjian*. Beijing: China Film Press [Zhongguo dianying chubanshe], 1983).
3. Conversation with Professor Cheng Jihua of the China Film Association and the Beijing Film Academy, Los Angeles, November 1983.
4. Cf. Metz's discussion of the distinctions between 'the filmic' and 'the cinematic', which constitutes the problematic of *Language and Cinema* (The Hague: Mouton, 1974). While my use of 'the cinematic' corresponds exactly to Metz's term, it should of course be noted that 'the filmic' may contain elements which are not representational, e.g. narrative structure.
5. Cf. Christian Metz, *The Imaginary Signifier* (Bloomington: Indiana University Press, 1982), and Jean-Louis Baudry, 'Ideological Effects of the Basic Cinematographic Apparatus', *Film Quarterly* 28:2, 1974/5.
6. Stephen Heath, 'Narrative Space', *Screen* 17:3, 1976.
7. Christian Metz, 'Problems of Denotation in the Fiction Film', in *Film Language: A Semiotics of the Cinema* (New York: Oxford University Press, 1974).
8. Laura Mulvey, 'Visual Pleasure and Narrative Cinema', *Screen* 16:3, 1975, and 'Mulvey on *Duel in the Sun*', *Framework*, vol. 6, Summer 1981; Raymond Bellour, 'To Segment, To Analyse', *Quarterly Review of Film Studies* 1:3, 1976; 'Hitchcock, The Enunciator', *Camera Obscura* no. 2, 1977 (on *Marnie*); and 'Psychosis, Neurosis, Perversion', *Camera Obscura* nos. 3–4, 1979. The same edition of *Camera Obscura* contains a complete bibliography of Bellour's work to 1979.
9. See illustrations. The numbers that follow in parentheses here refer to shot numbers as provided in the shooting script contained in the volume referred to in note 1 above.

Filmography

NB: s = scenarist, d = director.

Li Shuangshuang (*Li Shuangshuang*), s: Li Zhun, d: Lu Ren (Shanghai: Haiyan Studio, 1962).

Xi Ying Men (*The In-Laws*), s: Xin Xianling, d: Zhao Huanzhang (Shanghai Studio, 1981).

Two Hundred Flowers on China's Screens

PAUL CLARK

'Let a hundred flowers bloom, let a hundred schools contend' is a conventional Chinese expression which has been applied to intellectual and artistic discussion since the Warring States period (403–221 B.C.). Mao Zedong used the ancient phrase in 1956 to encapsulate an unconventional period for a Communist leader, in which he encouraged debate and criticism of his own regime. Mao was attracted to toy with liberalisation by the examples of de-Stalinisation in the Soviet Union and of the consequences of Communist ridigity in Hungary that year. After initial hesitation many scholars, writers and film-makers answered Mao's call with often bitter denunciations of aspects of life since the founding of the People's Republic in 1949. In 1957 the authorities responded in some alarm with an 'anti-rightist' backlash, and the flowers withered.

In the late 1970s, after recovery from the chaos of the 'cultural revolution' (1966–9) had got under way following the arrest of the 'gang of four' in October 1976, a new period of relative liberalisation began. Not inappropriately, it was labelled the 'second Hundred Flowers'. Again, film-makers were active in the discourse, their films reflecting the climate of the new cultural thaw.

Over twenty years apart, these two periods when artistic debate and relative boldness were encouraged reveal a great deal about the politics of Chinese film-making. The experience of the two Hundred Flowers also illuminates the place which film occupied in Chinese cultural life in the late 1950s and the 1970s. In both periods the tripartite relationship between Party, film-makers and audiences was directly discussed and in consequence modified, even if to a large extent unconsciously. The differences in the nature of these relationships in the 1950s and the 1970s is striking. In the late 1950s film-makers were closely tied to Party control and expectations, to a degree because of the weakness of linkages between artists and their audiences. At the time of the first Hundred Flowers the Party decided what audiences needed and how film-makers should cater to these needs. By the late 1970s the relationships had changed. Certainly the pre-eminent position of the Party as arbiter of cultural policy and censor had never been threatened. Film-makers' understanding of audiences, however, had matured considerably. Likewise audiences' and artists' views of the Communist Party had altered, allowing for a more sustained critique of the three-way connections. In this respect, the second Hundred Flowers reflected broader changes in Chinese society, for which Mao may have wished in the back of his mind in 1956. Ironically, twenty years later his successors were dismantling much of his legacy.

For the first Hundred Flowers period (1956–7) the following discussion will concentrate on the criticisms raised by the film-makers, since the brevity of the blooming allowed few new films to be completed and shown. The discussion of the second Hundred Flowers (1978–81), however, will centre on some of the films which typified the new climate and the advances made since the 1950s.

When the call came in the late spring of 1956 for one hundred flowers to bloom on China's screens, the film industry had recently passed through what was officially known as the 'transition to socialism' in both managerial and artistic terms. State ownership of the film studios, and much of the rest of the industry, had been achieved, and films put emphasis on socialist themes and styles. Inasmuch as this transition had been neither smooth nor complete, as we shall see below, the call for the type of discourse envisioned by Mao in the 'hundred flowers' expression promised to be a further unsettling factor in the art industry.

When the People's Republic was founded in 1949, most of the movies shown on China's screens were not Chinese. This situation remained little changed until the late 1950s, because the shortfall between the once dominant American features (not shown after 1951) and the few Chinese films which were being produced was made up with other foreign films, in the 1950s mainly from the Soviet Union and Eastern Europe.

Chinese film production was unable to fill the gap left by the disappearance of American movies for several years, largely because of political pressure on film-makers. The most celebrated example was the 1951 criticism of *The Life of Wu Xun*. Wu Xun was a nineteenth-century peasant who had begged and saved enough money to found a school for the poor in his native district. Although something of a cultural hero for socially conscious intellectuals in the 1930s and 1940s, Wu Xun was considered outdated, at least by Mao Zedong and other critics, when his film biography was finally completed in 1951. The film-maker's attempts at a 'critical biography' of Wu Xun did not disguise the fact that he had worked within the existing imperial social and political system with a reformist rather than a revolutionary ethos.[1]

The Life of Wu Xun was the product of a privately owned Shanghai film company, and the campaign against the film also indicated the attitudes of the new regime to such private studios and to the cosmopolitan, somewhat undisciplined Shanghai film world in general. While the film medium offered the greatest potential as a tool for the creation of a socialist mass culture, film artists were distrusted by the Communist Party cultural leadership as having bourgeois, cosmopolitan and elitist tendencies inimical to the new cultural policies. After the 1951 campaign, the uncertainty of film artists and the caution of managers of the studios, whether state-owned or private, caused a slow-down in production which extended to the mid-1950s. The last private studios, kept going for over a year by subsidies from the government, were nationalised in early 1953.

Political pressure on film-making came also in the period before the first Hundred Flowers in the form of strictures on the artistic content and style of films. The Chinese version of what the Italians called 'neo-realism' had been a feature of the 'golden age' of Chinese cinema in the late 1940s. 'Socialist realism' superseded neo-realism in the early 1950s, even if it received more lip-service in print than any clear articulation on celluloid. What the new artistic ideal meant in reality, however, was a narrowing of subject matter and styles in response to the simultaneous broadening of audiences to include working people and some peasants. Party cultural authorities felt that simplification and familiarity of film settings, stories and styles would make the new films more accessible for these new audiences who were unfamiliar with film. The urbane tragi-comedies and social melodramas of the late 1940s were replaced by socialist melodramas set in either urban workplaces or the countryside. Here again film-makers' adjustment to the new artistic conditions required time: writing on film in the period emphasised the need for film artists to 'go down' to familiarise themselves with the lives of the ordinary proletarian heroes they were now expected to portray.

Complicating the effect of these pressures on film-makers and their relationships with the Party and with audiences were divisions within the artistic ranks. Three major groups can be discerned. Those artists who had undergone the experience of socialist training in the wake of Mao's *Talks at the Yan'an Forum on Literature and Art* during the war years (1937–45) in the Communist Party headquarters in Yan'an tended to enjoy the greater confidence of the Party authorities and were often placed in positions of some responsibility in the film industry. The majority of film-makers did not spend the war under direct Party tutelage in Yan'an, but in Guomindang-controlled areas or in Shanghai under Japanese occupation. As in other artistic fields, these people were less trusted and less powerful, despite their considerable film experience. A third group were those new recruits to film-making, the majority coming to the studios after a few years in the armed forces' cultural groups, and who responded to their own lack of experience with disquiet and caution towards the cultural leadership above them and towards the artists in their charge.

The new atmosphere of the first Hundred Flowers was epitomised by the six weeks of 'blooming' in the summer of 1957, although it extended, albeit in attenuated form, from the previous spring. In some respects it ameliorated and in others it complicated the political pressures which had been at the root of the various problems of film-making hitherto. The criticisms of the film industry made by film-makers, viewers and other individuals towards the end of 1956 and through the Hundred Flowers spring and summer presented an unvarnished picture of the context in which film-makers operated and the nature of the art industry. The criticisms concentrated on two interrelated issues: the problem of leadership in the film industry, and the shortcomings seen in the films produced by this industry.

The reported criticisms directed against the leadership were expressed, when not with sarcasm, in two virtual codewords prominent in all types of Hundred Flowers critique: dogmatism (*jiaotiaozhuyi*) and sectarianism (*zongpaizhuyi*). The former was manifested, the critics argued, in unrealistic demands being made on film-makers by the Party leadership since 1949. Xia Yan, the most successful scenarist in the 1930s and 1940s, and now in charge of cultural work in Shanghai, himself noted how artists were expected to do a bit of everything: making films in the form of 'commemorative monuments' for the heroes of the past, while at the same time tying their work into current political movements and campaigns.[2]

Dogmatism was also reflected in excessive interference in artists' work, both from the studio-level management and from outside the studios, from the Film Bureau of the state Ministry of Culture and from the Party's Propaganda Department. At each level of the film production system – from the centre down to the studios – there was a parallel structure of Party and non-Party or managerial leadership. In reality, however, at all levels the voice of the Party – in a section of the studio, at the studio level, in the local cultural offices (for example, the Shanghai Film Bureau), up to the central Film Bureau in the Ministry of Culture – could override other voices. A film script or completed film apparently required approval at each level in this hierarchy, with central approval usually being pro forma. The Hundred Flowers critics complained that unnecessary delays were caused by scripts requiring higher-level approval.[3] Further interference came at later stages in production. One celebrated critique, soon the subject of a strong official backlash, cited the case of prolonged discussion of just when and in what manner the unfortunate heroine of *New Year's Sacrifice*, scripted by Xia Yan from the Lu Xun short story, should drop a sacrificial fish. Similar careful high-level censorial attention was paid to the behaviour of dogs, to whether characters should wear black-framed spectacles, and to how an actor should express thanks or even knock on a door.[4]

The Film Bureau and other cultural leaders acknowledged this problem of 'dogmatism', as indeed they had, though less emphatically, for the preceding several years. The most acerbic Hundred Flowers critics, however, were not satisfied by general statements that inexperience in how to manage a socialist cultural enterprise had caused the problems raised by the critics. The division of the huge Shanghai Film Studio in April 1957 into three feature film units (the Haiyan, Tianma and Jiangnan studios) was apparently motivated by an urge to placate the critics by decentralising some levels of leadership in Shanghai film-making.[5] The move did not persuade one commentator: 'They are changing the soup, not the main courses,' he complained.[6] Similarly, promises by the cultural leadership to take more account of the artistic peculiarities of film-making – for example by allowing scenarists to choose their own subjects, and directors the scripts they felt most comfortable with – and to give more autonomy to the studios and to the artistic personnel in the studios were treated with scepticism by many film-makers. Lü Ban, an actor since the 1930s in Shanghai and now a director at the Changchun studio in the north-east, reportedly saw little chance for one hundred flowers to bloom. 'There is no spring in Changchun: all seasons are winter.'[7]

A major reason for the chilly atmosphere in the film industry was the other main target of the critics, namely persistent 'sectarianism', especially in the tendency of the Communist Party cadres to distrust and discriminate against non-Party personnel. This was also acknowledged in part by cultural authorities. In the film-making context one object of such discrimination against non-Party personnel was those film artists who had been active before 1949. Although now outnumbered in film-making circles by newer recruits, the older, more experienced artists were a vital element in the art industry. But the Hundred Flowers criticisms still looked upon the former denizens of the Shanghai film world as tainted by unorthodoxy and cosmopolitanism. It was probably reasonable on the part of the authorities to presume that the makers of petit-bourgeois fantasies in the 1940s had not been uniformly transformed in the space of a few years into committed socialist artists. The 1956–7 voicing of criticisms about 'sectarianism', however, suggests that many in cultural leadership went further, holding on to a view of art and artists moulded in the mountain fastness of Yan'an. Film, perhaps the most alien and distant from the Yan'an experience, was therefore the most liable to intervention. This tendency was reinforced by an awareness of the potentially vital function of film (in Lenin's misquoted phrase, 'the most important art'), as the most accessible component in the new socialist culture.[8]

The Film Bureau of the Ministry of Culture, anxious to improve relations between the Party and film-makers, acknowledged its 'sectarianism' in a May 1957 reassessment of awards for the best films and film artists of the period 1949–56. *Crows and Sparrows*, made by a group of prominent leftist artists at the Kunlun Studios in Shanghai before the fall of the Guomindang and released after 1949, was added to the awards list. Its inclusion was a recognition of the contribution to Chinese film of non-Party artists. Apologies were also made for slighting the contribution of older actors who had been active before 1949 but had had little opportunity to practise their craft since then.[9] A similar gesture towards granting film-makers a measure of autonomy during the Hundred Flowers six weeks was the establishment of a formal, and nominally independent, organisation of film-makers, the Film Workers Association. Its list of aims made no mention of socialist realism, referring instead to 'new films of a socialist national nature'. The Association's executive included such experienced film artists as Sun Yu, the writer-director of the previously stigmatised *The Life of Wu Xun*.[10]

The relatively open discourse in 1956–7 (and the subsequent 'Anti-Rightist' accusations) revealed that, quite apart from the 'sectarianism' alleged by the critics to be pursued by the cultural leadership, there were considerable divisions and factions within film-making circles themselves. Encouraging expression of grievances made this clearer than ever before. Most notable were generational cleavages among film artists. The plight of under-employed younger actors associated with the Changchun studios were reported in a controversial article in the *Literary Gazette* in which details were offered of the failure to pay attention to the actors' problems on the part of Lu Dingyi, head of the Propaganda Department, Chen Huangmei, deputy head of the Film Bureau, and other high-level bureaucrats.[11] Disaffection was also apparent on the part of older film-makers, as was some sense of superiority towards less experienced or, in their view, less sensitive artists. Lü Ban, leader of a comedy-making group at Changchun, reportedly scoffed at those who had made earlier 'socialist realist' films. 'Just rely on Yan Xiucen and Han Lan'gen [two Shanghai comics hardly associated with socialist heroics] and you've got it made.'[12] Several artists who had been active before 1949 were said to have sought more power for experienced directors like themselves and their friends, and to have fanned the flames of discontent within film circles in Shanghai, where the cultural leadership was drawn from ex-Yan'an ranks. In contrast, a major proportion of older Shanghai film artists had spent the Anti-Japanese war years in Guomindang or Japanese-controlled areas.[13]

This factionalism within film-making ranks, like the weakness of connections between film-makers and their expanding audiences, made it easier for the third party in this tripartite relationship, the cultural authorities, to use 'divide and rule' policies to preserve their pre-eminent position. Events during the second Hundred Flowers two decades later showed that the Party could no longer count on the divisions and isolation of artists.

Moving on from the charges levelled at the leadership of the film industry in the form of 'dogmatism' and 'sectarianism', the second area of Hundred Flowers criticism in 1956–7 was cultural policy as applied to film art and the films which had been produced under this policy. Most of the criticisms singled out not socialist realism, which had never been emphatically endorsed, but the orientation to serve workers, peasants and soldiers (*gongnongbing*). This orientation in film had encouraged a concentration on proletarian subjects and simple styles based on linear narrative. Zhong Dianfei, soon to be condemned as a 'Rightist', approached the problem with a directness not seen since the *gongnong-*

45

bing artistic orientation was presented as Party policy by Mao in his 1942 Yan'an *Talks* on literature and art. Concern about box-office performance had been condemned since 1949, particularly when moves were made to abolish the popular American and other bourgeois films at the start of the 1950s. In his celebrated, and anonymous, critique, published in early December in the *Literary Gazette*, Zhong argued that the box-office record of many recent films was a warning about problems with this *gongnongbing* policy.[14] More than 70 per cent of the films made since 1953 (alluding to the year in which the last of the private studios had been nationalised) did not recoup their costs, with some earning a mere 10 per cent. Box-office returns like these indicated that the connection between audiences and art, a major concern of Mao in his Yan'an *Talks*, was in danger of being severed.[15] Zhong laid the blame for the imminent break on a tendency to treat the *gongnongbing* orientation of art and literature in an abstract yet ossified way. If the orientation deserved more than lip service, careful consideration on how it might best be put into effect needed to be done. However, four months later, on the eve of the Hundred Flowers six weeks, Xia Yan warned against confusing problems of leadership with the correctness of the *gongnongbing* orientation itself. While repudiating Zhong Dianfei's questioning of the *gongnongbing* orientation, Xia on the other hand implied that the cultural leadership should not use adherence to the orientation to divert or dismiss legitimate questioning of their actions.[16]

The results that could be seen on the screen of this general loosening of censorial standards and greater openness (*fang*, as opposed to *shou*, control), were more limited and less bold than the written and reported criticisms. This is not surprising, for film's potential to reach a wide audience made it more sensitive than long articles in newspapers or the *Literary Gazette*. The cost and other resources committed to a film also encouraged caution at all levels, and the time needed to produce a feature film was another contributing factor. Over twenty years later, in the late 1970s, these factors again meant that cultural liberalisation on China's screens was more circumscribed than in other media.

Nevertheless, the new elements in many 1956–7 films should not be underestimated. Comedy films were attempted for the first time in many years and subject matter became broader than it had been since at least 1949. The best known of the new comedies was *Before the New Director Arrives*, based on the play of the same name. Comedy is used in the film to satirise the false expectations of both cadres and workers in a government bureau. A new director will shortly take over. The present deputy uses the occasion to ostentatiously redecorate the offices, diverting manpower and other resources to this task. The new director turns up unannounced and observes all the fuss before revealing his identity, to the horror of his deputy and the delight of the young workers who had questioned the correctness of the preparations. The comparatively fast pacing of the film preserves the spirit of comedy while making sure the satirical points are made. The exemplary character of the new director is also made clear, but indirectly through his early arrival, unlike the direct presentation of the heroes of *gongnongbing* dramas.

In addition to style, the subject matter of the 1957 films also changed from the narrow concentration on usually dour worker, peasant and soldier heroes in the films of the previous half-decade. Typical of the new films was *Loyal Partners*, made at the Shanghai studios, which had intellectuals as its heroes. Hong Lieguang, the director of a microbiology research institute, invites an old friend, Huang Weiwen, to join him in researching a new antibiotic. Unfortunately, Huang's attitude to research is very conservative, causing delays in the project and anguish to his friend. Huang is forced to make bolder efforts, however, in order to save Hong's life when the latter becomes infected by the bacteria they are using in the experiment. Prompted by his affection for Hong and with the encouragement of his younger colleagues, Huang produces the new vaccine and all ends well.

While this bare plot outline suggests that the themes of *Loyal Partners* were little different from earlier films, the types of character who articulated these themes certainly were new. Dr Huang was played by Xiang Kun, who had until then specialised in portraying maniacal Guomindang generals and other unsavoury types. As if to compensate for the unfamiliar class-status of these new-style heroes, whose weapons were microscopes not machine-guns, and perhaps to indicate to audiences how they might respond to them, Shi Hui, a character actor well-known since the 40s, played the part of 'Old Zhou' (he does not have the benefit of a personal name in the script). A caretaker at the institute, Old Zhou respects and loves the younger and higher-ranking scientists, an introduction to the movie in *Popular Film* noted.[17] A viewer need not be an anti-intellectual left extremist to detect a patronising element associated with this character.

It may not be surprising, therefore, that several persons involved with *Loyal Partners* were condemned as 'Rightists' when the Party put an end to the Hundred Flowers discourse after June 1957. Xiang Kun and Shi Hui were so labelled. The film was said to make a case for friendship above class feeling by having Huang really apply himself to the research project only once his friend (and brother-in-law) must be cured. Such bourgeois 'sentimentalism' (*wenqing momo*) and the absence of the Party's leadership in scientific endeavours and care for scientists caused the film to be banned.[18] Shi Hui was also accused of using his considerable prestige in Shanghai to influence younger film-makers to support the now inflammatory aspirations for artistic autonomy expressed in the previous months.[19] However, the Party leadership was clearly sensitive to charges that they were singling out older artists for criticism, and divide and rule was now applied, with artists like director Cai Chusheng and actress Shu Xiuwen reportedly making criticisms of 'Rightists' who had been their colleagues in the 1940s.[20]

The strongest attacks in the 'Anti-Rightist' campaign during the second half of 1957 were directed at the comedies which had come out of the Changchun studios under the direction of another pre-1949 star, Lü Ban. Lü had taken great pains to publicly express foreboding that satirical comedy might get into trouble, seemingly with the intention of disarming the critics, when his movie, *Before the New Director Arrives*, was released in 1956.[21] A year later the critics responded, accusing Lü Ban and his colleagues of using satire to attack the Party and undermine socialist morality. Lü, a member of the Communist Party, was said to have added his own notions that 'the old society had not died, but was living healthily on in the new' to the script of the film. Lü's meddling with the film script helped explain why the 1954 play from which the film was drawn could have won national drama awards in that year. Slapstick and other farcical elements in this and two other film comedies, *The Man Unconcerned with Details*, and the prophetically titled *Unfinished Comedy*, were cited by the critics as evidence of taking satirical licence too far. One of the characters in the last-named film, for example, is 'an authority in literary criticism' with a name homophonous with 'A Bludgeon' (*yi bangzi*).[22] Other 'Rightists' condemned in 1957 included Party member Guo Wei, the director of a very orthodox 1955 soldier-hero biography, *Dong Cunrui*, and Wu Yin, who, like several other Shanghai 'Rightist' film artists, had her membership of the nominally independent political party, the China Democratic League, used against her by the 1957 counter-attackers. Wu Yin had played the hero's mother in the 1947 *A Spring River Flows East*.[23]

While the suffering and cultural loss caused by the 'Anti-Rightist' movement should not be underestimated, a curious epilogue in film circles provides a caution against making too bleak a reading of the event. In December 1958, *People's Daily* published a lengthy article titled 'Resolutely wrench out the white flag on the screens: a critique of mistaken ideological tendencies in 1957 films'. Written by Chen Huangmei, responsible for feature film production in the Culture Ministry's Film Bureau and a target of Hundred Flowers criticisms by Changchun actors, the article made a detailed and bitter analysis of the whole film industry, which it characterised as dominated by unrepentant bourgeois artists.[24] Given the passage of eighteen months since the 'Anti-Rightist' campaign began, Chen's acerbic tone seemed out of place in the rhetorical fervour of Great Leap Forward enthusiasm. Three months later the unusual joint publication of an open letter from the secretary of the Film Workers Association and what amounted to an apology by Chen himself showed that wilder interventionist urges on the part of the cultural authorities could encounter some limits.[25] If compromise is too strong a characterisation, something close to it was advisable if the Party was to have access to the special skills which film-makers, perhaps the most specialised of artists, possessed.

The temporary attainment of adjustment in the relationship between

48

Party political concerns, artistic sensibilities and what audiences seemed to want to watch was indicated by the relative popularity of many films made in the early 1960s. The 'let a hundred flowers bloom' slogan was never formally abandoned (indeed, because of the person who had used it, it was even referred to during the 'cultural revolution'), but it had little direct connection with the achievements of such films as *Third Sister Liu*, *The Red Detachment of Women*, *Early Spring* and *Serfs*. Three factors help explain these successes. First, direct political intervention from Party and cultural authorities lessened. The unproductive results of heightened intervention in the 'Anti-Rightist' campaign of 1957–8 and in the Great Leap Forward (1958–9) encouraged a pulling back by the more radical wing of the Party in culture as in other areas of Chinese life. Second, artists showed a greater willingness to work together within the new cultural boundaries and an ability to stretch them. With an increased tempo of production and more experience gained by younger artists, the divisions among film-makers which had been revealed during the Hundred Flowers criticisms seem to have become less obtrusive. Cultural policies became more flexible, both in response again to the failure of the late 1950s rigidity and as a reflection of the break with the Soviet Union. Socialist realism was replaced by a looser, more Chinese and all-encompassing slogan, 'Combine revolutionary romanticism and revolutionary realism.' This allowed considerable range, which some film-makers were bold enough to explore. Lastly, the films of the early 1960s evinced increased awareness by both these parties of the tastes and expectations of a third party, namely the film audiences, and a greater willingness to cater to these tastes. The new cultural slogan indicated an awareness of audiences by the cultural authorities. Film-makers' efforts at more variegated subject matters and styles were another indication.

These tripartite relations faltered in the mid-1960s, then ended with the coming of the 'cultural revolution' (1966–9 or, more broadly, 1966–76). The period from the slow resumption of feature film production in 1973 up to and including the late 1970s, when the second Hundred Flowers era began, was a time when the tripartite relationship between Party, artists and audiences was re-established and reconsidered. The progress accelerated, and indeed only became realisable, after the arrest of the 'gang of four' in October 1976. The strength of interventionism in film-making, as elsewhere in cultural life, markedly weakened after the fall of the 'gang'. After more than two years of restoration and uncertainty, comparative liberalisation was actively encouraged from the highest Party leadership in 1978. Referring to the years from 1978 to 1981 as the 'second Hundred Flowers' is not inappropriate, for both in 1956–7 and in the late 1970s a reconsideration of the three-way relationship between Party, artists and audience occurred.

The differences between the two Hundred Flowers periods, however, are obvious and more illuminating than the similarities. In 1956–7, for the first time since the establishment of the People's Republic (if not since the Yan'an *Talks*), the proper role of the Communist Party in creative enterprises had been candidly questioned by Party members and non-members alike. Artists and writers who had been active and prominent before 1949 were notable participants. In 1978–81 the questioning was more indirect, and probably more effective. Whereas the 1956–7 criticisms of aspects of Party policy could be condemned as an attack on the whole Party and its position, the late 1970s criticisms began with a narrower focus. The new Party leadership in fact encouraged the repudiation of their 'gang of four' predecessors in order to legitimate their own position. Accordingly, in its initial stages the late 1970s critique emphasised the destruction wrought by the 'gang of four' and, given this narrower and thoroughly repudiated target, was much bolder than the critique of 1956–7. Soon, however, the distinction between the aberrant wing represented by the 'gang' and the rest of the Party became blurred. The boldness of the criticisms encouraged by the narrow 'gang' target provided a momentum to discussion that went beyond the 'cultural revolution' years to include an increasingly explicit critique of the Party's cultural leadership in general during the previous three decades. The wide-ranging critique included discussion on the tripartite relationship between Party, artists and audiences and was reflected also in the subjects and styles of many of the new films.

The consciousness of history – both of the first Hundred Flowers and of the 'cultural revolution' – extended to all three groups, and meant that the ending of the second Hundred Flowers was less destructive and more ambiguous than the backlash of 1957.

The important part played in 1978–81 by younger critics was another difference from the earlier period. The so-called Democracy Wall movement which peaked in the spring of 1979 was a young persons' activity and subject to far fewer constraints than the formal criticism meetings of 1957 and publication of debates in a controlled press. In film-making itself, the younger generation was also a major element in the late 1970s blooming.

Much of the importance of youth in films' second Hundred Flowers can be explained by reference to the seven-year hiatus after 1966 in both recruitment and artistic creation. When the film industry attempted full restoration after 1976, the corps of film-makers consisted of two groups: older artists and technicians, some of whom had worked in the early 70s on screen versions of the Jiang Qing model performances, others of whom had been in political disgrace, and young recruits of limited experience. An effort continued to be made after 1976 to train a new generation of film-makers to succeed their older colleagues, many of whom had been active since the 1930s.

A parallel shift towards youth also seems to have occurred among film audiences, with younger persons making up a greater proportion of viewers in the late 1970s than they had in the early 60s. This impression may be partly false, encouraged by the tendency in many of the new films to cater to younger audiences more than the films of the pre-'cultural revolution' period had done. By the later 1970s, moreover, film attendance had become a more ordinary part of recreation for a greater part of the population, in both big cities and smaller centres.[26]

The concerns of youth were prominent in the themes of many of the films made during the second Hundred Flowers. Whereas in 1957 the major cinematic change had been an emphasis on comedy, after 1978 films featured often youthful love stories, not infrequently in a setting of the immediate, unhappy past.

The Legend of Tianyun Mountain combined these elements with a subtlety not often seen in more ordinary films made in 1980. Two love stories are intertwined, one happy and the other eventually hurtful. Ironically, one member of the happier couple is a young engineer condemned as a 'Rightist' in 1958 for his outspokenness during the first Hundred Flowers discourses. His exile in the Tianyun mountains is rendered more bearable by the love of a former colleague who makes great sacrifices for her husband and her support of his principles. The other couple consists of the engineer's former fiancée and one of the cadres who had criticised the engineer in 1958. In the late 1970s, when the story is narrated, this couple are both high-level cadres in the Tianyun district, having themselves undergone incarceration during the 'cultural revolution'. The cadre refuses, despite his wife's objections, to re-examine the case of the engineer with a view to reversing the 1958 verdict. The film ends with this marriage in ruins, the verdict reversed and the engineer's wife dead. The future lies with the engineer, the cadre's wife, and more particularly with two other characters: the inquisitive young woman who served as an initial narrator of the story, and the adopted daughter of the engineer.

Youth and love are thus prominent elements in *The Legend of Tianyun Mountain*. But director Xie Jin, who directed one of the three parts of the abortive *Unfinished Comedy* in 1957, along with *The Red Detachment of Women* (1960), *Stage Sisters* (1965), the model opera *On the Docks* (1972), and *Youth* (1977), combines these elements with a vivid re-examination of Chinese history since the late 1950s. The importance of the individual attitudes, guilts and courage of the characters is typical of the films of the second Hundred Flowers. Motivation for the cadre's wife and the engineer's wife, for example, seems to derive from a combination of socialist idealism and personal feelings. All the films made under the cultural dictatorship of Jiang Qing and perhaps most produced in the seventeen years before 1966 strongly discounted the importance of characters' individual emotions. Socialist man or woman acted only for socialist reasons. *The Legend of Tianyun Mountain* was an echo of the 1957 *Loyal Partners*' reminder of the limitations of this proposition.

Love and destruction during the 'cultural revolution' years were themes in a number of films from the second Hundred Flowers period. *Love and Inheritance* contrasts the experiences in love of the son and daughter of the head of an ophthalmology institute. The girl eventually marries her boyfriend, forgiving his earlier participation as a Red Guard in the wrecking of her home, and realising that her dedication to her medical work need not preclude other dedications. Her brother, on the other hand, went astray in the indiscipline of the 'cultural revolution' years and is being pursued by an ambitious and greedy young woman. The father, before his death, acknowledges that he and his late wife had tended to ignore the proper education of the children in their devotion to the revolution and their work. As his children's inheritance, he leaves an unpublished manuscript and a battered case of surgical instruments, given to him by a martyred comrade at Yan'an.

A more direct treatment of the 'cultural revolution' is made in *Reverberations of Life*, a cinematic representation of the Tiananmen Square demonstrations of 5 April 1976 which were a direct inspiration for the Democracy Wall movement during the second Hundred Flowers period. The black and white photography and the editing of some sequences distinguish this film from its more pedestrian contemporaries, notwithstanding its piety towards the memory of Zhou Enlai. *On a Small Street* is a better reflection of the uncertainties in Chinese attitudes, particularly among youth, which distinguish the late 1970s from the 1956–7 period. The film tells the story of a young woman in the 'cultural revolution' who, under pressure because of her class background, assumes the guise of a young man. Echoes of the traditional love story of Liang Shanbo and Zhu Yingtai, which involves the disguise of one partner, are noteworthy. *On a Small Street* presents the viewer with three possible present-day endings: one happy, one tragic, and the third, a mixture. Whatever the multiple ending does to the artistic integrity of the work (cinematic reference to Kurosawa's *Rashomon* is not unintentional), it amounts to a mutual acknowledgment by the film-makers and their audiences that the simple happy endings characteristic of 'socialist realism' are no longer satisfactory.

Other issues in socialist society and human relations were examined in *Longing for Home*, in which a young man who had grown up with a foster mother in the countryside goes to the city to be reunited with his real parents, who are important Party cadres and veteran revolutionaries. Differences between and prejudices about living in urban or rural areas are given a prominent place in the film, as are the privileges available to cadres and their offspring. The film's setting in the 1950s does not negate its relevance to the early 1980s. Lyrical evocation, clearly inspired by traditional landscape painting, of the boy's childhood spent tending water buffalo is contrasted with the bustle and ambition found in cities. The boy's mother finally sees the error of her ways, notably as with characters in *The Legend of Tianyun Mountain* because she recognises a direct personal debt to the countrywoman, whom she now remembers as the young peasant with whom she left her son in the 1930s. The film ends ambiguously, with the boy's decision about where to live unclear. As in *On a Small Street*, the incomplete ending is a new concession to the intelligence of post-'cultural revolution' audiences.

This second Hundred Flowers interest in human feelings and relation-ships extended also to films with a more distant historical setting. A film centred on the ruling circles of the new Chinese Republic in the 1910s represented a big change in cultural politics. That *Intimate Friends* should dwell on the love between Cai E, the Yunnan warlord, and Fengxian, a courtesan, as well as on their mutual patriotic efforts against President Yuan Shikai's monarchical ambitions, made the work typical of its time. The strengthening affection between warlord and courtesan indeed provides needed momentum for the film after early expository, more political scenes in Yuan's court. In the end, on the death of Cai E in Japan, Xie Tieli and his co-directors show considerable restraint. A single string on the zither Fengxian is playing on her way to refuge in Hunan suddenly snaps.[27] Where once, in another context, the film might have cut to shots of crashing waves accompanied by a heavenly chorus, *Intimate Friends* ends in a southern Chinese landscape, subtly underlining the patriotic theme and hinting at eventual change arising from the South. The placid watery context of the last scene also recalls the opening shots of water, a favourite directorial motif of Xie Tieli, which he used even in the 1972 model opera film *On the Docks*.[28]

Comedy was not neglected in the films of the second Hundred Flowers, most often in conjunction with a youthful love story. In 1979 the veteran film-maker Sang Hu directed *Twins Come in Pairs*, exploiting the comic confusion and cinematic trickery of two sets of identical twins who eventually fall in love. The contrast between the earnest, hard-working couple, giving their all for the Four Modernisations, and their less discip-lined siblings draws a lesson in social morality. A noteworthy element in this comedy, and many other films made and set in the late 1970s, is the atypical spaciousness and luxury of the characters' accommodations. While the so-called 'socialist realism' of the 50s and 60s has been highly modified, a similar idealisation of reality seemed to succeed it in the 1980s. This later idealisation, seen also in the new television dramas, may be a way to show audiences the putative rewards of achieving the Four Modernisations.

At the same time as new subject matter, themes and styles were being explored on screen during the cultural liberalisation of the late 1970s, as in 1956–7, well-publicised assessment was made by both artists and bureaucrats of the systematic problems of Chinese literature and art. The discussions of 1978–81 showed the extent of change after two decades in the three-way relations between Party, film-makers and audiences. The experience of the 'Anti-Rightist' campaign in 1957–8 and of the 'cultural revolution' had affected all three parties. In contrast to the confidence which had allowed the first Hundred Flowers to take place at all, the Party and cultural leaders by the late 1970s were less certain of their position and of their relations with the other two groups. The events of the 'cultural revolution' and its aftermath had also made clear that the

Party itself was a far from monolithic entity. The criticisms raised about film-making, and about all other aspects of Chinese life, could not easily be suppressed but could at least be ascribed to others, labelled 'gang of four'. The position of film-makers vis-à-vis the Party and audiences had changed considerably over the preceding two decades. While Party confidence had lessened, that of film-makers had grown. The two phenomena were interrelated: a less interventionist-minded cultural leadership made bolder experimentation and criticism by artists possible. The impact of the growth and increasing sophistication of audiences on Party-artist relations should not be overlooked. Film attendance had become a more established feature of cultural life by the late 1970s than it had been earlier. An awareness of audiences – their diversity, tastes and reception of particular films, reflected for example in film popularity polls – contributed to the confidence of film-makers that they should have a greater role than had been earlier granted by the Party, convinced that it knew mass audiences best, in determining what audiences could see. The late 1970s discussions of the proper distinction between politics and art are better understood in the context of this 'cultural revolution' sea change in Party, artist and audience relationships.

Like their colleagues at Democracy Wall, young persons in the film studios were active in these criticisms, which peaked in 1979 as the first of the new-style films began to be released. By this time discussion had gone beyond ritual condemnation of the 'gang of four' to include the previous three decades. The title of a seminal article by two young film-makers at the Changchun studios, Peng Ning and He Kongzhou, in January 1979 provided the column heading for further discussions over the following six months in the *People's Daily*. Peng and He responded to their title, 'What's wrong with the movies?', with the answer that artists had not been allowed a necessary degree of artistic autonomy to practise their craft.[29]

The different atmosphere of the second Hundred Flowers was epitomised in many of the speeches at the Fourth National Congress of Artists and Writers in Beijing, October–November 1979. Older cultural bureaucrats, newly returned to their former positions of influence, like Chen Huangmei who had criticised 'Rightist' films in 1958, came out at the Congress and elsewhere as exponents of greater liberalisation and of less interference in cultural life.[30]

At the Congress, one of the most outspoken proponents of a bold new effort to go beyond old caution and restrictions was a fifty-year-old army writer, Bai Hua, who had himself been labelled a 'Rightist' in 1957.[31] The fate of a 1980 film written by Bai Hua seemed to show the advances that had been made in Chinese film-making. As a war film, *The Stars are Bright Tonight* had a long cinematic pedigree in socialist China. But in his script Bai Hua did not present much of the Huaihai campaign of 1948. Instead, the film centres on the experiences of three young soldiers and a young peasant woman who falls into their midst.

This upset some viewers. Chen Yi, a former head of the Culture Section of the People's Liberation Army General Political Department who had been condemned as a 'Rightist' in 1958,[32] objected in the *People's Daily* that *The Stars are Bright Tonight* distorted and diminished the significance of the Huaihai campaign.[33] The response in defence of Bai Hua and the film was a vigorous affirmation of the new cultural atmosphere of the second Hundred Flowers. At a round-table discussion on the film organised by the editors of *Popular Film*, now China's largest-circulation magazine with an estimated readership of one hundred million, Chen Yi's objections were seen as representing a lingering tendency in the new age to fling about old 'anti-Party' and 'anti-socialism' labels. The film was endorsed as a 'healthy' one for young persons, a view shared by the Communist Youth League.[34]

Between 1978 and 1980 a lot of discussion was also reported, as in 1956–7, on the need to give the film studios and the creative artists in those studios greater autonomy to select scripts and approve completed films. However, only minor organisational changes in this direction seem to have been effected with a view to devolving more artistic control to directors and production groups. An editorial in the December 1980 issue of *Popular Film* raised the continuing need for systemic reforms.[35] But a considerable degree of change in policy, if not in practice, had been indicated earlier by the publication in the *People's Daily* in October 1980 of the artistic testament of the film actor Zhao Dan two days before his death. Under the blunt headline, 'Rigid control ruins art and literature', Zhao asked, 'Is there anyone who has become a writer because he was asked to by the Party? . . . And who asked Marx to write? . . . Convention is not truth. Still less should corrupt practices be followed as hard and fast rules. A good work can never be produced by many levels of scrutiny.' The publication of these blunt views indicated the considerable policy change of the late 1970s and suggested that some at least in the cultural leadership entertained the possibilities implied in Zhao's commentary. Zhao concluded with the question, 'Will this article of mine have any effect?'[36]

The answer to Zhao's deathbed question came in mid-1981, largely in relation to a new film, *Bitter Love* (or *The Sun and the Man*). The script was written by Bai Hua, who had been notably outspoken at the 1979 Fourth Congress of Writers and Artists, and Peng Ning, who himself had warned in his January 1979 article that the current policy of 'openness' (*fang*) might be succeeded by 'tightening up' (*shou*) when the cultural leadership decided to take more control of the second Hundred Flowers. Peng Ning also directed the unreleased film.

Like many of the current films, *Bitter Love* was set in the 'cultural revolution', recounting the experiences of an artist who had returned to China in the 1950s but later found his patriotism thwarted in the 'cultural revolution', when he became an outcast from society. After a primitive existence in swamp lands, the artist dies just before word of the arrest of the 'gang of four' reaches him. Prior to succumbing, he tramps out a huge question mark in the snow. The film ends, as it begins, with a flight of geese in the form of the written character for 'man' (*ren*).

While its setting and much else were typical of the second Hundred Flowers, the script and film attracted the concern of elements unhappy with the blooming of the early 1980s. These elements were associated particularly with the military. In late April 1981 a guest correspondent of the *Liberation Army Daily* objected that the script failed to draw adequate distinction between Guomindang and 'gang of four' times on the one hand, and the true socialist regime on the other. Also objectionable were the somewhat unsubtle parallels drawn between the Mao cult and idol worship portrayed in the hero's youth.[37] Here, as on many occasions before and after 1957, a film was vulnerable in reflecting a broader tendency in society thought by some as worthy of condemnation. The *Liberation Army Daily* critic made direct comparison between the writings of the Democracy Wall movement, long since banned, and the script of *Bitter Love*. At first, it seemed that the fate of the first Hundred Flowers movement would be repeated.

In 1981, however, the second Hundred Flowers did not immediately stop blooming, even if the cultural climate did become somewhat cooler. Two reasons for the comparative restraint at the end of the second Hundred Flowers can be delineated. The first was the apparent confusion of signals, to a greater extent than in 1957, coming from the Party and cultural leadership. While, as in other areas of Chinese life, there was undoubtedly a pulling back from the relative 'openness' of 1979–80, there was also obvious concern that history should not repeat itself. At a forum on film script-writing in early May, Central Committee General Secretary Hu Yaobang emphasised that defence of a work like *Bitter Love* should be encouraged, but not at the expense of spreading the issue over the pages of every newspaper and periodical. Hu hoped that the criticism of the film and Bai Hua could be brought to a speedy end.[38] But the *Bitter Love* issue was revived in October 1981 in an article by Huang Gang, best described as a hack film critic since the 50s, and the writer Liu Baiyu, a deputy chairman of the Writers Association but also head of the PLA General Political Department's Cultural Section. The April and October attacks on *Bitter Love* were thus closely associated with the army and its general discontent with the liberalising trends of the previous three years.[39] But those who wanted to continue the criticism of the film found little support. The summer critique of 'bourgeois liberalistic tendencies' (*zichanjieji ziyou qingxiang*) sputtered on but did not take hold as a full-scale movement: in 1982 concern focused on the role of films in fostering socialist morality, particularly among youth.

The second reason for the relative mildness of the critique of Bai Hua and *Bitter Love* was the obvious reluctance of many fellow writers and film workers to join in the campaign, and the insistence that the Party honour promises (renewed by Hu Yaobang in May 1981) that literary criticism should distinguish between an author and his or her work. The more open atmosphere of the second Hundred Flowers, the more vocal concern of a broad and largely youthful public opinion, and the leadership's concern to reassure artists and audiences could not now, in contrast to 1957, be so easily ignored.

This comparison between two periods of relative cultural liberalisation has indicated the extent of changes in the politics of Chinese film-making between the end of the 1950s and the beginning of the 1980s. What changed least was the formal structure of censorship and control, despite a lot of talk about the desirability of improvement: the film industry remained a centralised structure under Party control exercised through the Ministry of Culture at the top, local cultural offices in Shanghai, Changchun and elsewhere, down to studio-level Party committees. The attitudes, however, of those in control of this structure seemed different by the 1980s. Of course, care should be taken to avoid assuming that all cultural bureaucrats shared a single collective outlook and all artists likewise held another. The degree of factional bitterness evident in much of the discourse of the first Hundred Flowers and the ambiguities of the 1981 Bai Hua episode are warnings against such presumptions. Nor should the degree of real change be overestimated. A more liberal attitude from those in control may be simply a pragmatic response to a perceived diminution in the efficacy of control, even if pragmatism is not usually ascribed to ideologues.

This realisation of the limits of control was the most significant change between the first and second Hundred Flowers and was a perception shared by all parties in this and other areas of Chinese life at the beginning of the 1980s. While it would be misleading to talk of the autonomy of the literary and artistic enterprise as the People's Republic entered its fourth decade, a degree of unanimity had been achieved which contrasted with the factionalism of the 50s and 60s. This factionalism, particularly between former Yan'an residents and those who had spent the war years in Guomindang areas, had contributed to the implementation and consequences of the 'Anti-Rightist' and 'cultural revolution' campaigns. Such divisiveness, or at least that based on these particular historical cleavages, seemed less likely in the 1980s. Perhaps in the film world, as elsewhere in society, the shared national experience of the 'cultural revolution' helped obliterate older divisions.

For Chinese film-making, three new features gave the industry strengths which had earlier been lacking or less developed. First, a new generation of artists, more specialists in film than their predecessors who often worked in theatre, was emerging and gaining recognition in audience polls and film awards. Second, new styles of cinema were being explored, to be sure frequently with unsatisfactory results, when unsuitable styles vulgarised subject matter. There was wholesale copying, for example, of Taiwanese and Hong Kong styles in some movies, with flower-filled screens and slow-motion, nature-loving couples. Many more artistically integrated films from the second Hundred Flowers were characterised by bold use of flashback and less single-minded concern for unambiguous exposition. Some of these latter changes were a direct outcome of the third, and most important, development: closer understanding between film-makers and their audiences. Film had taken time to build audiences in the 1950s. In the 1960s, the 'cultural revolution' efforts at a forced, opera-based sinification of cinema submerged any longer-term moves towards a Chinese cinematic style that may have existed. By the 1980s, film was more securely a part of Chinese cultural life, and, like the films of the late 1940s, the new films were again a more direct reflection of changes in Chinese society. Film-makers and audiences had established linkages which would make the sort of intervention that ended the first Hundred Flowers more difficult to repeat.

Notes

1. Criticism of *The Life of Wu Xun* was not confined to the film itself, but extended immediately to a broader critique of intellectuals' attitudes to class struggle.
2. *Renmin Ribao*, 26 April 1957, p. 7.
3. 'Gongs and drums from the movies' (*Dianying de Luogu*), *Wenyi Bao*, no. 23, 15 December 1956, pp. 3–4.
4. Ibid.
5. Cultural commissar Zhou Yang's vigorous denial in 1957 that the studio was split up in response to criticisms of over-centralisation tends, ironically, to confirm the validity of the interpretation presented here: *Wenyi Bao*, no. 19, 11 August 1957, p. 8.
6. *Wenyi Bao*, no. 36, 15 December 1957, p. 11.
7. Quoted in *Wenyi Bao*, no. 36, 15 December 1957, p. 11, and in *Dazhong Dianying*, no. 17, 11 September 1957, p. 7.
8. Lenin was referring specifically to newsreel films when he made this remark.
9. See, for example, *Renmin Ribao*, 22 May 1957, p. 7.
10. Reported in *Renmin Ribao*, 22 May 1957, p. 4.
11. Luo Dou, 'First sound from Changchun' (*Changchun de Diyige Shengyin*), *Wenyi Bao*, no. 11, 16 June 1957, pp. 1–2. On Beijing actors' similar frustrations, see *Dazhong Dianying*, no. 12, 26 June 1957, pp. 23–4.
12. The quote read literally, 'You can eat for life' (*Keyi chi yibeizi*), *Renmin Ribao*, 2 December 1958, p. 7.
13. *Dazhong Dianying*, no. 1, 13 January 1957, pp. 32–3.
14. *Wenyi Bao*, no. 23, 15 December 1956, pp. 3–4.
15. See Bonnie S. McDougall, *Mao Zedong's 'Talks at the Yan'an conference on literature and art': a translation with commentary* (Ann Arbor: Center for Chinese Studies, University of Michigan, 1980).
16. *Renmin Ribao*, 26 April 1957, p. 7.
17. *Dazhong Dianying*, no. 6, 26 February 1957, pp. 26–7.
18. An early review of the film can be found in *Wenyi Bao*, no. 29, 27 October 1957, p. 14. For a criticism of the film, see *Renmin Ribao*, 3 December 1957, p. 7.
19. *Wenyi Bao*, no. 36, 15 December 1957, p. 11; *Dazhong Dianying*, no. 23, 11 December 1957, p. 26. Shi Hui died at about this time.

20. See, for example, *Dazhong Dianying*, no. 19, 11 October 1957, pp. 3–7. Attacks on the 38-year-old Zhong Dianfei for his December 1956 'gongs and drums' article (see note 3 above) began before more established film-makers such as Shi Hui were criticised. Zhong was even accused of presently writing a film script on the life of the Song dynasty reformer, Wang Anshi, a charge which would have appealed to any orthodox Confucian. Zhong's reported statement that 'we need not determine if a work of art is socialist or bourgeois. As long as the masses welcome it, it's good', has interesting parallels with Deng Xiaoping's celebrated remark that the colour of a cat was immaterial, so long as it caught mice.

21. *Dazhong Dianying*, no. 17, 11 September 1956, p. 7.

22. *Dazhong Dianying*, no. 18, 26 September 1956, pp. 5–7; *Dazhong Dianying*, no. 17, 11 September 1957, pp. 7–8. Lü Ban was even alleged, by an 'old party member', to have joined the Party in pursuit of a female member.

23. See *Wenyi Bao*, no. 36, 15 December 1957, p. 11, and *Dazhong Dianying*, no. 14, 11 July 1957, pp. 25–6.

24. *Renmin Ribao*, 2 December 1958, p. 7.

25. *Renmin Ribao*, 4 March 1959, p. 7. The secretary, Yuan Wenshu, dated his letter in Shanghai, perhaps signalling that his response could be seen as being on behalf of Shanghai film circles. Chen's letter carried no place name.

26. In 1980 over 11.4 billion attendances were recorded at films (*Dianying Yishu*, no. 4, 3 April 1982, p. 18). This compared with 2.86 billion in 1958, and 47.3 million in 1949 (*Wenyi Bao*, no. 19–20, 26 October 1959, p. 59).

27. The film's title, *Zhiyin*, is from an ancient poetic comparison of close friendship with two stringed instruments in harmony.

28. In the fifth annual readership poll conducted by *Dazhong Dianying* in 1982, *Intimate Friends* was the fifth most popular film of 1981. *Longing for Home* ranked second. *Dazhong Dianying*, no. 6, 10 June 1982, pp. 2, 4.

29. *Renmin ribao*, 21 January 1979, p. 3.

30. For translations of some of the speeches at the Congress and an informative introduction, see Howard Goldblatt (ed.), *Chinese Literature for the 1980s: the Fourth Congress of Writers and Artists* (New York: M.E. Sharpe, 1982).

31. For a brief outline of Bai Hua's life, see *Shikan*, no. 7, July 1981, p. 7. His words at a round-table discussion in late 1979 on the social function of literature can be found in *Wenyi Bao*, no. 1, 12 January 1980, pp. 29–37.

32. *Wenyi Bao*, no. 5, 11 March 1958, pp. 21–4.

33. *Renmin Ribao*, 30 July 1980, p. 5. For Bai Hua's response, see *Renmin Ribao*, 3 September 1980, p. 5.

34. *Dazhong Dianying*, no. 10, 10 October 1980, pp. 1–5.

35. *Dazhong Dianying*, no. 12, 10 December 1980, p. 1. *Dianying Yishu* carried a similar editorial in their December 1980 issue, pp. 1–3.

36. *Renmin Ribao*, 8 October 1980, p. 5. For an English translation, see *Chinese Literature*, no. 1, January 1981, pp. 107–11. Zhong Dianfei in 1957 had reportedly also argued that when leadership was strongest, no films were produced; *Wenyi Bao*, no. 19, 11 August 1957, p. 8.

37. The Hong Kong magazine *Zhengming*, no. 44, June 1981, pp. 82–98, reprinted the script of *Bitter Love*, originally published in *Shiyue*, no. 3, October 1979. The April criticism of the film was reprinted in the Hong Kong magazine *Dongxiang* (*Direction*), no. 32, May 1981, pp. 10–13.

38. Excerpts from Hu's speech were reported in *Zhengming*, no. 46, August 1981, p. 16. The original April article had not been reprinted in other newspapers. Concern expressed by readers, and by students in Beijing and Shanghai, prompted the *Beijing Evening News*, among other organs, to reassure its readers that Bai

Hua was continuing to write; *Beijing Wanbao*, 8 May 1981, p. 3.

39. The article, originally published in the *Literary Gazette*, was reprinted in *Renmin Ribao*, 7 October 1981, p. 5. Peng Ning was now named as co-author of *Bitter Love*.

Filmography

NB: s = scenarist, d = director.

A Spring River Flows East (*Yijiang chunshui xiang dong liu*), s/d: Cai Chusheng and Zheng Junli (Shanghai: Kunlun and Lianhua Studios, 1947).

Crows and Sparrows (*Wuya yu Maque*), s: Shen Fu, d: Zheng Junli (Shanghai: Kunlun Studio, 1949).

The Life of Wu Xun (*Wu Xun Zhuan*), s/d: Sun Yu (Shanghai: Kunlun Studio, 1950).

Dong Cunrui, s: Ding Hong, Zhao Huan, Dong Xiaohua, d: Guo Wei (Changchun Studio, 1956).

New Year's Sacrifice (*Zhufu*), s: Xia Yan, from a short story by Lu Xun, d: Sang Hu (Beijing Studio, 1956).

Before the New Director Arrives (*Xin juzhang daolai zhi qian*), s: Yu Yanfu, d: Lü Ban (Changchun Studio, 1956).

The Man Unconcerned with Details (*Buju xiaojie de ren*), s: He Chi, d: Lü Ban (Changchun Studio, 1956). Unreleased.

Loyal Partners (*Qingchang yishen*), s/d: Xu Changlin (Shanghai: Tianma Studio, 1957).

Unfinished Comedy (*Weiyou wancheng de xiju*), s: Lü Ban and Luo Tai, d: Lü Ban (Changchun Studio, 1957). Unreleased.

Third Sister Liu (*Liu Sanjie*), s: Qiao Yu, d: Su Li (Changchun Studio, 1960).

The Red Detachment of Women (*Hongse niangzi jun*), s: Liang Xin, d: Xie Jin (Shanghai: Tianma Studio, 1960).

Early Spring (*Zaochun eryue*), s/d: Xie Tieli (Beijing Studio, 1963).

Serfs (*Nongnu*), s: Huang Zongjiang, d: Li Jun (August First Studio, 1963).

Stage Sisters (*Wutai jiemei*), s: Lin Gu, Xu Jin, Xie Jin, d: Xie Jin (Shanghai: Tianma Studio, 1965).

On the Docks (*Haigang*), d: Xie Jin and Xie Tieli (Beijing and Shanghai Studios, 1977).

Youth (*Qingchun*), s: Li Yunliang and Wang Lian, d: Xie Jin (Shanghai Studio, 1977).

Reverberations of Life (*Shenghuo de chanyin*), s/d: Teng Wenji and Wu Tianming (Xi'an Studio, 1979).

Twins Come in Pairs (*Talia he talia*), s: Wang Lian, Sang Hu, Fu Jinggong, d: Sang Hu (Shanghai Studio, 1979).

The Legend of Tianyun Mountain (*Tianyunshan chuanqi*), s: Lu Yanzhou, d: Xie Jin (Shanghai Studio, 1980).

Love and Inheritance (*Aiqing yu yichan*), s: Li Yunliang, d: Yan Xueshu (Xi'an Studio, 1980).

The Stars are Bright Tonight (*Jinye xingguang canlan*), s: Bai Hua, d: Xie Tieli (August First Studio, 1980).

Bitter Love (*Kulian*), alternative title *The Sun and the Man* (*Taiyang he ren*), s: Bai Hua and Peng Ning, d: Peng Ning (Changchun Studio, 1980). Unreleased.

On a Small Street (*Xiaojie*), s: Xu Yinhua, d: Yang Tanjin (Shanghai Studio, 1981).

Longing for Home (*Xiangqing*), s: Wang Yimin, d: Hu Bingliu and Wang Jin (Pearl River Studio, 1981).

Intimate Friends (*Zhiyin*), s: Hua Ershi, d: Xie Tieli and Chen Huai'ai (Beijing Studio, 1981).

Yellow Earth
Western Analysis and a Non-Western Text

ESTHER C. M. YAU

1984. China. The wounds of the 'cultural revolution' have been healing for nearly a decade. After the hysterical tides of red flags, the fanatical chanting of political slogans, and militant Mao supporters in khaki green or white shirts and blue slacks paving every inch of Tiananmen Square, come the flashy Toshiba billboards for refrigerators and washing machines, the catchy phrases of 'Four Modernisations', and tranquillised consumers in colourful outfits and leather heels crowding the shops of Wangfujing Street. A context of Change. Yet contradiction prevails. Who are these people flocking to local theatres that posted *First Blood* on their billboards? Are they not the same group that gathered for lessons on anti-spiritual pollution? The Red Book and the pocket calculator are drawn from shirt pockets without haste, just like the old long pipe from the baggy pants of the peasant waiting for the old Master of the Heavens to take care of the order of things. In 1984, after the crash of the 'gang of four', when China becomes a phenomenon of the 'post-' – a nation fragmented by and suffering from the collapse of faith in the modern, socialist politics and culture – the search for meaning by the perturbed Chinese character begins to occupy the electric shadows of the new Chinese cinema.[1]

At the end of 1984, a few Chinese men who were obsessed with their history and culture – all of them had laboured in factories and farms during the Cultural Revolution and had just graduated from the Beijing Film Academy – quietly completed *Huang Tudi* in a very small production unit, the Guangxi Studio, in southern China. A serious feature that had basically eluded political censorship, *Huang Tudi* (which meant *Yellow Earth*) was soon regarded as the most significant stylistic breakthrough in new Chinese cinema. It won several festival prizes, started major debates at home about film-making, and interested international film scholars.[2]

Safely set in the 1930s, *Yellow Earth* tells the story of an encounter between a soldier and some peasants. Despite its ambitious attempt to capture both the richly nourishing and the quietly destructive elements of an ancient civilisation already torn apart in the late 19th century, the film's story and its use of folk songs/folktale as device and structure is deceptively simple and unpretentious. In fact, the film's conception and its musical mode were originally derived from one of the trite literary screenplays which glorified the peasants and the earlier years of socialist revolution: an Eighth Route Army soldier influenced a peasant girl to struggle away from her feudal family.[3]

Such a commonplace narrative of misunderstanding-enlightenment-liberation-trial-triumph or its variations would be just another boring cliché to the audience familiar with socialist myths, while the singing and romance could be a welcome diversion. Dissatisfied with the original story but captivated by the folktale elements, director Chen Kaige and his young classmates – all in their early thirties – scouted Shaanxi Province in northwestern China for months on foot. Their anthropological observations of the local people and their subcultures both enriched and shaped the narrative, cultural and aesthetic elements in the film.[4] Consequently, they brought on to the international screen a very different version of the Chinese people – hardworking, hungry and benevolent peasants who look inactive but whose storage of vitality would be released in their struggles for survival and in their celebration of living. The structure of the original story was kept, but *Yellow Earth* has woven a very troubling picture of Chinese feudal culture in human terms that had never been conjured up so vividly before by urban intellectuals.

The film's narrative. 1937: the socialist revolution has started in western China, but most other areas are still controlled by the Guomindang. Some Eighth Route Army soldiers are sent to the still 'unliberated' western highlands of Shaanbei to collect folk tunes for army songs. The film begins. Spring 1939. An Eighth Route Army Soldier, Gu Qing, reaches a village in which a feudal marriage between a young bride and a middle-aged peasant is taking place. Later, the soldier is hosted in the cave home of a middle-aged widower peasant living with his young daughter and son. Gu Qing works in the fields with them and tells them of the social changes brought about by the revolution, which include the army women's chances to become literate and to have freedom of marriage. The peasant's daughter, Cuiqiao, is interested in Gu Qing's stories about life outside the village, and she sings a number of 'sour tunes' about herself. The peasant's son, Hanhan, sings a bed-wetting song for Gu Qing, and is taught a revolutionary song in return.[5] The young girl learns that her father has accepted the village matchmaker's arrangement for her betrothal. Soon, the soldier announces his departure. Before he leaves, the peasant sings him a 'sour tune', and Cuiqiao privately begs him to take her away to join the army. Gu Qing refuses on grounds of public officers' rules, but promises to apply for her and to return to the village once permission is granted. Soon after his departure, Cuiqiao's feudal marriage with the middle-aged peasant takes place. At the army base, Gu Qing watches some peasants drum-dancing to soldiers going off to join the Anti-Japanese war. Back in the village, Cuiqiao decides to run away to join the army herself. She disappears crossing the Yellow River while singing the revolutionary song. Another spring comes. There is a

63

drought on the land. As the soldier returns to the village, he sees that a prayer for rain involving all the male peasants is taking place. Fanatic with their prayers, nobody notices Gu Qing's return, except the peasant's young son. In the final shots he runs to meet the soldier, struggling against the rush of worshippers. End of story.

Yellow Earth poses a number of issues that intrigued both censors and the local audience. The film seems to be ironic: the soldier's failure to bring about any change (whether material or ideological) in the face of invincible feudalism and superstition among the masses transgresses socialist literary standards and rejects the official signifieds. However, such an irony is destabilised or even reversed within the film, in the sequences depicting the vivacious drum-dancing by the liberated peasants and the positive reactions of the young generation (i.e. Cuiqiao and Hanhan) towards revolution. The censors were highly dissatisfied with the film's 'indulgence of poverty and backwardness, projecting a negative image of the country'. Still, there were no politically offensive sequences to lead to full-scale denunciation and banning.[6]

To the audience used to tear-jerking melodramas (in the Chinese case, those of Xie Jin, who is by far the most successful and popular director[7]), *Yellow Earth* has missed most of the opportune moments for dialogue and tension, and is thus unnecessarily opaque and flat. For example, according to typical Chinese melodrama, the scene where Cuiqiao is forced to marry an older stranger, and the one when her tiny boat disappears from the turbulent Yellow River, would both be exploited as moments for pathos. But here they are treated metonymically: in the first, the rough dark hand extending from off-screen to unveil the red head-cloth of the bride is all one sees of her feudalist 'victimiser'; in the second instance, the empty shots of the river simply obscure the question of her death. In both situations, some emotional impact is conveyed vocally, in the first by the frightened breathing of the bride, and in the second by the interruption of her singing. But the cinematic construction is incomplete, creating an uncertainty in meaning and a distancing effect in an audience trained on melodrama and classical editing. Nevertheless, when the film was premiered at the 1985 Hong Kong International Film Festival, it was lauded immediately as 'an outstanding breakthrough', 'expressing deep sentiments poured on to one's national roots', and as 'a bold exploration of film language'.[8] Such an enthusiastic reception modified the derogatory official reaction towards the film (similar to some initial Western reception, but for different political reasons), and in turn prompted the local urbanites to give it some box-office support.[9]

Aesthetically speaking, *Yellow Earth* is a significant instance of a non-Western alternative in recent narrative film-making. The static views of the distant ravines and slopes of the Loess Plateau resemble a Chinese scroll-painting of the Chang'an School. Consistent with Chinese art, Zhang Yimou's cinematography works with a limited range of colours, natural lighting, and a non-perspectival use of filmic space that aspires to a Taoist thought: 'Silent is the Roaring Sound, Formless is the Image Grand'.[10] Centrifugal spatial configurations open up to a consciousness that is not moved by desire but rather by the lack of it – the 'telling' moments are often represented in extreme long shots with little depth when sky and horizon are proportioned to an extreme, leaving a lot of 'empty spaces' within the frame. The tyranny of (socialist) signifiers and their signifieds is contested in this approach, in which classical Chinese painting's representation of nature is deployed to create an appearance of a 'zero' political coding. Indeed, the film's political discourse has little to do with official socialism; rather, it begins with a radical departure from the (imported) mainstream style and (opportunist) priorities of narrative film-making in China. One may even suggest that *Yellow Earth* is an 'avant-gardist' attempt by young Chinese film-makers taking cover under the abstractionist ambiguities of classical Chinese painting.[11]

To film-makers and scholars, then, *Yellow Earth* raises some intriguing questions. What is the relationship between the aesthetic practice and the political discourse of this film? In what way is the text different from and incommensurable with the master narratives (socialist dogma, main-stream film-making, classical editing style, etc.); in what way is it 'already written' (by patriarchy, especially) as an ideological production of that culture and society; and finally, how does this non-Western text elude the logocentric character of Western textual analysis as well as the sweeping historicism of cultural criticism?[12]

This essay will address the above questions by opening up the text of *Yellow Earth* (as many modernist texts have been prised open) with sets of contemporary Western methods of close reading – cine-structuralist, Barthesian post-structuralist, neo-Marxian culturalist, and feminist discursive. This will place *Yellow Earth* among the many parsimoniously plural texts and satisfy the relentless decipherers of signifieds and their curiosity for an oriental text. The following discussion of this text will show that the movement of the narrative and text of *Yellow Earth* involves the interweaving and work of four structurally balanced strands (micro-narratives) on three levels: a diegetic level (for the construction of and enquiry about cultural and historical meaning), a critical level (for the disowning and fragmentation of the socialist discourses), and a discursive level (for the polyvocal articulations of and about Chinese aesthetics and feudalist patriarchy).[13] In this way, I hope to identify certain premises of Chinese cosmological thinking and philosophy as related in and through this text. In this analytical process, the contextual reading of Chinese culture and political history will show, however, the limitations of textual analysis and hence its critique.[14]

I shall begin with a brief description of the organisation of the four narrative strands and their function on both diegetic and critical levels. The Lévi-Straussian structural analysis of myths is initially useful: the peasant father imposes feudal rules on Cuiqiao, the daughter (he marries her off to stabilise the kinship system), and the soldier imposes public officers' rules on her as well (he prevents her from joining the army before securing official approval). Thus, even though the host-guest relationship of the peasant and the soldier mobilises other pairs of antinomies such as agriculture/warfare, subsistence/revolution, backwardness/modernisation, the pattern of binaries breaks down when it comes to religion/politics, since both signify, in Chinese thinking, patriarchal power as a guardian figure. In addition, Hanhan, the young male heir in the film, counteracts the establishment (runs in the reverse direction of the praying patriarchs) in the same way Cuiqiao does (rows the boat against the Yellow River currents for her own liberation). Again, the antinomy peasant/soldier is destabilised, as myth is often disassembled in history – that is, the mythic glory of hierarchic dynasties and the revolutionary success of urban militia break down when confronted by the historical sensibility of the post-Cultural Revolution period.

There are four terms of description: brother, sister, father, soldier. While there is a relationship of consanguinity and descent, both are complicated by the problematic relation of affinity: Cuiqiao's intimacy with Hanhan and their distance from the peasant father is more excessive while romance is taboo and marriage is ritual in the film. The prohibition of incest among family members (Cuiqiao with her brother or father) is transferred to prohibition of romantic involvement between Cuiqiao and the soldier, enforced at the cost of the girl's life.[15] Hence the textual alignment of patriarchy with sexual repression. However, the film text is not to be confused with an anthropological account. As both Fredric Jameson and Brian Henderson point out, historicism is at work in the complex mode of sign production and in reading.[16] Hence this text would preferably be read with a historical knowledge of the Communist Party's courtship with the peasants and its reconstruction of man [sic] through the construction of socialist manhood – which reserves desire for the perfection of the ideological and economic revolution, while the liberation of women (its success a much debated topic) becomes an apparatus for the Party's repression of male sexuality, besides being a means for winning a good reputation. Hence the position of contemporary Chinese women, generally speaking, involves a negotiation between patriarchy and socialist feminism in ways more complicated than what one deduces from the Lévi-Straussian analysis of kinship systems.

Now I shall proceed to a more detailed (though non-exhaustive) discussion of what is at work in each of the micro-narratives as narrative strands, as well as the contextual readings relevant to the textual strategies.

First narrative strand: the peasant's story

The scenes assembled for the first narrative strand have a strong ethnographic nature: the material relation between the Shaanbei peasants and their land is documented through the repetitive activities of ploughing land on bare slopes, getting water every day from the Yellow River ten miles away, tending sheep, cooking, and quiet residence inside the cave home, while marriages and rain prayers are treated with a moderate amount of exotic interest – of the urban Han people looking at their rural counterparts. The peasants are depicted as people of spare words (Cuiqiao's father even sings little: 'What to sing about when [one is] neither happy nor sad?'). They have a practical philosophy (their aphorism: 'friends of wine and meat, spouse of rice and flour') and they show a paternal benevolence (Cuiqiao's father only sings for the soldier for fear that the latter may lose a job if not enough folk tunes are collected). Obviously, anthropological details have been pretty well attended to.

Meaning is assigned according to a historical or even ontological dependence of peasants on their motherly Land and River. This signifying structure is first of all spatially articulated: the Loess landscape with its fascinating ancient face is a silent but major figure both in Chinese painting and in this film. Consistent with the 'high and distant' perspective in scroll painting is the decentred framing with the spatial contemplation of miniaturised peasants as black dots labouring to cross the vast spans of warm yellow land to get to the river or their cave homes.[17] No collective farming appears in this film, and neither planting nor harvesting modify this relationship. The symbolic representation of an ancient agrarian sensibility is condensed in shots that include the bare details of one man, one cow and one tree within the frame in which the horizon is always set at the upper level and the land, impressive with deep ravines, appears almost flattened. In an inconspicuous way, the Yellow River's meaning is also contemplated: the peasants are nourished by it and are sometimes destroyed by it. A narrative function is attached: this is a place in dire need of reform, and it is also stubbornly resistant. The state of this land and people accounts for the delay of enlightenment or modernity – there is an unquestioning reliance on metaphysical meaning, be it the Old Master of the Heavens or the Dragon King of the Sea, but which is tied so closely to the survival of the village. The narrative refusal of and enthusiasm for revolution are motivated: the ideology of survival is a much stronger instinct than the passion for ideals. But to the peasants, the Party could have been one of the rain gods.

There is a vocal part to this cosmological expression as well, articulated dialectically for a critical purpose. We shall attend to three voices: the first, that of the peasant's respect for the land: 'This old yellow earth, it lets you step on it with one foot and then another, turn it over with one plough after another. Can you take that like it does? Shouldn't you respect it?' A classical form of deification born from a genuine, everyday relationship. Then it is countered by the second, the soldier's voice: 'We collect folk songs – to spread out – to let the public know what we suffering people are sacrificing for, why *we farmers* [my emphasis] need a revolution.' Gu Qing offers a rational reading of the agrarian beliefs; his statement contains a simple dialectic – the good earth brings only poverty, and the way out is revolution. Yet his statement and his belief are but a modernised form of deification: the revolution and its ultimate signified (the Revolutionary Leader) are offered to replace the mythic beliefs through a (false) identification by the soldier with the peasants ('Our Chairman likes folk songs,' says the soldier). Blind loyalty (of peasants to land) finds homology in, and is renarrativised by, a rational discourse (of soldier to his Leader). The ancient structure of power changes hand here; thereafter, the feudalist circulation of women and the socialist liberation of women will also remain homological.

As explicit contradiction between the first two voices remains unresolved, a major clash breaks out in the form of a third voice, which appears in the rain prayer sequence. Assembled in their desiccated land, the hungry peasants chant in one voice: 'Dragon King of the Sea, Saves Tens of Thousands of People, Breezes and Drizzles, Saves Tens of Thousands of People.' Desperation capsuled: the hungry bow fervently to the Heavens, then to their land, and then to their totemic Dragon King of the Sea, in a primitive form of survival instinct. At this moment the soldier appears (his return to the village) from a distance, silent. A 180° shot-reverse shot organises their (non)encounter: a frontal view of the approaching soldier, followed by a rear view of the peasants whose collective blindness repudiates what the soldier signifies (remember his song 'The Communist Party Saves Tens of Thousands of People'). In this summary moment of the people's agony and the film's most searing questioning of the Revolution's potential, the multiple signifieds are produced in and through a mirroring structure: the soldier's failure reflected by the peasants' behaviour and the peasants' failure in the soldier's presence.

At the outset, two dialectical relationships are set up explicitly in the text, one against the other: between peasant and nonpeasant, and between peasant and land. The roots of feudalism, through this first narrative strand, are traced to their economic and cultural bases, and are compared in a striking way to Chinese socialism. In this manner, the whole micro-narrative is historicised to suggest reflections on contemporary China's economic and political fiascos. But there is another relationship between the filmic space and the audience's (focal) gaze. The nonperspectival presentation of landscapes in some shots and sequences often leads one's gaze to linear movements within the frame, following the contours of the yellow earth and the occasional appearance and disappearance of human figures in depth on an empty and seemingly flat surface. The land stretches within the frame, both horizontally and vertically, with an overpowering sense of scale and yet without being menacing. In these shots and sequences, the desire of one's gaze is not answered by the classical Western style of suturing, indeed it may even be frustrated.[18] Rather, this desire is dispersed in the decentred movement of the gaze (and shifts in eye level as well) at a centrifugal representation of symbolically limitless space. Such an unfocused spatial consciousness (maintained also by nonclassical editing style) has a dialectical relation-

Yellow Earth: landscape and gaze

ship with one's pleasure-seeking consciousness. It frustrates if one looks for phallocentric (or feminist, for that matter) obsessions within an appropriatable space, and it satisfies if one lets the sense of endlessness/ emptiness take care of one's desire (i.e., a passage without narrative hold). In these instances, one sees an image without becoming its captive; in other words, one is not just the product of cinematic discourse (of shot-reverse shot, in particular), but still circulates within that discourse almost as 'nonsubject' (i.e., not chained tightly to signification).

Within the text of *Yellow Earth*, one may say, two kinds of pleasures are set up: a hermeneutic movement prompts the organisation of cinematic discourse to hold interest, while the Taoist aesthetic contemplation releases that narrative hold from time to time. Most of the moments are assigned meaning and absences of narrative image are filled, though some have evaded meaning in the rationalist sense. When the latter occurs, the rigorous theoretical discourses one uses for deciphering are sometimes gently eluded.

Second narrative strand: the daughter's story

Inasmuch as the sense of social identity defines the person within Chinese society, individuals in Chinese films are often cast as non-autonomous entities within determining familial, social and national frameworks. Ever since the 1920s, the portrayals of individuals in films have been

69

inextricably linked to institutions and do not reach resolution outside the latter. Hence, unlike the classical Hollywood style, homogeneity is not restored through the reconciliation of female desires with male ones, and the ways of looking are not structured according to manipulations of visual pleasure (coding the erotic, specifically) in the language of the Western patriarchal order. With an integration of socialism with Confucian values, film texts after 1949 have often coded the political into both narrative development and visual structures, hence appropriating scopophilia for an asexual idealisation. In the post-Cultural Revolution context, then, the critique of such a repressive practice naturally falls on the desexualising (hence dehumanising) discourses in the earlier years and their impact on the cultural and human psyche.[19]

The plotting of *Yellow Earth*, following the doomed fate of Cuiqiao the daughter, seems to have integrated the above view of social identity with the recent critique of dehumanising political discourses. Within the second narrative strand, the exchange of women in paternally arranged marriages is chosen as the signifier of feudalist victimisation of women, while the usual clichés of cruel fathers or class villains are replaced by kind paternal figures. The iconic use of feudal marriage ceremonies has become common literary and filmic practice since the 1930s, but compared with other texts, this one is more subtle and complex in its enunciation of sympathy for women.[20] In this regard, we may undertake to identify two sets of homological structures in the text that function for the above purpose. It is through the narrative and cinematic construction of these structures that *Yellow Earth* made its statement on patriarchal power as manifested in cultural, social and political practices.

The first set of homological structures involves the spatial construction of two marriage processions, each characterised by a montage in close-up of the advancing components (trumpet players, donkey, dowry, the red palanquin and its carriers) in more or less frontal views. In each case, the repetitive and excessive appearance of red, which culturally denotes happiness, fortune and spontaneity, is reversed in its connotative meaning within the dramatic context of the oppressive marriages. More significantly, the absence/presence of Cuiqiao as an intradiegetic spectator and her look become a linchpin to that system of signification. In the first marriage sequence, the bride is led from the palanquin to kneel with the groom before the ancestor's plate and then taken to their bedroom. Meanwhile, Cuiqiao as a spectator is referred to three or four times in separate shots, establishing her looking as a significant reading of the movement of the narrative. Yet she is not detached from that narrative at all. Seeing her framed as standing at the doorway where Confucius' code of behaviour for women is written, one is constantly reminded that Cuiqiao's inscription will be similarly completed (through marriage) within the Confucian code.[21] Her look identifies her with the scene of marriage, and also relays to the audience her narrative image as a young rural female. The victimising structure (feudalist patriarchy) and the

70

potential victim (Cuiqiao) are joined through a shot-reverse shot method, mobilised by her looking which coded the social and the cultural into the signifying system here.

In the second marriage sequence, the similar analysis in close-up of the advancing procession (by a similar editing style) performs an act of recall, which as a transformed version of the first marriage sequence reminds the audience of Cuiqiao's role as the intradiegetic spectator previously. In this instance, however, Cuiqiao is the bride, locked behind the dull black door of the palanquin covered by a dazzlingly red cloth. The big close-up of the palanquin, however, suggests her presence within the shot (hidden), in depth, and going through the process of 'fulfilling' the inscription predicted earlier on for her against her wish for freedom. The palanquin replaces her look but points to her absence/presence. At the same time Hanhan, her quiet brother, replaces Cuiqiao as an intradiegetic spectator looking (almost at us) from the back of the palanquin, figuring her absence and her silence. Hanhan as the brother represents an ideal form of male sympathy in that context, yet as the son and heir of a feudal system he is also potentially responsible for the perpetuation of this victimisation. In this manner, the text shifts from a possible statement on class (backwardness of peasants before the Liberation) to a statement of culture (the closed system of patriarchy) to locate the woman's tragedy. With an intertextual understanding of most post-1949 Chinese films presenting feudal marriages, this cultural statement becomes a subtle comment on the (pro-revolutionary) textual appropriations of folk rituals for political rhetorics.

The second set of homological structures appears in two pairs of narrative relationships between three characters (between Cuiqiao's father and Cuiqiao, and between Gu Qing the soldier and Cuiqiao) concerning the subject of women's (and Cuiqiao's) fate. Initially, one finds the first relationship a negative one while the second is positive, i.e. the father being feudal but the soldier liberating. This is encapsulated in a dialogue in which the soldier attempts to convince the peasants that women in socialist-administered regions receive education and choose their own husbands, and Cuiqiao's father answers: 'How can that be? We farmers have rules.' However, when one compares the peasants' exchange of women for the survival of the village and the revolutionaries' liberation of women for the promotion of the cause, then one finds both relationships being similarly fixated on woman as the Other in their production of meaning. Such a homology, nevertheless, is assymetrical in presentation. On the one hand, the film is direct about the negative implications of the patrilinear family, though without falling into a simple feminist logic (Cuiqiao's father sympathises with women's tragedy in the sour tune he sings for the soldier). On the other, there is no questioning about the socialist recruitment of women (Cuiqiao's failure to join the army is regarded as regrettable). The critique falls on another issue: Gu Qing's refusal to take Cuiqiao along with him because 'We public

71

Yellow Earth: Cuiqiao

officers have rules, we have to get the leader's approval.' Thus it is nongendered bureaucracy that is at stake here, and not exactly the patriarchal aspects of the feudalist and socialist structures, which can only be identified from an extratextual position.

The suspected drowning of Cuiqiao, then, can be read as the textual negotiation with the symbolic loss of meaning: she is to be punished (by patriarchy, of course) for overturning the peasants' rule (by leaving her marriage), for brushing aside the public officers' rule (by leaving to join the army without permission), and for challenging nature's rule (by crossing the Yellow River when the currents are at their strongest).

When Cuiqiao is alive, the sour tunes she sings fill the film's sound-track – musical signifiers narrating the sadness and the beauty of *yin*. Her death, though tragic, brings into play the all-male spectacles in the text: drum-dancing and rain-prayer sequences each celebrating the strength and attraction of *yang*, so much suppressed when women's issues were part of the mainstream political mores.[22] Here one detects the 'split interest' of the text in these instances – the nonpolitical assignment of bearers of meaning (rather than the nonsexist) prescribes a masculine rather than feminine perspective of the narrative images of man and woman. That is to say, since the position of men and women in this patriarchal culture has been rearranged for the last three decades, first

72

according to everyone's class background, then with a paternal favouring (as bias and strategy) of women, the text's critique of socialist discourses becomes its own articulation of a male perspective. In this way, this text does not escape being 'overdetermined' by culture and society, although in some ways by default.

Third narrative strand: the Eighth Route Army soldier's story

Since the Yan'an Forum for writers in 1942, literary writing in China has followed a master narrative that has privileged class consciousness over individual creativity.[23] In revolutionary realism, character types (and stereotypes) have been considered the most effective methods of interpellating the masses during economic or political movements. Literary and filmic discourses on the social being dictate a structure of dichotomies: proletariat/bourgeois, Party members/non-Party members, allies/enemies, peasants/landlords, etc. It was not until 1978 that 'wound literature' gave an ironic bent to the hagiographic mode for Party members and cadres. Still, such writing found shelter in specificity – for example, Xie Jin's *The Legend of Tianyun Mountain* and other adaptations from 'wound' literature were bold in questioning the political persecution of intellectuals during the terrifying decade, unmistakably attributing the causes of people's suffering to the influences of the 'gang of four'. Dichotomy, however, was basically maintained even though the introduction of good cadre/bad cadre did cause some reshuffling in the antinomies. Meanwhile, the master narrative remained intact, with authority diminished but the direct questioning of it taboo.[24]

The figure of an Eighth Route Army soldier and Party member in *Yellow Earth*, therefore, was not written without technical caution and political subtleties. A number of alterations to humanise the soldier were made during adaptation which to some extent decentralised his position in the narrative. Nevertheless, the rectitude of a revolutionary perspective and its influence on the peasants were not the least mitigated – that is to say, the third narrative strand sets the three others in motion. Thus, even when the representation of the Party member may be more in line with the popular notion, there is a level of operation that makes socialist interpretation plausible. One may say that with an audience used to being prompted by dialogue and behaviour, the figure of Gu Qing does not contest the proper image of a revolutionary military man.

As a signifying structure, the soldier's story functions as (in)difference and as metonymy, which is where the ironic mode works. The figures of that ancient agrarian subculture are no longer the same when Gu Qing, the outsider, enters – they are transformed under the soldier's gaze of bewilderment, which subsequently exerts its critical import. It is the third strand that begins the braiding process among the four and is responsible for the climaxes: the daughter no longer submits to her father's wishes, the son abandons the rain-prayer ceremony. Yet these changes take place virtually outside Gu Qing's knowledge: he is ignorant of Cuiqiao's dilemma (except about women's fate in a general way) and of the peasants' problem of survival (except in broad terms of their poverty). The Party's political courtship with the peasants is metonymically dealt with here, in the prohibition of romance (as lack of knowledge) between Gu Qing and Cuiqiao, and also powerfully in the last scene of rain prayer which brings into circulation 'hunger' as the peasants' signified (versus the power elite's lack of experience of it) for their rural, human-land and marriage relationships. Tension between history and ideology is again condensed, the three to four decades' national history of socialism contesting to little avail the five thousand years' national ideology of subsistence. The peasants' hospitable reception of Gu Qing and Cuiqiao's idealistic trust in the Party further reinforce the ironic mode – difference is not a simple dichotomy and often works in the areas least expected. Then, none could go very far: Cuiqiao disappears in the Yellow River, the peasants are dying of drought, while the totemic figure of the Sea Dragon King dominates the scene, lifted by worshippers who want their lives saved. The discourse here is historicist: the cultural and epistemological barriers (of both Party and people) to the capitalist market economy in the 1980s motivates this myth of survival. Yet it is also historical: the gods, emperors, leaders, all have been sought after by people in disaster, and made disasters by people.

Yellow Earth: revolutionary soldier and peasant family

'The silent, blank face': Hanhan and the soldier in *Yellow Earth*

Fourth narrative strand: Hanhan's story

A quiet young boy with a blank facial expression, Hanhan moves almost inconspicuously as a curious figure in the scenes. One may even ponder a Brechtian address made possible by this marginal but conscious presence. Almost uninscribed by culture, and, to some extent, by the text itself, Hanhan has the greatest degree of differentiation (i.e., Hanhan = X) and exists to be taken up by the three other narrative strands for signification.[25]

As a peasant's son, Hanhan is heir to land, feudalism and patriarchy. As a brother to Cuiqiao, he is the displaced site of her repressed feminine love and its failure. As a little pal of Gu Qing's, he is the first person to learn the song and spirit of revolution. Yet his story is also underdeveloped. In other words, Hanhan is neither unconnected nor fixated in the textual generation of meaning. Contrary to the marked positions of other song singers (of either sour tunes or revolutionary songs), Hanhan is more ambiguous with his short 'bed-wetting song' (which makes unrefined jokes with both the Sea Dragon King and the son-in-law) before the soldier recruits his voice for the revolutionary song, which he sings only once. In the scene where he is already made part of the fanatic horde of worshippers, Hanhan turns towards the sight of the soldier as the source of possible change in an act of individual decision.

However, it is not Hanhan the literary figure that escapes inscription. Indeed, pressured by political demands, the textual movement of Hanhan is along the trajectory of 'liberation', though there is no intention of completing it. The circulation of Hanhan (as X) along the various narrative strands is, significantly, a production of textual interweaving. When conventional meaning in that society has been fragmented and questioned within the text, Hanhan (as a textual figure) functions as the desire for meaning. One may venture to say Hanhan is the signifier of that meaning – an insight for history and culture with an urge for change, portrayed as a childish moment before inscription, before meaning is fixed at the level of the political and agrarian institutions. Therefore the silent, blank face, because to speak, to have a facial expression, is to signify, to politicise.

A braid? Perhaps, as one woven by culture in society, and not flaunted as a fetish. Since the 19th century, major historical events in China (wars, national calamities, revolutions, etc.) have made four topics crucial to national consciousness – feudalism, subsistence, socialism and modernisation – and discourses are prompted in relation to them in numerous literary and cultural texts. In 1984, when contemporary China struggles with the evil spells of the Cultural Revolution and begins flirting once again with the capitalist market economy, discourses related to the four topics reappear in terms of current issues. Will the agrarian mentality of its people prevent China from becoming a modern nation? Will feudal relations persist in spite of the lure of individualist entrepreneurship? Will the country's recent radical economic move (as in the Great Leap Forward) bring another large-scale fiasco? Is the Communist party leadership still competent for the changing 1980s? Will a second Cultural Revolution occur soon? As technology and business turn corporate and global, the answers to these questions can no longer be found in an isolated situation. The China that partakes in the world's market economy no longer operates in an 'ideological context' that is uniquely Chinese (as it had during the Cultural Revolution). Inevitably (and maybe unfortunately), this changing, modernising 'ideological context' in China also informs the 'avant-gardist' project of *Yellow Earth* which has focused its criticism only on the patriarchal and feudal ideologies of that culture. Arguably, then, *Yellow Earth*'s modernist power of critique of Chinese culture and history comes from its subtextual, noncritical proposition of capitalist-democracy as an alternative; it is (also arguably) this grain in the text that attracts the global-intellectual as well.

A historicist reading of texts and contexts is a powerful analytic practice. In the case of *Yellow Earth*, such a reading enables one to relate the film's textual strategies to the specific political and cultural context, while at the same time exposing some of the text's symptoms. However, there still remains a need to locate *Yellow Earth*'s difference from the other interesting Chinese films made during the same period. Wu Tianming's *Life* (1984), for example, deals with the disparity between intellectual and agrarian life as an important subcultural dichotomy in Chinese identity and boldly pits individual motivation against class issues. Again, such a film was possible in China only in the 1980s. Yet one may argue that discursive constraints are not fully watertight in their operations. With respect to *Yellow Earth*, there is a presence of a certain 'negative dialectics' that seems to run counter to its grain of modernist activities and does not yield to a historicist reading. It is, again, the simple Taoist philosophy which (dis)empowers the text by (non)affirming speaking and looking: 'Silent is the Roaring Sound, Formless is the Image Grand.'[26] There are many such instances in the film: when the human voice is absent and nobody looks, history and culture are present in these moments of power(lessness) of the text. With this philosophy, perhaps, we may be able to contemplate the power(lessness) of our reading of the text.

Notes

1. For detailed discussions of the conflicts and contradictions involved in recent political and economic formulations of Chinese socialism, see Bill Brugger (ed.), *Chinese Marxism in Flux, 1978–84, Essays on Epistemology, Ideology and Political Economy* (New York: M.E. Sharpe, 1985).
2. In 1985, *Yellow Earth* won five festival prizes – in China, Hawaii, Nantes, Spain and Locarno. This film's impact on film-makers and critics in China and Hong Kong was documented in *Talking About Huang Tudi (Hua Shuo Huang Tudi)*, (Chen Kaiyan, ed., Beijing: China Film Press, 1986). For an English discussion, see Tony Rayns' discussion of the dissident 'Fifth Generation' of PRC directors, and also his review of *Yellow Earth* in *Monthly Film Bulletin*, October 1986.
3. A number of melodramatic and political clichés in the original essay *Echoes of the Deep Ravine (Shen gu hui sheng)* were dropped in Chen Kaige's adaptation into the screenplay titled *Silent is the Ancient Plain (Gu yuan wu sheng)*. The impressive colour tones of the first work-print inspired the film's final title, *Yellow Earth*.
4. According to director Chen Kaige, Cuiqiao's father in the film is close to a *vérité* version of a local peasant he met during the walking reconnaissance of Shaanxi Province, and the bachelor singer in the first marriage sequence was also a local recruit. Yet according to official views, the film's representation of peasants was ethnocentric and derogatory. One may understand this disparity by noting that Chinese socialism has always favoured a more progressive image of peasants. Interview, Beijing, August 1985.
5. '*Xintianyou*', the folk songs sung in the northern Shaanxi region, provide a rich form for metaphoric expressions and direct telling of the singers' sentiments.
6. The first film completed by a group of Beijing Film Academy '82 graduates, *One and Eight (Yige He Bage*, 1984) was directed by Zhang Junzhao. Cinematographer Zhang Yimou's contribution was already regarded as the major reason for the film's aesthetic excellence. However, the film's entire ending was altered due to censorship and it was still banned. *Yellow Earth* also had several censorship problems, but with its ambiguities it had better luck with the Film Bureau.
7. Examples from Xie Jin's most popular films include *The Red Detachment of Women (Hongse Niangzijun*, 1961) in which a serf girl reacted positively to a soldier's influence and turned herself into a brave red soldier, and *The Legend of Tianyun Mountain (Tianyunshan Chuanqi*, 1981), in which two women were emotionally entangled with a persecuted Rightist intellectual. Xie Jin has successfully dealt with topical issues in melodramatic form shot with classical style which has made most of his works tearjerking successes in China.

8. All drawn from the collection of Hong Kong reviews in Chen Kaiyan, ed., op. cit., pp. 301–15.
9. According to Tony Rayns, the triumph of *Yellow Earth* in film festivals prompted the official accusation of its bad influence on local aspirations to 'compete with the ideology of the bourgeoisie at foreign film festivals'. On the other hand, it is the film's international reputation that silenced established film-makers and officials.
10. Originally from Lao Tzu (Lao Zi)'s *Daode Jing*, this Taoist concept of representation was developed in two seminal discussions on Chinese aesthetics, 'On the Origins and Bases of Chinese and Western Painting Techniques' ('*Lun zhongxi hua fa de yuanyuan yu jichu*', written in 1936), and 'The Spatial Consciousness Expressed in Chinese Painting and Poetry' ('*Zhongguo shi hua zhong suo biaoxian de kongjian yishi*', written in 1949) by Zong Baihua and collected in Zong's *A Stroll in Aesthetics (Meixue Sanbu)* (Shanghai: The People's Press, 1981), pp. 80–113.
11. Some of the principles of Chinese spatial representation have been taken up by the West for interrogation of its own norms, e.g. Beijing opera by Brechtian theatre, and hence what is classical for one cultural system can be appropriated for avant-gardist reasons in another. Here, I would quickly add (with reference to Edward Said's discussion on 'Travelling Theory' in *The World, the Text and the Critic*) that while critical consciousness is the issue, classical Chinese painting as the borrowed theory itself is not free of institutional limitations in the local context. On the other hand, the aestheticisation of nature in *Yellow Earth* could also be quickly seized on by Western audiences for sentimentalised retreats to a pre-industrial corner of the world.
12. Culturalist or neo-Marxist criticisms of mass culture focus mostly on sign systems produced within bourgeois capitalism. In general, hardcore propaganda is taken to be characteristic of socialist sign systems, which is a gross simplification of the complicated mediations and processes at work in those economies and cultures. With reference to China, a more complicated view of socialist mass cultures is called for, and Bill Brugger's *Chinese Marxism in Flux* can be read along with Victor F. S. Sit (ed.), *Commercial Laws and Business Regulations of the PRC, 1949–1983* (London: Macmillan, 1983) to see that utilitarian individualism, for example, is functional within recent Chinese economic discourses.
13. For substantial discussions of the interweaving of Confucianism, socialism and patriarchy in contemporary China, see Richard Madsen, *Morality and Power in a Chinese Village* (Berkeley: University of California Press, 1984) and Judith Stacey, *Patriarchy and Socialist Revolution in China* (Berkeley: University of California Press, 1983).
14. Refer to Said's discussion of Derrida's and Foucault's approach to texts in 'Criticism Between Culture and System', *The World, the Text and the Critic*, op. cit., pp. 183–225.
15. The largely asexual representation of revolutionary characters was a major practice in the Revolutionary Model Plays, the only films made during 1970–73. In the post-Cultural Revolution era, the hagiographic mode of representation was debated as suppression of 'true human character' in literary and film circles.
16. Both Brian Henderson's '*The Searchers*: An American Dilemma' (Bill Nichols, ed., *Movies and Methods*, vol. II, pp. 429–49) and Fredric Jameson's *The Political Unconscious* (Ithaca: Cornell University Press, 1981) have informed the historicist reading of this essay. I am also thankful to Nick Browne of UCLA who introduced me to them and gave valuable advice, and to David James of Occidental College for his inspiring comments.

17. The term 'Chinese Westerns' was used recently in China to describe films that took to northwestern China for location shooting (e.g. Tian Zhuangzhuang's *On the Hunting Ground* [*Liechang Zhasa*], 1984). Yet while the American frontier appealed to the immigrants' evolutionist expansion of social and political organisation over inanimate nature (according to Frederick J. Turner in *The Significance of The Frontier in American History*, ed. Harold P. Simonson [New York: Frederick Unger, 1963]), the Chinese west evoked a non-aggressive self-reflection; or according to Wang Wei, 'The sage, harbouring the Tao, responds to eternal objects; the wise man, purifying his emotions, savours the images of things'. For further discussion of the Tang dynasty poet Wang Wei, see James Liu's article in Richard J. Lynn (ed.), *Language – Paradox – Poetics: A Chinese Perspective* (New Jersey: Princeton University Press, 1988).

18. While I agree with Heath's critique of Oudart-Dayan's definition of 'suturing' in filmic discourse as 'narrow', I still refer here, for convenience, to the privileged example of shot-reverse shot as the suturing approach to spatial articulation.

19. In this respect, Laura Mulvey's 'Visual Pleasure and Narrative Cinema' would not be relevant to many Chinese films, especially those made during the Cultural Revolution which prohibited erotic codes in its representation of women.

20. One may suggest, in terms of Teresa DeLauretis' 'Desire in Narrative' in *Alice Doesn't* (Bloomington: Indiana University Press, 1984), pp. 139–46, that there are instances in which the girl in *Yellow Earth* moves as 'mythical subject' in narrative while men became her topoi; the marriage sequence and the river-crossing sequence are arguable examples.

21. The four Chinese characters in the shot are '*San Cong Si De*', meaning 'three obediences and four virtues'. The 'three obediences' for a Chinese woman are obedience to her father at home, to her husband after marriage, and to her son in her widowhood.

22. *Yin*, the female element; *Yang*, the male element. These two elements in Chinese cosmology involve symbolic systems and economies present both in the male and the female gender.

23. 'Talks at the Yan'an Forum on Literature and Art', *Mao Zedong on Literature and Art* (Beijing Foreign Languages Press, 1977).

24. Recently, the citing of Mao's 'Talks at the Yan'an Forum' as the standard literary and artistic creation in China is usually indicative of a tightened literary policy. In 1987, with the 'anti-bourgeois liberalisation' (*Fan Zichanjieji Ziyouhua*) movement, China celebrated the 45th anniversary of the 'Talks'.

25. This concept is taken from Gilles Deleuze's 'A Quoi Reconnait-on le Structuralisme?' (1973). Hanhan's name in Chinese means simple and lacking the ability to talk well.

26. '*Da xiang wuxing, da yin xisheng*', from the *Daode Jing*, Chapter XLI. For a standard English translation, see Arthur Waley, *The Way and Its Power: A Study of the Tao Te Ching and Its Place in Chinese Thought* (New York: Grove Press, 1958), p. 193 ('Great Music has the faintest notes, The Great Form is without shape').

Filmography

NB: s = scenarist, d = director.

Yellow Earth (*Huang Tudi*), s: Zhang Ziliang, d: Chen Kaige (Guangxi Studio, 1984).

Red Sorghum
Mixing Memory and Desire

YUEJIN WANG

For some Chinese, watching *Red Sorghum* could almost be a traumatic experience. Strikingly rough, forthright, rugged, bold and unrestrained both stylistically and morally to Chinese tastes, the film is a shocking affront to many cherished and received formulae of Chinese cultural praxis; to the deep-rooted Confucian ethical and moral codes of sobriety and decorum; to the ingrained artistic codes favouring strategies of concealment and restraint; and to the aesthetic taste which prioritises emotional delicacy and refinement. Never before has the medium of Chinese cinema been so unquestionably given over to the countenancing containment of an unbridled and abandoned manner of life and visual wantonness and crudity.

Hence its controversial Chinese reception that amounted to a '*Red Sorghum* Phenomenon'. Over-shooting itself, a film originally meant as a modest stylistic and aesthetic exercise has been taken as seriously as any other product that addresses certain cultural images in the socialist ideological scaffolding. The film has been forced to transcend itself and grow into a nationwide cultural phenomenon. Everyone could not care more. But how is it that the film scandalises and offends the public's not-too-delicate taste? How come so many people find it so hard to swallow, absorb and 'buy'? By measuring the negative critical response against what the film shows, we will not only come to a better understanding of the true power of the film, but also lay bare the way in which regressive ideology masquerades as a self-righteous rhetoric that represses desire and against which desire seeks to find itself.

The film is based on Mo Yan's already controversial novella of the same title. A voice-over narrator tells the legend of his grandparents. Set in northern China, the narrative begins with the arranged marriage of Jiu'er, a young girl, also known as 'my grandma', to a leper thirty years her senior, a winery boss, in exchange for a mule. The marriage procession breaks into a 'tossing-the-sedan dance', where the crude sedan-bearers want to have fun with the pathetic bride whose sobs, however, silence the revellers. The procession is unsuccessfully waylaid by a masked bandit who is killed by the sedan-bearers, led by 'my grandpa-to-be'. It is elliptically suggested that the wedding night does not end with consummation, as the bride defends herself with a threatening pair of scissors. She spends three subsequent days at her parents' home, according to local custom. On her journey back to her husband, she is kidnapped by 'my grandpa' and carried off into the depths of the sorghum field, where she happily acquiesces and they make love. Her return to the leper's winery is greeted by the news that the leper has been mysteriously killed. She recovers from the shock and persuades the workers to stay and help her run the winery. The narrator's 'grandpa' returns, drunk, to claim Jiu'er. His tipsy manner wins him a beating instead, and he is thrown into a vat where he stays groaning for three days. Meanwhile, the real local bandit has kidnapped Jiu'er, who is ransomed for 3,000 pieces of silver. Grandpa awakens and goes to seek revenge for the disgracing kidnap, only to be disgraced himself. The winery is now in full swing. Grandpa reappears, and defies the ensemble there by pissing into the wine vat, and with a powerful demonstration of strength. He claims Jiu'er and nine years pass. The Japanese come, rounding up the local people to trample down the sorghum field, and to witness the flaying of an anti-Japanese bandit and Luohan, once a helper at Jiu'er's winery. After the event, the furious group at the winery resolve to seek revenge for Luohan by ambushing a Japanese truck. They succeed at the cost of almost all their lives except those of the narrator's grandfather and father. The latter appears on screen as a small child whose chant for his dead mother ends the film.

Red Sorghum's detractors in China dismiss the film as mindless sensationalism, a libidinal impulse for 'the ugly', a regressive effort at 'the uncivilised and the savage', and a stylistic horror indulging in moral and visual 'crudities'.[1] For a Chinese film, a narrative blatantly addressing issues of desire, sexuality and transgression is itself already a transgression, even in an age of radical transformation of values. The film transgresses a lot of boundaries and codes, moral and cinematic, in a Chinese context where the two are traditionally yoked intimately together. The charges brought against the film cluster round its indulgence in boorishness, forthrightness and a savage lifestyle in defiance of refinement, inwardness and civility, all traditional Chinese virtues. Surprisingly, the central antithesis around which sound and fury erupt simply implicates a sexual difference: favouring femininity over masculinity. The pejorative epithets attached to the film are almost exclusively masculine, while the attributes detractors find lacking are mostly feminine restraint, introversion, refinement and so forth. This critique betrays a cultural priority given to femininity, a priority embedded in the deep structure of an ideology that seems contradictory to itself. In the feudally informed hierarchy of the Chinese ideological superstructure, women have traditionally been scaled down to the lowest stratum, so how is it that this traditional subordination is reversed? By examining this paradoxical contradiction, we will see how the masculine send-up of *Red Sorghum* confronts, challenges and transgresses ideological boundaries.

In search of man: the politics and aesthetics of masculinity

In the Chinese cultural context, gender is a rich node couched in a panoramic intertextuality produced out of the entire historical intellectual canon. In the ancient Chinese metaphysical framework, the two fundamental metaphysical entities *yin* and *yang* create, define, perpetuate and perfect the cosmic mode of existence or essence of the world (referred to as '*taiji*' in the *Yi Zhuan* or '*yuan*' by Dong Zhongshu). Provided they are coordinated and in equilibrium, as with any of the other semantically undefined notions in the intuitive system of Chinese thought, this dichotomy is amorphously polysemic to the extent that its ultimate meaning seems to reside in a structure of shifting dialectic relationships that project themselves on to diverse categories and spheres. Hence the unanimously accepted reluctance to pin these two words to specific English equivalents in any context. Here, however, for a working clarity, some simplification is licensed. Among the commonly accepted connotations attached to *yang* are light, warmth, summer, daylight, masculinity, ascent and action; while attributes clustered around *yin* include the opposites: darkness, cold, winter, night, femininity, descent and inaction.[2] 'The *yang* and strong becomes the male, the *yin* and smooth becomes the female.'[3] In Dong Zhongshu's interpretative text, probably the most comprehensive after the *Yi Zhuan*, *yin* and *yang* are rendered mutually exclusive in that the presence of one means the absence of the other, as seen for example in seasonal change and temperature alternation. Moreover, the dichotomy enters the moral spectrum in his explication: 'The *yang* is benign while the *yin* is malign, the *yang* means birth while the *yin* means death. Therefore, *yang* is mostly present and prominent; *yin* is constantly absent and marginal.'[4] From this isolated text alone, it would be too far-fetched to press for a consciously misogynistic vision. Yet considering that Dong is one of the most significant interpreters and disseminators of Confucian ethics, and in view of the Confucian ethical dictum 'the noble male and base female', it is easy to see how the very structure of the phrases allows an easy equation with the 'noble male and base female'.[5]

Dong is known for disclaiming plurality of thought in favour of Confucian ethics, which has been officially privileged, hermeneutically tamed and politically congealed to form the canonical bedrock of Chinese feudal ideology ever since. The 'noble male and base female' became not only a feudal moral value, but was also displaced into the feudal social structure. The dichotomy of, and tension between, masculinity and femininity was no longer only a matter of sexual difference; it began to figure class difference, too. The hierarchical feudal order sought to structure itself around the figure of gender, with the ruler as the dominant male and the ruled as the submissive female.

Moreover, despite the diversity of undercurrents that may provide alternatives to dominant Confucian ethics, for example Taoism and Buddhism, there is one thing almost universally embraced by the Chinese mentality: the belief in internal stillness and passivity as a positive way to appropriate external reality. This has been affirmatively rhetoricised in various ways, and the ruling classes have been only too happy to appropriate it into ideology to consolidate the existing class structure. As the aspired-to stillness and passivity have touches of femininity, femininity itself becomes a condition highly aspired to. Instead of being afflicted by castration anxiety, the problematic of the lack is quite reversed in the Chinese cultural context. It is the man who lacks. If anything, a femininity complex would be a more appropriate form of the unconscious in the Chinese psyche. All those historical figures which, once filtered through ideological refracture, are mythicised into cultural archetypes that partake in masculinity, are also shown to be born with fatal flaws usually associated with braggarts and bigots. Even though they may be basically humane, they are always objects of ridicule, such as Li Kui and Lu Zhishen from *Water Margin*.[6] Well-known dynastic struggles for the throne always end up with overblown masculine warriors outwitted by feminine quasi-warlords (their femininity hardly earning them the name of a warlord at all).

'The fair beauty and the fragrant plant' (*Meiren Xiangcao*) is a clichéd classical poetic figure that ancient poets, mostly male, identify with to embody their yearning for spiritual purity and loyalty:

> And I thought how the trees and flowers were fading, and falling,
> And feared that my fairest's beauty would fade, too.
> Gather the flower of youth and cast out the impure! ...
> All your ladies were jealous of my delicate beauty;
> They chattered spitefully, saying I lived wantonness.[7]

It does not follow, however, that the femininity complex relieves women of their inferiority, nor is the curse of the 'lack' lifted from woman as her place is elevated. What happens is that men usurp women's proper space so that women are pushed aside, marginalised, expelled, suspended, bracketed, and exiled into the realm of the imaginary to become icons and absences. It is interesting to note how persistent is the Chinese poetic convention of a male poet figured in his own poems as a sentimental woman who waits and longs for her/his lover's overdue arrival or return from a long journey. In 'Song of Yan' (*Yan Ge Xing*), allegedly the first complete poem in the seven characters per line format, the emperor-poet Cao Pi assumes the role of a neglected woman pining away in her lonely chamber:

> Autumn winds whistle sadly, the air grows chill,
> Plants wither, leaves fall, dew turns to frost,
> Swallows fly homeward, geese wing south;
> I think of your distant wandering and am filled with love.
> Longingly you think of returning to your old home,
> Why linger on in remote places?

Forlorn, your wife keeps to the deserted room;
Misery cannot make me forget my love.
Unaware of the tears that moisten my gown,
I play zither tunes in the *ch'ing shang* mode,
The songs are brief, the breath, weak – nothing lasts ...[8]

Working in conspiracy with this practice is the enduring moral value that 'for woman, ignorance is a virtue.' Thus men not so much speak for women as stand in their place to speak, thereby replacing women's linguistic space, usurping their world of consciousness, and depriving women of their right to speak. According to Barthes, the denial of speech is the ultimate deprivation of existence, as speech is the final mode of proving one's existence.[9] Female subjectivity is out of the question. Women have no way of articulating 'I'. Worse still, they live in a limbo: they cannot even inhabit the place of 'thou' as the 'thou' addressed in poems, since that place is male when the speaker is a textual female.

Femininity is seen by Lin Yutang as an overriding descriptive figure that brings together a set of otherwise loosely associated characteristics of the Chinese, including the priority given to intuition and a common-sensical way of thinking, and the tendency towards stability and non-aggression.[10] Temperamentally, it may have its positive side, but the loss of masculinity necessarily creates a blank in the cultural body. Even from the perspective of the ancient dialectic of *yin* and *yang*, balance between the two is a prerequisite for a wholeness of the cosmic order. The 'sick man of Asia', a curse that haunted China during the semi-colonial era, suggests the diseased cultural body then at its worst. Spiritual feebleness, moral spinelessness, silent suffering and absorbing passivity certainly betray a loss of spiritual masculinity.

This loss is even reflected in Griffith's *Broken Blossoms*, a Hollywood narrative about a feminised 'chink' and a 'chinkised' woman – an equation implicitly drawn by the Western colonial ideology that informed Hollywood cinematic discourse. Cheng, an idealistic young Chinese, comes to London with the hope of teaching 'the Western white man of the peace and inner tranquillity of the Buddha'.[11] The values Cheng embodies are already categories of *yin*/femininity according to the classical Chinese taxonomy of *yin* and *yang*. *Broken Blossoms* is blatantly critical of the abusive and sadistic *yang*/masculinity, and sympathetic to the oppressed *yin*/feminine side, physically figured by Lucy (the Lillian Gish character), and metaphorically figured by Cheng, the 'chink'. Both are immature, fragile victims of male dominance and power. Battling Burrows, the masculine paradigm, is strong, militant, overpowering, menacing, and tall; the girl and the 'chink' are fragile and vulnerable. Instead of facing up to Battling with an equal amount of masculine strength, Cheng is seen to be as femininely vulnerable as the girl. The 'chink' and Lucy become mirror-images of each other. Hence his inadequacy as her potential lover, as if he has been castrated. By appropriating him into the female side, the film politicises sexual difference, a meta-phorical site onto which are collapsed class difference and racial difference.

Feminisation of men as a form of the cultural collective unconscious is manifested in traditional models of Chinese artistic representation. The exchange of sexual identity is a conventional theatrical licence. In Beijing opera, men play women by seriously masquerading as women in every way. In Shaoxing opera, an extremely popular variant among people in Shanghai, Zhejiang and Jiangsu provinces, male characters are played by women because of generic imperative: the stock-in-trade of Shaoxing opera is a love story between a young woman and a 'tender' male scholar or potential scholar good at poetry and painting. The tenderness is required to the extent that only women seem able to portray it. Yet by having women impersonate men, the convention creates a theatrical illusion that stands in for an illusion of reality: desirable male prototypes fit for such romantic slots should be, and are, feminised men. These cultural praxes have created an ingrained aesthetic taste in Chinese audiences for feminine male icons on stage, and consequently on screen.

In the early 1980s, the speculation on the past, on our cultural history, and on the structure of the Chinese mentality, led to a radical change in taste. The intelligentsia were awakening to the ideological implications of feminisation, while average theatregoers became fascinated by the char-isma of 'tough guys' in Japanese and Western movies. Suddenly there was an excruciating realisation of the fundamental 'lack'. There was a 'mas-culinity' anxiety which culminated in a stage play, *In Search of Man*. Once popular delicate, 'cream-puff' male stars lost audience favour, and even became despised.

Before *Red Sorghum*, the Chinese 'dream factory' had already been diligent about churning out new masculine icons to meet the new appe-tite for masculinity. These were usually rough-featured, lip-biting, brow-knitting types. However, the overtly self-conscious cinematic evocation of masculinisation betrayed the essential lack and the anxiety of that lack all the more. The clumsiness also came from the awkward imitation of Japanese or Western tough types that appeared preposterous in Chinese diegetic milieux, and hence unconvincing.

Red Sorghum is a cinematic milestone that proposes a powerful Chi-nese version of masculinity as a means of cultural critique. The film creates a masculine world rather unselfconsciously and cavalierly. It is unmistakably a male world (though itself problematic, as we shall see), with its boisterous swing and with only a minimum female screen presence (there is only one full-fledged female character). The intimida-tion, the subversive potential, and the sense of a cultural relevance in the creation of masculinity derive from its harking back to the under-repre-sented genealogy of historical male archetypes and mythical prototypes, with a perennially historicised undesirability dogging their presence/absence in historical textuality. The pre-*Red Sorghum* self-conscious concoction of 'perfect male icons', given their lack of credibility, posed no threat. The audience's consciousness of their imitative 'foreignness' and fictional status rendered their presence on the Chinese screen harmless. Any immediate political consequences and cultural implications they may have had were comfortably suspended and bracketed. Yet once an unaffected earthier version of masculinity took shape, the audience was frightened. For them, the experience of watching Japanese tough guys could safely lock them in an enclosure of distanced aesthetic pleasure. They were screened off from a culturally irrelevant world. *Red Sorghum* screens them in. Their fear of some particular version of native masculinity is the unease with, if not fear of, the return of the collectively repressed and the recuperation of historically exiled outlaws: the masculinity in *Red Sorghum* is a reiteration of the outlaws, drunkards and rebels who were historically marginalised and expelled from official historical documents, and survived only in folk tales, romances, myths and historicised fictional narratives. These characters could be enjoyed for their beauty of characterisation from the safe distance of another age without the need to fall into moral speculation, though the moral overtones are already congealed into them.

Red Sorghum is therefore a return of the collectively repressed, an evocation of the cultural unconscious, a remembrance of the forgotten, and a tapping of intertextual memories.

One historical/fictional narrative readily collapses into the film: the well-known *Water Margin*, a 16th-century novel about outlaws and rebels based upon a real historical event, a peasant uprising in the Northern Song dynasty. This fictional world is inhabited by a galaxy of 108 idiosyncratic outlaw-warriors. Mostly male, they shape a spectrum of masculinity with one end bordering on femininity (for example, Yanqing the Dandy) and at the other end, macho (Li Kui, Lu Zhishen, and others). This spectrum is also a moral taxonomy. The group inhabiting the more feminine end are talented and clever, whereas the motley crew clustered around the more masculine end share a certain lack: represented as boorish, crude in manner and speech and rash in action, as bare-bellied, shaven-headed and swaggering. They are boozers, most daring when drunk. It is this end of the spectrum that *Red Sorghum* sub- or unconsciously evokes. 'Grandpa' is a continuation of the masculine outlaw type. He kidnaps a woman, drinks heavily, is dauntless in defying everything, and given to occasional mischief such as pissing into the wine vat.

The problematic of drinking, along with its reiteration of historical narrative implications, is foregrounded in *Red Sorghum*. The red sorghum, the central image, connotes both the awe-inspiring landscape of the wild sorghum field and the raw material used to brew wine. In the Chinese historical memory, heavy drinking can be a transgression of decorum, an act of defying convention, a route to visionary intensity for transcendental possibilities and poetic ecstasy, or a way of achieving autonomy. It also bears the burden of moral condemnation for spiritual

degradation, over-indulgence, moral corruption and social irrespon-
sibility. Dialectically, the former derives its strength from the moral
overtone of the latter. The most memorable feats of the masculine heroes
in *Water Margin* are all one way or another the aftermath of drinking.
The celebrated narrative about Wu Song single-handedly killing a tiger
persistently emphasises the effect on him of the strong local liquor. Lu
Zhishen's dramatic defeat of Zhen Guanxi, a bullying butcher, and his
later mischievous and fearless defiance and blasphemy in a Buddhist
temple are also shown to be the side-effects of a drop too much.

It is interesting to note how in Chinese texts, past and present, drinking
is a way to attain masculinity. This betrays ideology: it presupposes a
sober state of mind which is other than masculinity. It is as though
masculine courage and defiance were impossible while in one's 'right
mind'. Therefore, masculinity is a self-deluded state. *Red Sorghum* is
both parasitical and critical of this historical tradition.

The sorghum wine, named by Jiu'er as '*Shibali Hong*' ('Eighteen Mile
Red') is the central constituent of the film's symbolic colour scheme. The
film is ritualistically motivated, with the power of wine as a central
dynamic. The drinking of the red wine derives its meaning from a
network of red motifs: the red wine, red marriage dress and decor, the
blood, the sun, etc. They combine to evoke a world of visualised passion,
a topology of fertility, a cinematically articulated life force, an iconographic presence of creativity and destruction, and death and rebirth.
Placed within this system, the ritualistic celebration of the red wine
radically transcends the traditional moral dichotomy of defiance and
debauchery attached to heavy drinking. In a way, the film appropriates
Western values such as the Nietzschean celebration of the Dionysian
spirit, and indeed the 1980s in China saw the revival of a Nietzschean
wave.

The chant that accompanies the sacrificial offering to the wine god,
however, narrows down the meaning and returns to a familiar historical
echo, politicising and defining the wine-drinking as an externalisation of
masculinity: a way of coming into one's own and the bold defiance of
authority. 'Drink our wine, the *yin* and *yang* will be strengthened'; 'one
dares to walk through the Black Death Gorge ... one does not kowtow
even at the sight of the emperor.' This echoes the historical motif of
drinking as a way of challenging authority, as in Lu Zhishen's one-man
riot in the Buddhist temple in *Water Margin*.

The equation of drinking with masculinity in the film points to an
ideological taxonomy: masculinity means transgression, which presupposes femininity as propriety and decorum in the Chinese political
unconscious. Masculinity is defined therefore as what Bakhtin calls
'carnival', which is 'sensuous', 'life turned itself out', suspension of
'hierarchical structure, and all the forms of terror, reverence, piety and
etiquette connected with it'; 'profanation: carnivalistic blasphemies, a
whole system of carnivalistic debasings and bringings down to earth,

Red Sorghum: the sedan-bearers

carnivalistic obscenities linked with the reproductive power of the earth and the body'; shifts and changes in the 'joyful relativity of all structure and order', crowning and uncrowning, birth and death, blessing and cursing, praise and abuse, face and backside, stupidity and wisdom, negation and affirmation.[12]

Red Sorghum is a cinematic carnival enacting almost every aspect of Bakhtin's scenario. As Bakhtin says of the carnival, it 'absolutises nothing'. The potentially pathetic opening exposition about the heroine's miserable marriage to a leper immediately careens into the hilarious tossing-the-bridal-sedan dance. The solemn ritual of sacrificial offering to the wine god is yoked to the comic scene of 'my grandpa', the intruder, pissing into the wine vat. The climactic moment of the tragic death of the heroine is matched on the soundtrack by a celebratory wedding tune. A more sustained carnival moment is an earlier sequence in the winery yard. The heroine, having recovered from the shock of her husband's mysterious death, persuades the workers to stay on. Disclaiming the title 'Mistress', she suspends the social hierarchy. But the moment she gives orders, she is 'crowned', while simultaneously 'uncrowning' the dead boss and his patriarchal order. At her wildly imaginative suggestion, which borders on perversion, the winery men gleefully splatter the wine on the ground 'three times' and then set the wine on fire to purge the curse on the winery. This is immediately followed by the drunken intrusion of 'grandpa' whose obscene account of the ravishment in the sorghum field disrupts the temporary reign of matriarchal order. Jiu'er is thus as easily 'uncrowned' as she was casually 'crowned' a moment ago. Under the rapid alternation between 'crowning' and 'uncrowning' lies 'the core of the carnival sense of the world – the pathos of shifts and changes'. As Bakhtin puts it:

> Crowning/uncrowning is a dualistic ambivalent ritual, expressing the inevitability and at the same time the creative power of the shift-and-renewal, the joyful relativity of all structure and order, of all order, of all authority and all (hierarchical) position. Crowning already contains the idea of immanent uncrowning: it is ambivalent from the very start. And he who is crowned is the antipode of a real king, a slave or a jester ...[13]

Soon grandpa is 'uncrowned': at the embarrassed Jiu'er's order, the newly 'crowned' is, as in Bakhtin's scenario, 'ridiculed and beaten'[14] while giving out a cry of joy and pain (itself a carnivalistic gesture), and is then thrown into a big vat. The hero who once bravely took the lead against the kidnapper and later became a kidnapper himself (another carnivalistic shift of crowning/uncrowning) – fulfilling what the first kidnapper failed to do, carrying away and ravishing the woman – is now rolling in the dust, his face masked with mud just as he masked it with cloth to capture the woman. The film 'introduces the logic of mésalliances and profanatory debasings'[15] of the hero in order to renew him. Nothing is absolute in the film, either negation or affirmation, in accordance with the imperative of carnival.

The uncrowning of 'grandpa', future boss of the winery, is replaced by the sudden menacing descent of a mob of local bandits. What ensues is 'a striking combination of what would seem to be absolutely heterogeneous and incompatible elements',[16] the yoking together of generic narrative elements. The accelerated montage of the gangster head descending from the roof to surprise Jiu'er clearly establishes a gangster-genre strand of suspense. Yet it is soon relativised and temporarily/partially negated by juxtaposition between gangster narrative and comic narrative: in the midground is the drunk, obliviously and ridiculously groaning and grumbling; in the background, high on the surrounding hills, is a line of gangsters menacingly hemming in the winery. As described by Bakhtin:

> Carnivalisation constantly assisted in the destruction of all barriers between genres, between self-enclosed systems of thought, between various styles, etc.; it destroyed any attempt on the part of genres and styles to isolate themselves or ignore one another; it brought closer what was distant and united what had been sundered.[17]

The comic undermines the threat posed by the gangsters; the gangster presence negates the comic element. Out of the dialectic interplay characterised by carnival levity and rapid change emerges the fundamental impulse of defiance and transgression that underlies or figures the film's vision of masculinity.

A discourse about masculinity in the Chinese context is in a way some version of what Mary Ann Doane would call the 'medical discourse', as it is pitched against disease. *Red Sorghum* echoes certain motifs recurrent in the literary 'search for roots' that surged in China in the early and middle 80s. Set in an imagined faraway, long ago world where naked human existence is every bit as crude as it is unpretentious, this new literary genre has as one of its leitmotifs the poetic celebration of masculine potency. D.H. Lawrence was a great source of inspiration. Masculine potency is often defined not so much around physiology as it is dialectically posited against the aging, disabled and diseased, for example the master well-digger in Jia Ping'ao's 'Heaven Dog' (*Tiangou*), who has to pull a wall down onto himself to give his wife away to his apprentice and son-figure.[18] Masculine potency becomes therefore a figure of coming into one's own being, of spiritual independence of authorial power. As an antithesis to 'disease', masculinity is an ideologically charged critique of a past cultural psyche afflicted with moral and spiritual disease.

Red Sorghum also sets up its masculinity as an antithesis to disease. The diegetic set-up is the potential victimisation of the heroine by Big Head Li, whose only boast is wealth. He 'generously' pays in the form of a big mule to acquire a beautiful young girl. Big Head Li is, both fortunately and unfortunately, a leper. He is figured on screen as a lean, old and haggard sulk whose sole action consists of smoking a water pipe (itself a culturally loaded signifier of addiction). The wedding does not appear to be consummated. Instead of approaching his bride with menacing desire, the misfit bridegroom is seen yards away wrapped up in the screen of his own smoke. One feels a lack, an impotence implied. Later we learn from the voice-over that the heroine kept her virginity with a pair of scissors, which again suggests the man's cowardice. He is also ridiculed in the sedan-bearers' song when they toss the bride by dancing along.

The medical discourse is also conducted at a deeper level. The masculinity posited as an antithesis to disease constitutes a critique of some essential lacks in the cultural body. Insensitivity to suffering, in a Western scenario of sexual difference, would mostly be categorised as a pretentious gesture towards masculinity. In Chinese historical and cultural codes, however, insensitivity to others' suffering in the form of passivity, indifference and evasion would have been considered an 'unmanly' attitude. In a classical narrative about outlaws or a martial arts legend, 'real men' would 'pull out the knife at the mere sight of injustice on the road'. Yet that masculine spirit seems to have disappeared, remaining only in the realm of the imaginary, in narrative utopias, whereas in the recent historical period of semi-colonisation there developed a 'national disease' of insensitivity and numbness which points to an inner cowardice and weakness.

Red Sorghum recuperates this issue. Yet the very recuperation through a melodramatic scene, while putting the presupposed spectatorial attitude under critique and proposing a *cause* of masculinity, at the same time creates a critique of itself.

A Japanese officer orders the butcher to flay two anti-Japanese heroes, one of whom happens to be the butcher's own gang leader. To do or not to do becomes a highly suspenseful narrative dynamic that is prolonged, deferred and twisted. The butcher kills the gang leader to relieve him of pain and is killed immediately. The suspense resumes when a kid, his apprentice, is ordered to do what is left undone. The torturing sequence ends with a prolonged shot of the boy approaching the hanging Luohan, once the foreman in the winery, reaction shots of the anxious spectators and a brief shot of the boy slicing Luo's eyelids.

This action may be meant as a visual stoicism to test the limit of human tolerance, to justify the inevitable masculinity as a Darwinist imperative and an ultimate survival strategy, and to buttress the cinematic representation of the masculine mood. The sadistic reification of the cruelty of reality may shatter any illusions about a feminine utopia of receptiveness, positive passivity, tenderness and harmony. The scene, however melodramatic it may seem, does have its cultural grounds: under the cultural surface of feminine tenderness and modesty, the satanic dark side of sadistic praxes such as flaying, branding, fragmenting and frying alive living humans – probably the cruellest on earth – was once a realised nightmare. The positive shock value of the scene may lie in its potential to jolt the audience out of their self-delusion about a tranquil feminine utopia, and out of their collective and private insensitivity to all kinds of massive social horror – a deep-rooted collective stupor characterised by Lu Xun, our most relentless and scathing cultural critic of the century, as one of the 'rotten diseases' of the Chinese cultural psyche.

Lu Xun is worthy of some attention here not only as an intertextual index on cultural attitudes towards the reality of violence and as a cultural frame of reference, but also because his work is generically significant. A number of his crucial narrative moments involve the problematic of spectatorship. The pivot in Lu Xun's physician-turned-writer career was a singular experience of movie-watching. On the screen were Japanese soldiers slaying a Chinese charged with spying for the Russians. The intradiegetic spectators – mostly Chinese – witnessed the scene in absorbing numbness and disinterested interest. Outraged and deeply hurt, Lu Xun walked out of the theatre with the painful documentary footage that was to surface and resurface in his literary imagination inscribed in his memory.[19] He resolved to cure the nation of its cultural disease with his scalpel-like pen. Lu Xun's most famous fictional character is Ah Q. He has become a prototype in the taxonomy of cultural archetypes, and an embodiment of all stupidities and insensitivity. When

Ah Q is sent for public execution, we have the most ironic narrative in Chinese fiction. Ah Q's last visual impression is of 'the crowds of spectators thronging both sides of the street' to witness a breathtaking spectacle. Their eyes seem to merge into a mass that starts to sink its teeth into his soul, and his last auditory memory is the spectators' 'Bravo!' that 'sounded like wolves howling'.[20] In *Medicine*, one of his short stories, the spectators watch a revolutionary's head being chopped off, their necks stretched 'as if they were a flock of ducks being gripped by an invisible hand and lifted upward'.[21] What Lu Xun deplores is not only the inhuman torpor attending such occasions and the selfish, unsympathetic coldness, but also the tragic mechanism implicating all the insensitive spectators: the victim of their visual pleasure may actually be a mirror, a flash-forward to their own future fates.

What we infer from these cultural narratives is the dichotomy of public moral insensitivity and private visual pleasure that lies at the heart of spectacle-watching as a deplorable cultural practice motivated by a diseased imagination. If we take this to be a cultural and historical given, we begin to feel an implicit critique of the contemporary Chinese mentality by Zhang Yimou's cinematic treatment of the spectacle of flaying in *Red Sorghum*. The sequence is almost a cinematic transcription of the Japanese soldiers slaying a Chinese in Lu Xun's memory. There is, however, a radical difference: the intradiegetic spectators are not those numb creatures that outraged Lu Xun. They are shown to be angry, only they have to suppress their helpless silent rage and defer its outburst to the narrative denouement. But for this sequence the locus is not in the intradiegetic spectators, though the main protagonists are among those who are given a few sporadic reaction shots. The vested cinematic interest here is in *showing* the spectacle for us, the spectators outside the screen world.

Zhang has publicly announced his interest in trying to steer a middle way between art cinema and the commercial blockbuster.[22] He does not want to lose audiences. Therefore *Red Sorghum* is motivated not only by cultural urgency, historical imperative and aesthetic vision, but also by a desire to act out the audience's spectatorial desire. This double aim could only be achieved through a bond dependent on tapping the depths of the audience's unconscious. Zhang's generous attention to the prolonged and profuse cinematic elaboration of the flaying as a privileged narrative moment betrays his awareness of the audience's private interest in violence. If violence is a universal, perennial stimulus that feeds on the audience's fantasy, then Zhang Yimou, while partly in complicity with that masochistic desire, politicises and historicises the violence so it cannot be taken comfortably as a mere visual thrill by a Chinese audience with a collective World War II trauma in their memory. The violence is pushed to extremes to jolt the audience out of their cowardice and insensitivity. This *presupposes* the continued existence of the pervasive insensitivity and torpor lampooned by Lu Xun half a century ago. Zhang therefore both acquiesces in and challenges the spectators' private desire.

Red Sorghum: heroine and lover in the sorghum field

On the other hand, there is always a danger that the audience will temporarily bracket the political, racial and historical significance of the scene for vicarious sado-masochistic pleasure. Even if the jolting effect exists, its cinematic elaboration may work in conspiracy with the audience's secret visual pleasure. In this way, the film encourages an insensitivity as well as discouraging it. And in so far as insensitivity has the potential to fall into an equation with passivity – as with the 'chink' in *Broken Blossoms* – which could be problematically attributed to femininity, it may subvert Zhang's project. In other words, the mass-culture motivations behind the film – the search for the melodramatic, for the visual stimulus – may deconstruct the texture motivated by a consciousness of high culture.

Autonomous ecstasy: a new version of female sexuality

One central dynamic in the cinematic narrative of *Red Sorghum* is men's kidnapping and ravishing of women, whether successful or not. Jiu'er is carried off by men four times in the film: first, as an unwilling bride carried by a group of lusty sedan-bearers to the leprous bridegroom; second, as a potential rape victim in the sorghum field; third, as a willing mate on her second trip through the sorghum field; and last, as a kidnapped victim to be ransomed by the local bandit. Even when 'grandpa' returns to assert his identity as her one-time love, he does it by the ritualistic act of carrying her off under his arm. As a regression and reversion to ancient myth, like the Western myth about carrying off Sabine women, described by Barthes as a masculine act in opposition to modern man's motionlessness which implies femininity, this diegetic impulse towards masculinity is unmistakable.[23]

Should we then dismiss the film as a blatant discourse privileging patriarchal order? Is female subjectivity jeopardized in this ostensibly masculine universe? A Barthesian dialectic is more than illuminating here. The subject/object paradigm in the problematic of the ravishment could well be reversed: 'It is the *object* of capture that becomes the *subject* of love; and the *subject* of the conquest moves into the class of loved *object*.'[24] The traditional scenario of subjective/active/aggressive male versus the objective/receptive/passive female is appropriated into the diegetic body, yet highly problematised, transfigured, challenged and subverted in the film. Jiu'er has to *wait* for men to initiate her. Yet passive waiting, the traditional fate of women in the Chinese narrative and scenario, attains a dialectic reversal in the film.

Red Sorghum transgresses the conventional Chinese melodramatic narrative pattern of the vulnerable woman intimidated by bullying men. As 'surprise' constitutes the heart of what Barthes calls the 'ancestral formality' of capture, the film subverts that by positing the woman as anything but panic-stricken or surprised prey to male desire. Jiu'er's first encounter with the masked kidnapper, or actually with a man, is one of the most transgressive and ambiguous moments in Chinese cinema. The shot-reverse shot structure establishes the woman's defiant confrontation with an unknown intimidating male presence, a diabolic male power. The filmic constraint of her explicit outward response signals her inner stability. The conqueror becomes the conquered. The frontal shot of Jiu'er is held still, correlating to the stupefied daze/gaze of the spiritually daunted and overwhelmed kidnapper. The reverse shot of the man, from Jiu'er's point of view, allows the camera the leisure and ease of tilting down from the mask to his body. The camera, as suggested by Christian Metz, can caress by tilting down the body, thus fetishising it. The camera that holds the bride could have conformed to Metz's formula, and it would be diegetically appropriate though symbolically different. Instead, we have the reverse. It is the woman's point-of-view shot 'fetishising', or rather exploring and sizing up, the man which is highly unexpected in such a situation. The bride's break into a smirk is even less expected. Her giggle neutralises the moral implication of the situation. The kidnapper's identity is temporarily bracketed; he is just an uncertain man desiring a woman who has an equal undiscovered and unchannelled desire.

A frontal treatment of female sexuality is almost a taboo in Chinese moral codes on representation. Female sexuality is traditionally split between moral denunciation and stylistic enunciation in Chinese texts. Women have been morally denounced as vamps and scapegoats bearing the historical burden of being roots of corruption and curses on imperial solidarity. Daji and Yang Guifei are just two examples.[25] At the same time, they have been stylistically enunciated as objects of desire with their subjectivity at stake. This duality itself bespeaks the inner workings of Chinese ideology: the mechanism of putting desire under erasure through which desire peeps.

Red Sorghum not only deletes that erasure, thereby unleashing the repressed desire, but also attempts to articulate an autonomous female sexuality/subjectivity. This is very rare in Chinese cinema. The film opens with a close-up of the bride. The ensuing shots put her among an undifferentiated male group, vaguely establishing an 'I-thou' relationship with the woman as 'I'.

The celebrated tossing-the-bridal-sedan sequence could superficially be taken as a scene of vulnerable woman at the mercy of lusty men. Yet the womb-like interior of the sedan, the condition of the Freudian 'oceanic self' where she floats as an effect of being tossed about, is symbolically self-sufficient and self-creative. The frontal close-up of her against a shrouding interior darkness not only frees her from the menacing male world, but also simulates the topology of interiority, an inner world. Its relationship with the outside world becomes tenuous. Her anxiety is indeed a response to the frightening picture of the feudal marriage awaiting her, sung out loud by the sedan-bearers. Yet by frequently registering the ballad as an offscreen auditory presence, and in view of the situation where she is the enunciated character – the 'I' amidst an undifferentiated male ensemble – it is easy to see that it is through her consciousness that the song enters.

But this is not an enclosure of narcissism. In this sequence, we are offered both the interior view of the sedan and the exterior view outside. A reiterated point-of-view shot by the bride looks out through the slightly open curtain on to a sweating, half-naked and muscular male body swaying in the dust. The following shot is the heroine's faintly dazed and desiring look. We may accept that the female gaze in classical cinema is often undermined, deflected, framed, erased by the male gaze catching the act of the female gazing, through *mise en scène* or editing, 'a strategy which is a negation of her gaze, of her subjectivity in relation to vision'.[26] However, the bride's gaze here is undistracted and subjectively autonomous. The interior is almost a figurative extension or externalisation of her subjectivity. Imprisoning as it is, it nevertheless resembles Kaspar's cave corresponding to Freud's 'oceanic self' or what Lacan calls 'l'hommelette'.[27] The slightly raised curtain offering the female heroine a keyhole-like or telescopic glimpse of the male body is almost a reversal of the classical formula for a male voyeuristic experience.

The group of sedan-bearers tossing a bride, while singing a lurid song or their own sexual fantasies out loud, is a displacement of sexual energy. The tossed woman panting and gasping is easily read as a sign of physical nausea, her emotional discomposure a mixture of fright and thrill. Yet the prolonged and repeated shots, cinematically rhetoricised here, are not so much sadistically motivated as a way of articulating a hitherto undiscovered female sexuality, both in the film and in historical textuality. The ruffled and confused look, heavy breathing and distractedness all suggest an overtone of sexual ecstasy, if not orgasm.

The establishment of autonomous female ecstasy, though a cinematic illusion, is highly subversive politically. In the context of Western Lacanian algebra, this might be yet another proof of female narcissism that impedes woman's stepping into subjectivity. In the Chinese scenario, however, posited against the deeply ingrained myth of female passivity and incompleteness, the twist in *Red Sorghum* is certainly a welcome cinematic gesture with its ideological effect, and it is not brought about by man's contact/act. Rather, we see the woman working herself into an ecstatic state through the agency of the structure of shot-reverse shot editing. Rather than falling into the conventional scenario of female sexual dependence on male initiation, the film maps out an autonomous space to foreground the world of her subjective consciousness. Female sexuality is represented not through the frank sexual scenes, which are kept off-screen, thus denying male spectators' voyeuristic impulses, but rather by focusing on the female presence as the locus of discourse. Gong Li, who plays Jiu'er, has a look of rapture and ecstasy that is always there. This assumes its most expressive form in the sequence where 'grandpa' shovels the distiller's grain out of the boiler. The grain falls on Jiu'er, who remains where she is, doused by the grains as if under a shower. She looks raptured and dazed. The shot carries a strong sexual overtone, as sexual intercourse is euphemistically alluded to as 'clouds and rain' in traditional Chinese texts. This allusion is visually recuperated here. What is important is that the shot concentrates on her while marginalising the male character, now an agent, who pours that shower off-screen.

The sequence where Jiu'er is shot unawares by a machine-gun from the approaching Japanese truck and her struggling on the verge of death is also highly stylistically transfigured and displaced into a non-diegetic moment of agony and dance. The slow motion plus the unexpected wedding music transform the scene into a moment of death and transfiguration, of death as a form of ecstasy (as if unconsciously echoing the Elizabethan equation of death with sexual ecstasy). In this way, the film could again be seen as a narrative return of the historically and culturally repressed. The idea of female sexual autonomy, probably derivative of the primitive matriarchal imagination, has survived more as a fantasised construct of desire and defiance against feudal patriarchy, in myths, legends, romances, folk tales, and various (sub)cultural Chinese texts.

These mythological narratives about autonomous female sexuality are diversely contained and reiterated in various historical/mythical narratives, such as *Huai Nan Zi, Shan Hai Jing, San Guo Zhi,* and *Hou Han Shu.*[28] Though imaginatively perverse, they fall into two basic categories: the myth of autonomous maternity, and the myth of a female utopia. In these female utopias, women become pregnant through immediate contact with the elements and forces of nature, for example through naked exposure to the 'South Wind',[29] or by dipping into the 'Yellow Pool',[30] or by dreaming of the white elephant.[31] These fantastic constructs project utopian visions of imagined realities in which even mere male existence is not to be tolerated; the female sex, self-reproductive, reigns all by itself.

One may argue that these narratives are the products of underlying Chinese feudal ideology privileging the homogeneity of femininity as a figure for class identity and a model for submissive consciousness. Yet considering the formal imaginative perversity of these fantasies that transgress the decorous mode of feudal discourse, the repressed desire sublimating into creative displacement is almost unmistakable.

These narratives also establish a scenario in which female sexuality and maternity are fused together. *Red Sorghum*, despite its predominant male presence, articulates an all-embracing female subjectivity which, in the same mythic fashion, destroys the distinguishing line between female sexuality and maternity, a line that is usually drawn in classical cinematic narrative, for example King Vidor's *Stella Dallas* (1937).

The film, ostensibly about the uninhibited manners of masculinity, is, however, ironically and structurally contained or cocooned in a discourse about the maternal, narrated by a first-person voice-over: 'Let me tell you a story about my grandpa and grandma. Where I come from, they still talk about it to this day. It has been a long time, so some believe it, some don't.' This opening dissolves into a medium close-up of a beautiful young woman and we hear the voice-over: 'This is my grandma.' The discrepancy between the connotations of the grandma and the actual iconographic figuration establishes a version of pre-oedipal attachment. The very first frontal shot of 'my grandma' could thus be seen as a mirror structure, the pre-Lacanian mirror-phase mirroring, inviting the unseen 'I' – whose very absent gaze towards the scene of his dreamscape also implicates us, the spectators in the dark theatre – towards a primary identification. 'Knowledge of the maternal is constituted as immediacy (one has only to look and see).'[32] In the cinema, according to Gaylyn Studlar, we all regress to the infantile, pre-oedipal phase, submitting ourselves to and identifying (fusing) with the overwhelming presence of the screen and the woman on it.[33] The device in *Red Sorghum* only accentuates that state of mind.

The voice-over frequently punctuates the cinematic narrative and reminds us that the screen presences, the young man and the young woman, are my 'grandpa' and 'grandma'. The first-person narrator, however, is absent throughout; at best he is figured on screen by a small boy spoken of as 'my father'.

The maternal discourse is, as it were, a framing structure and a strategy of containment: the film begins with the shot of 'grandma'/beautiful young woman, a fantasised image envisioned in the mind's eye/'I' of the voice-over narrator, and ends with a child's incantation and evocation of the maternal soul. The whole narrative is thus enclosed by this maternal discourse. One may even argue that this narrative strategy can be seen as a cinematic variant on the 'fort/da' game played by Freud's grandson, in an auditory form, experiencing the pain of the loss of his mother and the evocation of her recovery. The very beginning frontal shot of 'my grandma', a fiercely beautiful young woman – a frontal shot that resembles a still picture (and still pictures have an inherent pastness) – can thus be seen as recuperated from the historical/cultural memory, evoked by the child's incantation towards the end of the film.

Hence the film is a cinematic utopia, a dream narrative in which the speculative male 'I' of the narrative projects his desire and wishfulness onto a female/maternal world and ends up being contained by the final silent maternity: the voice-over narrator becomes absent towards the end of the film, replaced, or figured, by his father, iconographically represented on the screen as an infant who longingly chants after his dead mother. This narrative strategy holds the absent past in the cinematic present, while at the same time punctuating the illusion of presentness with a sense of the historical past. What is most interesting is that it is through 'my grandma'/young heroine's point of view that the past is mediated, reconstructed and totalised. In other words, it is through a feminine vision of totality that the masculine past is reconstructed and obtains coherence and meaning.

It follows that the death of Jiu'er, the 'grandma'/young heroine, in the diegetic space means the loss of perception, consciousness and meaning, since she has hitherto been the pivot around which the cinematic universe evolves. That traumatic blackout is cinematically enacted: 'grandpa'/young sedan-bearer, the survivor, turns into a stone as if without the female character's gaze he is one of the living dead.

The climactic denouement is actually an externalisation of Jiu'er's subjective consciousness on the verge of extinction. The shrieking *suona* (Chinese horn), playing the wedding song, projects her inner flashback of the moments of her past life. The agonised ecstasy and the ecstatic agony, the sexuality and death, are all (con)fused together. The death of the female's subjective consciousness means therefore a non-differentiation of everything, symbolised by the sweeping wash of red that dominates the screen – the dispersion of her entire being. Redness bespeaks desire, passion, blood (itself signifying birth and death), beauty and cruelty, and destruction and construction (in that the homogeneous colour scheme destroys the previous world of colour and re-orders a new world). The eclipse of the sun and moon defies any verbal formulation here, yet it is at least an emblem of Jiu'er's blackout, of a state of non-differentiation into which are collapsed the *yin* and *yang*, masculinity and femininity, day and night, self and other, warmth and coldness, war and peace. The haunting incantation praying for the soul of the mother is at once the echoes heard by the dying and echoes that reverberate in the corridor of historical memory, resounding Qu Yuan's poetic evocation for lost ancestral souls.[34]

The ending of the film is therefore the moment of cinematic *jouissance* in which we experience the loss of meaning as well as the birth of an infinite myriad of meaning. It is an orgastic and maternal synthesis, a maternal enclosure and mastery of narrative that proposes to construct a masculine identity.

Maternity is closely related to the natural, the unquestionable. 'Paternity and its interrogation, on the other hand, are articulated within the context of issue of identity, legality, inheritance – in short, social legitimacy. To generate questions about the existence of one's father is, therefore, to produce an insult of the highest order.'[35] The maternity of 'my grandma'/Jiu'er is an absolute given in the narrative while the paternity of 'my grandpa'/sedan-bearer is narratively 'mediated ... it allows for gaps and invisibilities, of doubts in short'.[36] 'My grandpa' is often an intruder onto the scene, which posits him outside of the maternal discourse and to be recuperated. The primal scene with 'my grandma', which admits the sedan-bearer into the narrative as 'my grandpa', is suggested but is only present as a narrative ellipsis. Ravished and sexually fulfilled, 'grandma'/young bride resumes her journey on a donkey, and 'my grandpa's' song, a barbarous yelp, is heard, designating his screen absence and offscreen presence. The sexual encounter is thus internalised into the heroine's consciousness and becomes a blank in the memory of the first-person narrator who has been denied the complete primal scene, a blank that may question its actuality and credibility in a later sequence when he appears from nowhere, drunk, and retells in a fragmented and crude manner what has taken place between him and Jiu'er. The narrative blank consequently puts the identity of the voice-over narrator at stake. Paternity in *Red Sorghum* is therefore frequently represented as absence, as the questionable, as the other. The irreverent attitude implied in the way the cinematic narrative comically contains him betrays not only an Oedipal complex with which the narrator tries to evince the paternal, but also the anti-patriarchal mastery of the narrative by maternity.

Red Sorghum also rewrites the maternal discourses of Chinese textuality. Identified with the mother earth, the motherland and the mother Party,[37] mother as a figure of identification in socialist ideology is traditionally evoked to elicit absolute unthinking allegiance, as maternity is related to the natural, the unquestionable. By positing the spectator vis-à-vis the sexuality of the maternal, the film not only pulls down all that is on the pedestal, but also revisions history as embodied in the dead grandma by setting free the repressed, figured as sexuality.

It is consequently tempting to fix *Red Sorghum* in a Freudian algebra as a narrative about the return of the repressed; or to water down the film into a Lacanian phraseology as the liberation of desire. Even director

Zhang Yimou's own confessional statement seems to favour that formulation: 'My personality is quite the contrary to the mood of the film. I have long been repressed, restrained, enclosed and introspective. Once I had a chance to make a film on my own, I wanted to make it liberated, abandoned.'[38] But there is also a difference. *Red Sorghum* is fundamentally a liberation of repressed collective desire. A lot of psychoanalytic categories, when placed in the Chinese context, cannot be embraced without some reorientation. The patterns of masculinity and femininity, dominance and submission, repression and desire are bound up with other cultural praxes in the Chinese context, and acquire new dimensions. In this way, *Red Sorghum* can be said to teeter on the borderline of the Western psychoanalytic scenario. And from this, we can come to feel the relevance of Fredric Jameson's critique of Western psychoanalysis in cultural criticism:

> The object of commentary is effectively transformed into an allegory whose master narrative is the story of desire itself, as it struggles against a repressive reality, convulsively breaking through the grids that were designed to hold it in place or, on the contrary, succumbing to repression and leaving the dreary wasteland of aphanasis behind it. At this level it is to be wondered whether we have to do with a mere interpretation any longer, whether it is not a question here of the production of a whole new aesthetic object, a whole new mythic narrative.[39]

Western allegories of desire and wish-fulfilment, according to Jameson, are 'locked into the category of the individual subject' and are therefore in need of expansion by transcending individual categories and tapping the political unconscious in terms of the collective and associative. This strategy remains comparable to a psychoanalytic one only in the persistence of just such a valorisation of desire.[40] Also, the Western psychoanalytic scenario of the male/female problematic, given its social implications and collective relevance, is equally motivated towards individual existence and finalised in the private realm.

One essential distinction that marks the contemporary Chinese New Wave cinema is its propelling sense of cultural urgency couched in the collective consciousness, and the impossibility of private isolation in a critical moment of historical transformation that will eventually implicate every individual. Issues of masculinity and femininity acquire more social symbolic resonance than the consequences they may have in the West. The problematic of sexual difference is politically more displaced, more often figured as signifiers of social and ideological entities than the immediate reality it denotes. Therefore Fredric Jameson's critique of the individualistic psychoanalytic critical paradigm seems especially relevant to the current cultural scenario of which Chinese cinema is a ramification. The strong repercussions *Red Sorghum* invoked confirm the public insistence on the wider collective implications of the cinematic narrative and the denial of any individual categories.

It is here, however, that Jameson's effective critique also becomes problematic. The very denial of the individual categories, given its cultural and historical imperative, has been shown to be regressive and repressive in the Chinese cultural context. In this way, the very placement of private categories, psychoanalytic or other, given their displacement in an urgently collective cultural landscape, can be seen as politically positive, affirming values that are nevertheless absent. In this sense, the culturally irrelevant psychoanalytic formula can be politically relevant.

In the ideological circumstances and cultural context of China, the narrative of psychoanalysis itself needs rewriting. In the case of *Red Sorghum*, repression and revolt – two fundamental events of psychoanalytic narrative – meet each other only through a tension across the threshold of the screen. The cinematic absence of repression renders the revolt undirected and dispersed into the ideological space outside the screen. The perennial offscreen reality as an antithesis to the screen world is *presupposed* and the cinematic world is an alternative to the offscreen world we inhabit. We see the importance of presupposition – the presupposition of a cultural presence registered on the screen as absence. Here we come to a critique of the simple-minded mimetic assumptions that sometimes go unquestioned in the rhetoric of cross-cultural studies (e.g., a culturally specific film is an iconographic representation of that culture). *Red Sorghum* and many other culturally specific texts do *not* reflect the *appearances* of a culture; they mirror what the actual cultural landscape *lacks*. They reflect fantasies and imagined memories – that which society expels. Any attempt to picture the Chinese cultural scene from this film requires an imaginative approach – in the same way one infers an image from a film negative.

Notes

1. For an example of negative critical response, see Zhu Shoutong, 'The Increasingly Ugly "Savage" Sensationalism' ('*Yuyi choulou de "man" ciji*'), and Zhong Youxun, 'They Lack Emotion', ('*Tamen queshao "qing"* '), in *Film Art* (*Dianying Yishu*), no. 192, Beijing, July 1988, pp. 35–40.
2. Cf. Li Zehou, *Zhongguo Gudai Sixiangshi Lun* (*A Critique of Chinese Intellectual History*) (Beijing: People's Press [*Renmin chubanshe*], 1985), pp. 161–2.
3. Zhang Dainian, *Zhongguo Zhexue Dagang* (*An Outline of Chinese Philosophy*) (Beijing: China Social Sciences and Humanities Press [*Zhongguo Shehui Kexue chubanshe*]), p. 34.
4. Dong Zhongshu, 'The Noble *Yang* and the Base *Yin* ('*Nanzun Nübei*')', quoted from Zhang Dainian, op. cit., p. 31. Dong Zhongshu (179–104 B.C.) founded the orthodox Confucian school of the Han dynasty (206 B.C.–A.D. 220). A civil servant in the reign of Emperor Wu, he was also an influential scholar who politicised, secularised and canonised Confucianism, turning it into a dominant

feudal ideology. The *Yi Zhuan* is a compilation of Confucian texts. Once attributed to Confucius himself, it is now thought to have been written by a group of scholars over a period from the beginning of the Warring States period (475 B.C.) to the end of the Han dynasty (A.D. 220).

5. This common saying may have its origins in the *Liezi*, a classical work of philosophy; see Zhang Zhan (ed.), *Liezi; Zhuzi Jicheng III* (Shanghai Shudian 1986), p. 6.

6. *Water Margin (Shuihu Zhuan)* is an extremely popular classical novel about a peasant uprising during the Northern Song dynasty (960–1127). Li Kui and Lu Zhishen are exemplary macho characters familiar to all Chinese.

7. Qu Yuan, *Ch'u Tz'u: The Song of the South – An Ancient Chinese Anthology*, ed. and trans. David Hawks (Boston: Beacon Press, 1962), pp. 22–5.

8. In Wu-chi Liu and Irving Yucheng Lo (eds.), *Sunflower Splendor: Three Thousand Years of Chinese Poetry* (New York: Anchor/Doubleday, 1975), p. 46.

9. Roland Barthes writes: 'I am wiped out more completely if I am rejected not only as the one who demands but also as the speaking subject (as such, I have at least the mastery of the formulas); it is my language, the last resort of my existence, which is denied.' *A Lover's Discourse: Fragments*, trans. Richard Howard (New York: Hill & Wang, 1978), p. 149.

10. Lin Yutang, *My Country and My People (Wutu yu Wumin)* (Taibei: Lin Bai Press, 1978), pp. 97–101. Lin Yutang (1895–1947) was a Chinese scholar who, with others, fashioned a Chinese equivalent of the English genre of familiar essays, with an emphasis on wit and brevity, which earned him a wide readership.

11. Martin Williams, *Griffith: First Artist of the Movies* (New York and Oxford: Oxford University Press: 1980), p. 109.

12. Mikhail Bakhtin, *Problems of Dostoevsky's Poetics*, trans. Caryl Emerson (Minneapolis: University of Minnesota Press, 1984), pp. 122–37.

13. Ibid., p. 124.

14. Ibid., p. 125.

15. Ibid., p. 124.

16. Ibid., p. 134.

17. Ibid., pp. 134–5.

18. Jia Ping'ao, 'Heaven Dog' (*Tiangou*), *October* (*Shiyue*), 2 (Beijing, 1985), pp. 6–29.

19. Lu Xun, 'Preface to *Call for Arms*', *Selected Works of Lu Xun* (*Lu Xun Xuanji*) I (Beijing: China Youth Press [*Zhongguo Qingnian Chubanshe*], 1956), p. 2.

20. Lu Xun, 'Ah Q' ('*Ah Q Zhengzhuan*'), op. cit., p. 89.

21. Lu Xun, 'Medicine' ('*Yao*'), op. cit., p. 20.

22. Li Xing, '*Red Sorghum*: A Journey to the West' ('*Hong Gaoliang: Xi Xing Ji*'), *People's Daily* (*Renmin Ribao*), overseas edition, 14 March 1988.

23. Roland Barthes, 'Ravissement/ravishment', *A Lover's Discourse*, p. 188.

24. Ibid.

25. Captured and taken as a favourite concubine by the last emperor of the Shang dynasty (1600–1100 B.C.), Daji is portrayed in various classical works as a vicious *femme fatale*, responsible for innumerable cruelties, perversities and corruptions. Named Royal Concubine in 745, Yang Guifei's elevation brought various of her brothers and sisters powers which they abused. This provoked an insurgency in which the emperor had to let Yang commit suicide to appease his own soldiers. The story forms the basis for Mizoguchi's 1955 film, *Princess Yang Kwei-fei*.

26. Mary Ann Doane, *The Desire to Desire: The Woman's Film of the 1940s* (Bloomington: Indiana University Press, 1987), p. 100.

27. Kaja Silverman, 'Herzog's *Kaspar Hauser*', *New German Critique*, Summer 1982, p. 74.
28. Also known as *Huainan Honglie*, *Huai Nan Zi* is a philosophical work compiled by Liu An (179–122 B.C.) and typical of a school known as the Eclectics, which flourished at the end of the Warring States period (475–221 B.C.) and the beginning of the Han dynasty (206 B.C.–A.D.220). The *Shan Hai Jing* is an ancient fantastic geography of China and its surrounding lands. It remains a major source of Chinese mythology. The *San Guo Zhi* is a 65-volume chronicle of the Three Kingdoms period (220–265), compiled by Chen Shou (233–297) of the Western Jin dynasty (265–316). The *Hou Han Shu* is a chronicle of the Eastern Han dynasty (25–220), compiled by Fan Ye (398–445). The latter two works are canonical examples of classical Chinese historiography.
29. 'The Female Kingdom', *Yi Yu Zhi* (*The Exotic Places*), quoted from Yuan Ke, *Zhongguo Shenhua Cidian* (*Encyclopedia of Chinese Mythology*) (Shanghai: Cishu Press, 1985), p. 45.
30. Guo Pu, *Shan Hai Jing*, *Jingyin Wenyuange Siku Quanshu*, ed. Ji Yun *et al.* (Taibei: Taiwan Shangwu Yinshu Guan, 1986), vol. 1042, p. 47.
31. Ji Yun, op. cit., vol. 254, p. 542.
32. Doane, op. cit., p. 70.
33. Gaylyn Studlar, 'Masochism and the Perverse Pleasures of the Cinema', *Movies and Methods*, vol. 2, ed. Bill Nichols (Berkeley and Los Angeles: University of California Press, 1985), p. 616.
34. Qu Yuan, '*Guo shang*' and '*Zhao Hun*', in *Ch'u Tz'u*, op. cit., pp. 43–4, 103–9.
35. Doane, op. cit., p. 70.
36. Ibid.
37. 'Sing a folk song to the Party', a popular song widely circulated in the 1960s in China, explicitly equates Mother with the Party: 'Sing a folk song to the Party, I liken the Party to Mother.' This identification has been wholeheartedly embraced by the Chinese since 1949, and has become almost a clichéd figure in various kinds of emotional rhetoric.
38. Li Xing, op. cit.
39. Fredric Jameson, *The Political Unconscious* (Ithaca: Cornell University Press, 1981), p. 67.
40. Ibid., p. 69.

Filmography

NB: s = scenarist, d = director.

Broken Blossoms, s/d: D. W. Griffith (Triangle Film Corporation, 1919).

Red Sorghum (*Hong Gaoliang*), s: Chen Jianyu, Zhu Wei, Mo Yan, d: Zhang Yimou (Xi'an Film Studio, 1988).

Breakthroughs and Setbacks
The Origins of the New Chinese Cinema

TONY RAYNS

The Chinese cinema was both product and participant during the remarkable and impressive transformation of Communist China brought to a dead halt in the Tiananmen Massacre of 1989. A dozen of the most innovative and exciting films made anywhere in the world in the last few years have come from China. As many already know, this 'new wave' has a lot to do with the arrival in the film industry of a number of young directors, most of them 1982 graduates from the Beijing Film Academy, China's film school. (They were the fifth class to graduate from the school's Directing Department; hence their tag 'The Fifth Generation'.) These films have won Chinese cinema a much higher international profile than it has ever known before.

The irony underlying these gains is that several of the 'new wave' films are now better known abroad than they are at home, where they have been attacked both for their failure at the box-office and for their suggestions of ideological deviation from CP orthodoxies. The following notes aim to set the 'new wave' films in the larger Chinese cultural context, and to clarify the debates that have been raging around them since the summer of 1986. The word 'debates' is probably already inducing yawns in some readers, and so I should stress that these are not academic squabbles but serious attacks and counter-attacks that put many entire careers on the line.

What makes the 'Fifth Generation' different from earlier generations in the Communist Chinese cinema? The short answer is: the life-stories of its directors. But the question is fundamental, and answering it properly involves sketching the general development of the film industry since the Communist victory of 1949.

Film has been a vitally important medium to the Chinese Left almost since the inception of the CP. Infiltrating the Shanghai film industry of the 1930s was a top Party priority, because film was seen as one of the most effective ways of opening up social divisions and promoting anti-Japanese resistance. Most of the films now thought of as 30s classics were written and directed by underground Leftists. And the film industry was an equally important battleground during the civil war years of the late 1940s, when left-wing film companies like Kunlun ('The Peak Film Industries Corp') and Wenhua regularly bribed government censors to let them make and release films that implicitly demanded radical solutions to social problems. It followed that the Party began establishing a new film industry as soon as it came to power in 1949. A studio built by the Japanese in Manchuria in the late 1930s was renamed the North-East Film Studio; despite terrible shortages of equipment and film stock, it managed to produce six features for 'New China' in 1949 alone. New studios were founded in Beijing and Shanghai in 1950. Meanwhile, the six existing left-wing film companies in Shanghai were allowed to continue operating independently of government control, although their films came under increasingly heavy ideological attack (led by Mao himself) and they were finally assimilated into an enlarged Shanghai Film Studio in 1953.

Films of both political colours made in Shanghai before 1949 had been addressed to a comparatively sophisticated and educated urban audience – for the simple reason that the cinemas to screen them existed only in the cities. The CP, needing to win hearts and minds in the vast rural hinterland, required a very different kind of film from the new, state-run studios. The new cinema was addressed primarily to the rural audience and the urban working class; it was couched in simple, didactic terms and was designed both to overturn centuries of feudal tradition and to pave the way for a huge programme of reforms, ranging from the new marriage law to campaigns to eliminate specific diseases. The model for this new cinema was, of course, the Soviet line in 'socialist realism', as developed under Stalin in the 1930s and still very current in the 1950s – as the Chinese film-makers sent to study at the VGIK film school in Moscow discovered. The Party took all necessary steps to bring this new cinema to the people: cinemas were built in every township and village, and small-gauge distribution was pioneered to enable films to be carried to the remotest areas of the country.

Although the Soviet influence was strong in the early years, the shortage of trained and competent film-making personnel was initially a problem. Many experienced veterans of the Shanghai film industry had fled to Hong Kong during the civil war or in 1949, and the Beijing authorities did not trust those who stayed to make the kind of films required in the new circumstances. China thus founded its own film school in 1956, under the aegis of the Ministry of Culture. From the start, the Beijing Film Academy opted against having an annual intake of new students, and instead accepted 'blocks' of students for training over a number of years. Like their present-day successors, the students of the first, second, third and fourth generations were taught not only film practice, theory and history, but also political economy, ideological theory and CP history. They were trained, in short, to make the kind of film that the government needed. The results were often none too distinguished as cinema; most of the best Chinese films of the 1950s and 1960s were actually made by older directors like Xie Jin, Ling Zifeng, Shui Hua, Lü Ban and Sun Yu, all of whom were active in the industry before the Academy was founded. (In the case of Sun Yu, long before; he began directing in the late 1920s, after studying in the USA.)

Like every other institution in Chinese cinema, the film school was closed down in 1966 by the early battles of the 'cultural revolution'. (The studios cautiously began to resume production in 1970, initially to film 'model revolutionary works' from the stage. The range of subjects gradually broadened, but the form remained straitjacketed by the Stalinist precepts laid down by Mao in his 1942 *Talks on Literature and Art*, as interpreted by his wife Jiang Qing. Levels of production returned to normal in 1976, the year of Mao's death, but it took several more years for China's film-makers to 'unlearn' the habits of the 'cultural revolution' years.) The school reopened in 1978, and the block of students who graduated as 'The Fifth Generation' in 1982 were part of its first post-'cultural revolution' intake. Their years in the Academy were marked by important developments at the national level: the short-lived 'Democracy Movement' of 1979, which left a permanent mark on the poetry and literature of the younger generation; the reopening of China to tourism; and the beginning of Deng Xiaoping's economic reforms, which quickly began to bring unprecedented levels of prosperity to some areas of the countryside. In the school, the students were able to see a much broader range of world cinema than preceding generations, partly because the Archive had also reopened and was beginning to recatalogue its collection, partly because the various foreign embassies in Beijing were much readier than before to loan prints for study purposes.

These students were different from their predecessors in several significant ways. For one thing, they had all been born *after* 1949, which meant that they had no first-hand experience of the 'old society' and that they were more or less immune to all the propaganda messages about things being better now than then. Like all other educated young people of their age, they had been sent to remote areas of the countryside in the late 1960s, to 'learn from the people'; they had consequently laboured in the fields and quarries alongside peasants for many years. For all of them, the competitive entrance exam to the Film Academy represented a lifeline back to urban society. The only 'culture' that had been available to them during their adolescence had been the ultra-didactic and endlessly monotonous theatre, cinema, fiction and painting of the 'cultural revolution', along with the notorious anthologies of Mao's *Thoughts*. The massive heritage of pre-Communist culture was as completely as possible suppressed. None of this was true for earlier generations of students at the Academy, who entered as younger men and women (their education having been uninterrupted) and who had neither first-hand experience of life with China's peasants nor the comprehensive grasp of China's realpolitik provided by the 'cultural revolution'.

There turned out to be another important difference between the Fifth Generation and earlier graduates: they were able to begin work as directors almost as soon as they graduated, instead of having to wait the usual

One and Eight

ten-to-twenty years. The long hiatus of the 'cultural revolution' makes it hard to generalise accurately, but the usual career-path for previous generations had been to serve long apprenticeships as assistant directors and then to direct first features around the age of 40. There were several reasons that the Fifth Generation directors didn't have this long wait. One was that many of them were assigned to small, regional studios, which didn't have hordes of directors on their books already. Another was that the rapidly burgeoning TV industry offered a lot of work to underemployed directors at all film studios. Yet another was the election of the middle-aged director Wu Tianming as head of Xi'an Film Studio at the end of 1983. Wu made it a matter of studio policy to give opportunities to young directors, with excellent (if controversial) results.

The initial breakthrough was made at the tiny Guangxi Film Studio in 1984. (Guangxi is the province that borders Vietnam in the mid-south-west of China.) Three Fifth Generation graduates assigned to the studio – director Zhang Junzhao, cinematographer Zhang Yimou and designer He Qun – formed a 'Youth Film Unit' within the studio, and made the film *One and Eight*. Faithful to its source, the film depicts an episode in the Anti-Japanese war: the chain-gang of prisoners, who include a falsely accused officer from the Communist army, demand their freedom so that they can protect themselves – and get it, in the process discovering unexpected reserves of patriotic feeling. The film neither looked nor sounded like any Chinese film before. Brutal behaviour and brutal language were matched by Zhang Yimou's brutally grimy and unsentimental images, and the film had a conspicuously unreverential attitude to the role of the Communist army. Inevitably, the Film Bureau in Beijing objected, particularly to the representation of the wronged Communist officer. Many changes were demanded before the film was cleared for release; some were simply cuts, but others involved reshooting entire scenes. The revised version (which preserves the original 'look' of the film but crucially alters much of the meaning) was released in China with fair commercial success, but banned from export until 1987. Its major impact was in critical circles: it demonstrated that a Chinese film could break the usual mould.

One and Eight was quickly followed by other 'new wave' films. At the Xiaoxiang Film Studio in Hunan Province, Wu Ziniu directed *Secret Decree*, another film that combined formal and tonal innovations with a certain thematic candour. It, too, is set during the Anti-Japanese war, and it shows an officer in the KMT (nationalist) army who refuses to cover up an embarrassing document signed by Chiang Kaishek; the depiction of a KMT officer as a 'good guy' was a first in Communist Chinese cinema. Meanwhile, Chen Kaige (who had been working as assistant to middle-aged director Huang Jianzhong in Beijing Film Studio since his graduation) was urged by his friend Zhang Yimou to apply for a transfer to Guangxi Film Studio. His request was granted, since Guangxi needed more directors and Beijing had too many. As a result, Chen was able to team up with his former classmates Zhang Yimou and He Qun and make the seminal *Yellow Earth*. At the same time, Tian Zhuangzhuang (who had cut his teeth on a TV film and a co-directed film for children) got invitations to direct features for the equally small regional studios in Kunming and Inner Mongolia. The Kunming Film Studio gave Tian the freedom to make *On the Hunting Ground*, a tough and mysterious film that could only be read as a devastating critique of China's traditional 'national minority' films.

This essay is not intended as a full-scale history of the Chinese 'new wave', and so subsequent developments must be summarised with telegrammatic terseness. *Yellow Earth* was received with considerable hostility by the older members of the film establishment, but its triumph at the 1985 Hong Kong Film Festival (with a 99 per cent Chinese audience) meant that it could not be dismissed as an aberration. In the film press and among the jury for the annual 'Golden Rooster Awards', the film was attacked for being obscure, incomprehensible and above the heads of the mass audience; the film-makers were also accused of trying to deal with a subject they were too young to know anything about. The China Film Association has since published a book of essays and reviews of the film, the only such book on a single film to appear in recent years.

Despite the controversies, the 'new wave' continued to gain ground in 1985 and 1986. Wu Ziniu continued directing innovative films for the

Xiaoxiang Studio, Tian Zhuangzhuang moved to Xi'an Film Studio to make his third feature, *Horse Thief*, and was soon followed there by Chen Kaige and Zhang Yimou. More new directors began work: Zhang Zeming in the Pearl River Studio in Guangzhou; Huang Jianxin, Zhang Zi'en and the man-woman team Zhou Xiaowen and Guo Fangfang in Xi'an; Hu Mei in the army-run August First Film Studio. Equally conspicuous was the influence of the younger directors on some directors of the older generations. Huang Jianzhong and Zhang Nuanxin, who had previously directed orthodox, theatrical-style melodramas, began making films that tackled unusual subjects and relied less on expository dialogue than on imagery to express themselves. The most striking evolution was in the work of the Xi'an Studio head, Wu Tianming, whose films *River Without Buoys*, *Life* and *Old Well* show a steady move away from ideological certainties and towards moral, psychological and political complexities.

By 1988, these and a few other Chinese directors had amassed a quite considerable body of work in the new vein, although it represents a very small proportion of the overall output of the film industry. Since the summer of 1986, however, it has attracted criticism on a scale and of a ferocity out of all proportion with its actual status in the industry.

The opening shot was fired by a young critic called Zhu Dake in the Shanghai newspaper *Wenhui Bao* (18 July 1986). Zhu wrote a viciously worded attack on the veteran director Xie Jin, whose films virtually embody the Shanghai Studio spirit. (They include *Stage Sisters*, *The Legend of Tianyun Mountain* and most recently *Hibiscus Town*.) Zhu accused Xie of 'cinematic Confucianism', by which he turned out to mean using blatant emotional manipulation to put across dated moral points. Published alongside a rebuttal by Jiang Junxu, Zhu's polemic sparked off a lively debate that soon spread right across the Chinese cultural press. Zhu Dake himself didn't say what he wanted to see in place of Xie Jin's melodramas, but the timing and placement of his attack strongly implied an endorsement of 'new wave' films like *Yellow Earth* and *Horse Thief*. Most of those who came to Xie Jin's defence certainly read such an endorsement between the lines. Whether the endorsement was intended or not, the backlash soon brought 'new wave' films into the firing line. Like the anarchic student demonstrations of December 1986, Zhu's polemic was a godsend to the hard left in the Politburo (most notably, the veteran ideologues Deng Liqun and Hu Qiaomu) and to the conservative mainstream of the film industry, which feared the new cinema and resented its success abroad.

The next important development was a speech given by Wu Yigong, head of Shanghai Film Studio and a talented director in his own right, in March 1987. A digest of Wu's speech was printed in the national newspaper *Guangming Ribao* (30 April 1987), and a translation accompanies Chris Berry's 'Market Forces' in this volume. Wu did not defend Xie Jin's films in specific detail, but argued for all films and film-makers to be

109

On the Hunting Ground

taken on their own merits; implied comparisons between directors of different ages and backgrounds were misguided and unhelpful. But he then went on to attack those in the film industry who contented themselves with a 'salon' success in foreign markets, thereby dismissing as insignificant the foreign sales of 'new wave' films. On the face of it, Wu's major concern was with the financial well-being of the film industry, which lost one-third of its domestic audience in the 1980s. He objected to the failure of the 'new wave' films to recapture this lost audience, and called for the production of a new type of conscientious entertainment cinema that would supposedly be capable of satisfying the home audience *and* of winning new audiences for Chinese cinema overseas. (Wu's speech was made just after Steven Spielberg's visit to Shanghai to shoot exteriors for *Empire of the Sun*.) However far-fetched Wu's dreams of international success seem, he cannot be accused of failing to put his money where his mouth is. At the time he made the speech, he was putting the finishing touches to his own new film *The Tribulations of a Chinese Gentleman*, a period adventure-comedy based on a Jules Verne novel, which exemplifies the kind of cinema he has in mind. The jury is still out on the film's prospects of achieving record foreign sales.

Tangled in with Wu Yigong's argument was a strong thread of nationalism: a desire for international prestige based on strictly Chinese terms. This evidently touched a chord in the hearts of those industry figures who suspected the 'new wave' films of being somehow 'un-Chinese', partly because they appealed to foreigners more than other Chinese films. But before anyone had time to ask themselves if there could possibly be a more specifically Chinese film than *Yellow Earth*, the debate took a more sinister turn. Disagreements about the merits of individual films were suddenly subsumed into the revived campaign against 'bourgeois liberalism', a campaign deliberately defined so vaguely that it allows the hard left to snipe at virtually *anything* it objects to. The campaign raged unchecked for most of 1987 (it was finally subdued to some extent by the Party Congress in October), with immediate, drastic effects in the literary and theatre worlds and effects on the film industry that will become apparent only in the longer term.

China's 'new wave' films have not uncritically embraced Western forms, nor have they turned their backs on Chinese themes and issues. On the contrary, if there is one factor that links directors as disparate as Chen Kaige, Huang Jianxin and Zhang Zeming, it is precisely their faith in a purely Chinese film aesthetic and their determination to deal with the immediate problems in Chinese society that they know at first hand. *Yellow Earth* re-examines one of the most cherished myths in CP history (the Communist army's encounter with backward village communities in the 1930s) and concludes that Communist ideology did not supplant feudal traditions as cleanly as the mythology holds. Zhang Zeming's

Horse Thief

111

Swan Song chronicles what has and what has not changed in China under Communist government, tracing a pattern of disappointments and betrayals across the life of an elderly Cantonese musician. Wu Ziniu's *The Last Day of Winter* is the first film to show China's *gulag*, a vast prison labour-camp in the north-western desert. Tian Zhuangzhuang's *On the Hunting Ground* and *Horse Thief* show the physical and spiritual lives of 'national minorities' in Inner Mongolia and Tibet, minus the usual mediating presence of Han Chinese. Hu Mei's *Army Nurse* calculates the emotional cost of sacrificing personal considerations to the greater good of the country. Huang Jianxin's films have brought satire back into Chinese cinema; although set in the present, *The Black Cannon Incident* shows a high-tech China from which all social problems except bureaucratic incompetence have been eliminated.

Taken as a group, these films have an impressive range and diversity. But they do have certain underlying elements in common. All of them reject the theatrical conventions that played so large a part in the 'socialist realism' tradition. They all minimise dialogue and trust their images to carry the burden of constructing meaning. They deliberately seek out subjects and angles of approach that have been missing from earlier Chinese films. As noted above, they are founded on a desire to forge a distinctively Chinese cinema, free of Hollywood and Mosfilm influences alike. Most important of all, though, they stand united against didacticism. They interrogate their own themes, and they leave their audiences ample space for reflection. After three decades of ideological certainty in Chinese cinema, they have reintroduced *ambiguity*. None of this means that they have made a radical break with the Chinese cinema of the past; nothing suggests that such a break would be either possible or even desirable. It would be truer to say that they are founded on a radical reassessment of the Chinese film tradition from a specifically modern perspective. They may have more in common spiritually with the left-wing classics of the 1930s than with the Maoist line in 'socialist realism', but that doesn't make them any less culturally specific to China.

Filmography

NB: s = scenarist, d = director.

Stage Sisters (*Wutai Jiemei*), s: Lin Gu, Xu Jin, Xie Jin, d: Xie Jin (Shanghai: Tianma Studio, 1965).

The Legend of Tianyun Mountain (*Tianyunshan Chuanqi*), s: Lu Yanzhou, d: Xie Jin (Shanghai Studio, 1980).

River Without Buoys (*Meiyou Hangbiao de Heliu*), s: Ye Weilin, d: Wu Tianming (Xi'an Studio, 1983).

Life (*Rensheng*), s: Lu Yao, d: Wu Tianming (Xi'an Studio, 1984).

One and Eight (*Yige he Bage*), s: Zhang Ziliang, Wang Jicheng, d: Zhang Junzhao (Guangxi Studio, 1984).

Secret Decree (*Diexue Heigu*), s: Cai Zaisheng, Lin Qingsheng, d: Wu Ziniu (Xiaoxiang Studio, 1984).

Yellow Earth (*Huang Tudi*), s: Zhang Ziliang, d: Chen Kaige (Guangxi Studio, 1984).

Army Nurse (*Nü'er Lou*), s: Kang Liwen, Ding Xiaoqi, d: Hu Mei (Beijing: August First Studio, 1985).

Black Cannon Incident (*Heipao Shijian*), s: Li Wei, d: Huang Jianxin (Xi'an Studio, 1985).

Horse Thief (*Daoma Zei*), s: Zhang Rui, d: Tian Zhuangzhuang (Xi'an Studio, 1985).

On the Hunting Ground (*Liechang Zhasa*), s: Jiang Hao, d: Tian Zhuangzhuang (Inner Mongolia Studio, 1985).

Swan Song (*Juexiang*), s/d: Zhang Zeming (Guangzhou: Pearl River Studio, 1985).

Hibiscus Town (*Furongzhen*), s: Zhong Ahcheng, d: Xie Jin (Shanghai Studio, 1986).

The Last Day of Winter (*Zuihou Yige Dongri*), s: Qiao Xuezhu, d: Wu Ziniu (Xiaoxiang Studio, 1986).

Old Well (*Laojing*), s: Zheng Yi, d: Wu Tianming (Xi'an Studio, 1986).

The Tribulations of a Chinese Gentleman (*Shaoye de Monan*), s: Yi Mingzhi, Qi Minsan, Hans Burger, chief director: Wu Yigong, d: Zhang Jianya (Shanghai Studio, 1987).

Market Forces
China's 'Fifth Generation' Faces the Bottom Line

CHRIS BERRY

Major changes have been occurring for quite some time now in the economics of the Chinese cinema, but it is only in the last year or two that they entered the written discourses surrounding the medium. I have translated a few examples of the new discourses here (see below, pp. 125–40), and the purpose of this commentary is to introduce but also to denaturalise the economic crisis they all assume. I do not doubt that money problems exist, but the questions are why it has taken so long for them to be written of, and why they have been taken up and deployed in the way they have.

The profitability of individual films at the box-office was not a major issue in the public discourses of the People's Republic from its establishment in 1949 to the 1980s. This was partly because such concerns would have been bourgeois thinking in the ideology of the times, and partly because, in a society where there were few other forms of recreation available, it was unlikely that films could lose money anyway.

All this has changed in the last few years. In 1979, Deng Xiaoping came to power and a programme of changes now referred to as 'the reforms' (*gaige*) was instituted step by step. Among other things, emphasis is now put on the financial accountability of individual economic units, which are expected to pay attention to efficiency, increased production and profitability. A whole genre of reform films has appeared to promote these policies. In place of the worker-peasant-soldier heroes of yore we now have the sort of technocrats and yuppies Mr Reagan and Mrs Thatcher would have been proud of.

For the film industry itself, these new demands have come at a time when it is less and less able to meet them. First, the range of recreation options has greatly increased. 'Swinging Nightlife in Guangdong' is the title of an approving article in Beijing's English-language newspaper, *China Daily*.[1] It announced that Guangdong province, which borders Hong Kong, now has 4,680 pool rooms, 510 video game arcades and more than 3,300 video theatres, visited by 150,000 people every day. Other alternatives to the cinema springing up all over China's major cities include discos, Japanese-style *karaoke* bars, teahouses and fast food restaurants. Beijing has China's first Kentucky Fried Chicken restaurant, situated within easy walking distance of the Chairman Mao Mausoleum.

Of possibly even greater importance than these outside-the-home options has been the advent of television as an entertainment medium. Less than ten years ago, few individual households had TV sets, and the medium was mostly regarded as an educational vehicle, whether in the sense of political lectures, news, or the teaching of academic and vocational skills ('education' has all these significations in Chinese). Now, fully 48 per cent of households have sets,[2] and the schedule has expanded greatly to include Mexican telenovellas, Italian league soccer matches, and innumerable home-produced mini-series.

As alternatives to the cinema have been multiplying, the film audience has been falling off steadily. Getting meaningful national-level statistics that can be compared year to year is very difficult in China. However, one 1987 article states that in urban areas between 1979 and 1985 there was a 17 per cent fall-off in the number of screenings and a 43.5 per cent decline in admissions. In the countryside, over 40,000 of the 150,000 mobile projection teams that serve the area have folded up.[3] The same article states that 1986 saw a rise in admissions, while another specifies a 14.7 per cent rise in urban admissions and a 15.38 per cent rise in urban box-office take during the first seven months of that year, although it also notes that rural audiences were continuing to fall.[4] In 1987, there seemed to be a switch, with urban audiences down 200 million in the first six months of the year and rural audiences up 620 million,[5] and a slight overall rise was recorded for the whole year,[6] but despite these hiccups long-term prospects seem to offer at best a bottoming out rather than a recovery.

To make matters worse, as the number of admissions has been falling, and with it box-office income, the costs of film production have been rocketing. One late 1986 article reports that the costs of hired extras have doubled, and lists all sorts of other apparently exorbitant location fees.[7] Another article published late last year states that since 1980 the costs of raw materials used in film production have gone up between 15 per cent and 36 per cent.[8]

As a result of all this, in 1986 only 20 per cent of films made back their investment.[9] As early as February 1987, the sense of crisis was so all-pervasive and well-publicised that an article could be headed 'Are Epics the Way Out?' (*Jupian Shi Chulu Ma*) without any fear that readers might ask, 'the way out of what?'[10]

Although a discourse of economic crisis was developing by 1986, this was quite a few years after the economic changes themselves had got under way (around 1980 according to the reports I have just cited). At that time, traditional discourses were still firmly in place, and it has taken a long time for them to shift. They derive mostly from the Yan'an Forum dictum that art must serve politics, a Maoist formulation that meshes well with the ancient Confucian precept of art as a form of education.[11] Since the establishment of the People's Republic, a pattern has developed whereby films, and indeed all literature and art, are supposed to reflect

115

and publicise Party policy and its achievements, and if they don't, periodic campaigns are launched to discipline the film-makers.

These campaigns are always launched in the name of the broad masses of the people. However, the box-office fall-off that began in the very early 1980s indicated that perhaps the broad masses were less desirous of education than the cadres assumed. In response, the studios began to produce *kung fu* (*gongfu*) films, detective films, and other forms of entertainment-oriented material that hardly fitted the traditional bill.

These films were part of an overall cultural loosening up and commercialisation. Whether directly because of the ideological misfit between this and existing critical demands, or because the misfit provided an avenue of attack for conservative forces within the establishment, in late 1983 the 'anti-spiritual pollution' (*fan jingshen wuran*) campaign was launched. Short-lived though it was, it now stands as the last example to date of a traditional campaign lining up the Party/state versus the filmmakers in defence of didactic art.[12]

However, although it was the last traditional campaign, 'anti-spiritual pollution' was not the last effort at a traditional campaign. That came late in 1985. In the years between, there was no let-up in the production of 'vulgar' (*su*) films to attract audiences back, or to attract new audiences, given that television was destroying family audiences and replacing them with more socially specific groupings. Furthermore, the appearance of a film called *One and Eight* in 1984, rapidly followed in the same year by the better known *Yellow Earth*, marked the appearance of a whole other category of films not obviously in the service of politics, or at least not the right politics. These were the 'Fifth Generation' films.

The term 'Fifth Generation' (*Diwu Dai*) is derived from a periodisation of Chinese film directors that started to make its way around soon after the appearance of *One and Eight* and *Yellow Earth*. Basically, it refers to directors trained since the end of the 'cultural revolution' in 1976. At least one of the reasons prompting the appearance of the term must have been the startling and immediately apparent dissimilarity of their films from what had gone before. Their topics were not the officially sanctioned issues of the day, as peddled endlessly in the *People's Daily* and almost every other mass medium. *One and Eight*, for example, is about prisoners held by the Communists during the Anti-Japanese War, including suspected traitors from their own ranks, something the authorities had hitherto preferred not to mention. Furthermore, the films looked very different from the marriage of 1940s Hollywood and Soviet socialist realism that had become the norm in mainland Chinese film-making. Darkness and asymmetry replaced centredness and full lighting in both *One and Eight* and *Yellow Earth*. Later Fifth Generation films such as *Horse Thief*, *The Big Parade*, *Black Cannon Incident* and *Swan Song* also kicked against the old norms in an astonishing variety of ways, including non-narrative forms, pitting the individual versus the collective, expressionism, satire on Party paranoia and personal film-making.

As the rapid coining of the term 'Fifth Generation' itself indicates, these new films had an immediate impact on Chinese film critics. Other terms that began to be used to characterise their highly distinctive work included 'the academy school' (*xueyuan pai*) and 'exploratory' (*tansuoxing*).[13] In the sudden vogue for art films, traditional Yan'an values seemed largely forgotten. The critical success of the 'Fifth Generation' inside China was repeated when *Yellow Earth* was sent abroad in early 1985, but reviews and discussion during its first outing at the Hong Kong Film Festival alerted officials that the film could be read as a criticism of the failure of the Party to transform the chronically impoverished lives of ordinary rural Chinese. In the autumn of 1985, repercussions against both the 'Fifth Generation' and the continuing flood of entertainment movies began.

At first, the new drive was not apparent in public discourse, but various films were withheld from distribution. This ban could apply either within China (for example, a *Flashdance* rip-off called *Superstar*), outside China (no more copies of *Yellow Earth* were to be sold abroad), or both (the 'Fifth Generation' satire on government bureaucracy called *Black Cannon Incident* was critically acclaimed but not distributed at all for quite some time). The only public evidence of this effort to launch a new cultural/ideological campaign was heavy publicity for two films called *Fascinating Musical Band* and *Our Demobbed Soldier*.

These films were typical examples of traditional didactic film-making, both eulogising aspects of the government's reform programme in classical style. In January 1986, a report appeared on the front page of the *People's Daily* that *Fascinating Musical Band* had been seen by various Party leaders, all publicly known to be cultural conservatives. Some, notably Deng Liqun and Hu Qiaomu, were heavily associated with the previous 'anti-spiritual pollution' campaign. They were reported to have liked the film. Hu Qiaomu was alleged to have commented: 'Everybody should give the green light to films that are healthy and in the interests of socialism, but everybody should also give the red light to bad films.'[14] Within the week, *Our Demobbed Soldier* was teamed with *Fascinating Musical Band*, and the two were released as the big films for the lunar New Year holiday. An unusual nationwide release advertisement for eight New Year films appeared in the *People's Daily*, including photographs for *Fascinating Musical Band* and *Our Demobbed Soldier* only.[15]

Despite this aggressive start, the effort to launch a new 'red light, green light' campaign, as I will call it, never got further than a publicity drive. Precisely what the broad political reasons for the failure were is largely a matter of guesswork. However, it was noticeable that the film industry stuck together in their opposition to what was going on, and not even the directors of *Fascinating Musical Band* and *Our Demobbed Soldier* got involved in calls for heavier censorship and 'healthy' films.

With the complete failure of the 'red light, green light' campaign even to get off the ground, state/Party insistence on didacticism seems to have

117

Fifth Generation films: *Black Cannon Incident* ...

reached the end of the road, at least for the time being. The public acknowledgment of the financial crisis that had beset the film industry for some years already is a mark of this in itself. No longer was the discussion of money and profits beyond the pale. The economic policies that had been pushing studios to keep an eye on the bottom line since the turn of the decade were finally out in the open. Complaints about studios who made commercial films being money-minded also disappeared. As early as March 1986, an article appeared pushing the old principle of 'appealing to both popular and refined tastes' (*Ya Su Gong Shang*).[16] Although stressing the middle road and not giving way to 'vulgarity', it also affirmed the need to entertain the audience more strongly than had been done for some time.

However, although this was a setback for conservative forces in the state/Party, it also put new pressure on the 'Fifth Generation'. Although their films have won critical plaudits, they have not been commercially successful. The average Chinese movie sells about 100 prints, but only a few of the 'Fifth Generation' films have reached this level. *Yellow Earth* only sold thirty prints within China, and many others have sold even less. Particularly notorious in this regard have been the almost non-narrative ethnic minority films of the iconoclastic Tian Zhuangzhuang. *On the Hunting Ground*, his account of traditional Mongolian life, only sold two prints, both to the head offices of China Film Corporation for reference purposes, not for distribution. His follow-up on Tibet, *Horse Thief*, only sold seven prints.[17]

118

... The Big Parade

However, Tian made himself more notorious than poor sales of his films alone could ever have done with a September 1986 interview in China's most widely read magazine, *Popular Cinema*.[18] Tian appeared remarkably unconcerned about his lack of fans, and declared that he was making films for audiences of the next century. It was this latter remark that everyone latched on to. The November and December issues of the magazine carried responses to the interview, most of them furious. If failure to serve politics had become a poor position from which to attack the 'Fifth Generation' or any other group of film-makers, failure to serve the immediate needs of the broad audience clearly commanded broader support.

The fuss about Tian's remarks was interrupted by the 'anti-bourgeois liberalism' (*fan zichanjieji ziyouhua*) drive, started at the beginning of 1987 in response to student unrest at the end of the previous year. Launched on a society-wide scale, it was conducted in discourses on the cinema in a way that reveals a lot about the readjustments and regroupings that had already taken place since the aborted 'red light, green light' campaign. First, it was almost entirely absent from discourses on the cinema at all. I can find almost no articles that go beyond the general mouthing of support to discuss what sort of films should be made and what should not. 'Anti-bourgeois liberalism' could only be interpreted in cultural spheres as a return to traditional opposition to 'vulgar' entertainment. This position was largely exhausted, as we have seen, and furthermore did not lend itself well to a film world now represented as facing financial crisis because of its failure to cater to the tastes of the masses.

However, when it did come, the one major film article produced out of the 'anti-bourgeois liberalism' drive confirmed a new conservative strat-

119

egy and an attempt to consolidate the new constellation of forces emerging against the 'Fifth Generation'. Wu Yigong's 'We Must Become Film Artists Who Deeply Love the People' was published in March 1987.[18] It was republished nationwide a month later, which indicated wide political support by the conservatives who were still riding high then.

The first important feature is that Wu is a film-maker, and a very prominent one. In the last few years, film professionals have presented a united front in response to government moves, not permitting a divide-and-rule strategy to be deployed against them. Wu's remarks, which were mostly directed against the 'Fifth Generation' and the young critics who support them, signalled an end to that. For his pains, he has won the undying hatred of much of the Chinese film-making community, who now see him as a traitor. Even some of those who agree with him have told me privately they resented his speaking out publicly at such a time.

Why would Wu be willing to break ranks and attack the 'Fifth Generation' in this way? The 'Fifth Generation' must bear some of the blame for this themselves, because they have been completely unabashed about their opposition to traditional mainland Chinese film-making. Zhang Yimou, cinematographer on *One and Eight* and *Yellow Earth* and director of *Red Sorghum*, has said quite frankly about the first 'Fifth Generation' film, *One and Eight*: 'One thing was clear – it had to be different from what had gone before. ... There was a lot of falseness in the Chinese cinema then, and we didn't like it very much.'[20] Even without remarks like this and Tian Zhuangzhuang's interview, just looking at their films it was obvious that the 'Fifth Generation' were determined to distinguish themselves from the older generation.

Furthermore, Wu Yigong belongs to a generation of Chinese film-makers some of whom have special reason to resent the 'Fifth Generation' – the 'Fourth Generation'. Trained before the outbreak of the 'cultural revolution' in 1966, this group of directors had little chance to practise their craft until after the fall of the 'gang of four' in 1976. No sooner had they hit their stride and made names for themselves as innovators than the 'Fifth Generation' came along. For the more adventurous among them, this was not a problem, but for the likes of Wu Yigong it spelt eclipse. His *My Memories of Old Beijing* and *Elder Sister* were considered groundbreaking, but by the time *University in Exile* was released, he had been overtaken completely. He had neither critical nor box-office success. Most recently, he has shot an extremely low-brow slapstick comedy called *The Tribulations of a Chinese Gentleman*, adapted from a story by Jules Verne. Going by his article, he has not taken eclipse well.

Second, although with this article Wu had been positioned as the mouthpiece of the 'anti-bourgeois liberal' line in the cinema, it includes none of the old attacks on 'vulgar' film-making.[21] The language of Wu's argument is a contradictory amalgam of the old and the new, almost deserving of close textual analysis in its own right. One moment, Wu is sneering at young critics who use the word 'explore', the next moment he is using it himself to boast about his studio's films.

However, despite lapses like these, he does work towards a consistent new position on the relationship between the old values and the newly acknowledged economic situation. On the one hand, Wu trots out the usual Yan'an line about cinema's 'essential value as a medium for popularising things with the masses'. But instead of setting this up against 'vulgar' films, he opposes it to 'salon art', arguing that greatness cannot be attained unless one's works are liked by the 'broad masses of the people'. While not going so far as to say that box-office success equals greatness, Wu makes it clear that in his book greatness is impossible without box-office success, a stance very different indeed from Tian Zhuangzhuang's idea that he is making films for the audiences of the next century.

In this article, then, a very significant reorganisation of forces is attempted, lining up audiences newly empowered by effective consumer choice, traditional film-makers and, presumably, the political conservatives behind 'anti-bourgeois liberalism' all on one side. This is very different from the past, when the forces of the state/Party tended to be isolated in the face of a united front of film-makers. This article attempts to isolate one fraction of the film-making community against everyone else: the 'Fifth Generation'.

Although the 'anti-bourgeois liberalism' drive waned quickly, the rest of 1987 saw a great number of articles discussing the need for 'entertainment' films and how to produce them. *Popular Cinema* devoted a whole issue to the discussion of comedy films, long felt to be a weak point in Chinese cinema but 'the genre that sells most seats abroad'.[22] They followed that up by publishing an imploring letter demanding to know why Chinese people always preferred foreign films to Chinese films.[23] In reply, they received over 150 manuscripts, some of which were published in the November and December issues of the magazine. Although some suggestions were made that the vulgarity of foreign films might have something to do with it, more emphasis was put on the idea that Chinese films lacked something. Flick through any national newspaper or film magazine of this period, and you will find more articles along these lines. In case anyone missed what all this was getting at, one newspaper article made it quite clear by suggesting that the 'fever' for 'exploratory' films of the last few years was giving way to an 'entertainment film fever' (*Yulepian Re*):[24] it meant continued pressure on the 'Fifth Generation'.

Any lingering doubts that this is the main direction in which the discourse of economic crisis has been developed can be met by consideration of some striking, and possibly structuring, absences in this discourse. First, and most noticeable, with the exception of Tian Zhuangzhuang's vigorous self-defence there has been very little consideration of why loss-making films might be worth funding, even though this was never a problem before economic crisis was finally discovered in 1986. After all, vanguardism could be argued to be an honourable Leninist tradition. The idea of subsidising art film production from commercial films has not been publicly debated much either, even though it is the *de facto* practice at studios willing to produce art films. Nor has there been much discussion of reforming the distribution system to allow for different patterns of release and the development of arthouse audiences.[25]

Perhaps most important of all, as accusations against 'Fifth Generation' films and film-makers in the name of the box-office have snowballed since the Tian Zhuangzhuang interview, there has been no discussion of the fact that 'Fifth Generation' films are far from the only loss-making movies in China. This is not surprising when one realises what the other box-office failures are. Wu Tianming, head of Xi'an Film Studio, explains: 'There are three audiences that have to be satisfied in China. One is the government, one is the art world, and one is the ordinary popular audience.' He goes on to say that although the studio is supposed to satisfy all three at once, that is rarely possible, and so it often shoots different films for different audiences.[26] For ordinary audiences, it is *kung fu* and detective films; for the art world, it is 'exploratory' films; and for the government, at the moment it is reform movies.

It is an open secret in China today that reform movies are no more successful with audiences than 'Fifth Generation' films, although there are no published statistics to verify this, and this is one topic that has not entered the debate about satisfying the box-office.[27] Furthermore, where 'Fifth Generation' films probably take up no more than 10 to 15 per cent of annual production and are usually made with low budgets, reform films command full budgets and take up 40 per cent of annual production. They are a far heavier burden on the studios than 'Fifth Generation' or 'exploratory' films, but studios dare not refuse to make them and no one has dared attack them for failing to attract audiences yet.

As I write, in early 1988, the deployment of economic crisis against the 'Fifth Generation' has begun to take its toll. The translation of an interview with 'Fifth Generation' director Zhang Junzhao (see below, pp. 130–3) is an example of that. Headed 'A Changed Director', it is in clear counterpoint to the interview with Tian Zhuangzhuang, which was headed 'A Director Who is Trying to Change the Audience'. It is also as heavily negotiated as the Wu Yigong text. On the one hand, Zhang claims to support 'formal experimentation', as he puts it, but on the other hand he wants to get closer to the audience and seeks a crossover point between art and the box-office. Zhang certainly isn't as unabashed in the face of box-office failure as Tian.

Zhang had in fact given up the iconoclastic path long before many other 'Fifth Generation' film-makers. He has made purely commercial films since his debut, *One and Eight*, and more recently other 'Fifth Generation' film-makers have been forced to follow suit, however reluctantly. Woman director Hu Mei has made two psychological character portrait movies, *Army Nurse* and *Far from War*. Although both were critical successes, neither did well at the box-office. 'Apart from anything else, when your film doesn't make money, your crew doesn't get a bonus,' she explains. 'I want to make a film that earns money for the studio now.'[28] Even Tian Zhuangzhuang has been cornered into shooting a BBC-style adaptation of a classic short story, *Travelling Players*. When I expressed surprise to him on reading the very conventional script, he explained why he had taken the project on: 'It's like when you go out shopping. Whatever you're looking for, you can't find it, so you end up buying radishes.' Even the ever-optimistic Zhang Yimou had to admit that he could not see any exciting films coming up in 1988.[29]

However, China is in a permanent state of flux, and at the same time as the 1987 box-office attack on the 'Fifth Generation' is having its effect, more positive signs have been appearing. Most important is Zhang Yimou's Golden Bear at the 1988 Berlin Film Festival for *Red Sorghum*, unquestionably the highest award any Chinese film has ever received. The event was covered extensively by the press in China, and, more important, *Red Sorghum* has been a major box-office success in China itself. Tickets in Beijing sold at 60 to 70 cents, well above the average urban price of 20 or 30 cents, and there was a brisk trade in black market tickets. Ironically enough, and contrary to the expectations of many, it may be a member of the 'Fifth Generation' who is showing the way to appeal, once again, to 'both popular and refined tastes'. Furthermore, the press coverage and official trumpeting indicated that there are other forces in the state/Party than just conservative ones.

All in all, the last few years have seen a series of shifts in which economic crisis has been taken up to bolster the weakened position of conservative Party/state forces and undermine the 'Fifth Generation' film-makers. That this strategy has been temporarily successful is evident from changes in film production. *Red Sorghum*, on the other hand, is evidence that the 'Fifth Generation' may be fighting back. What is unclear at this point is whether other 'Fifth Generation' directors will be equally able to find large audiences, and what price they will have to pay to do so. Whatever happens, whether things work out to the benefit of conservatives or cultural radicals, *Red Sorghum* also signifies that this struggle will now be played out according to the values of a new discourse of box-office demands that has replaced and taken over certain elements of the old Yan'an discourses.

Notes

1. *China Daily* (Beijing), 25 November 1987.
2. *China Daily*, 27 January 1988.
3. 'Film Market Studies Urgently Needed' (*Jianli Dianying Shichang Xueke Bu Rong Huan*), *China Film Times* (*Zhongguo Dianying Shibao*; Shanghai), 28 February 1987.
4. 'Urban Audience Grows in the First Seven Months' (*Tou Qige Yue Chengshi*

Guangzhong Da Sudu Shangsheng), *China Film Times* (Shanghai), 18 October 1986.

5. 'Cinemas losing viewers', *China Daily* (Beijing), 14 August 1987.

6. 'Thrills and spills win movie fans', *China Daily* (Beijing), 21 January 1988.

7. 'The Uncontrolled Demanding of Fees in Film and TV Shooting Must be Stopped' (*Yingshi Shezhizhong de Luansuofei Xianxiang Bixu Zhizhi*), *China Film Times* (Shanghai), 15 November 1988.

8. 'Film Studios Need Policy Support' (*Dianyingchang Xuyao Zhengce Fuchi*), *Wen Hui News* (*Wenhui Bao*; Shanghai), 11 November 1987.

9. 'The Reform of the Film System Has Become an Urgent Issue' (*Dianying Tizhi Gaige Chengwei Jinpo Keti*), *Wen Hui News* (Shanghai), 23 November 1987.

10. *Wen Hui News* (Shanghai), 6 February 1987.

11. Bonnie S. McDougall, 'Mao Zedong's "Talks at the Yan'an Conference on Literature and Art": A Translation of the 1943 Text with Commentary', *Michigan Papers in Chinese Studies* no. 39 (Ann Arbor: 1980).

12. Various reasons for the rapid failure can be guessed, ranging from the lack of response among the population at large to fears of another 'cultural revolution' and a withdrawal of the foreign investment and cooperation China's reformers were relying on for the success of their economic policies.

13. 'Exploratory' has taken hold rather more firmly than 'Academy school', and, along with 'Fifth Generation', appears without any explanation in some of the articles that follow. 'Academy school' refers to the Beijing Film Academy, China's only film school and the main training ground for the 'Fifth Generation'. Strict interpretations of the term limit membership to the Academy's 1982 graduates only. The appearance of terms like these must be seen as part of the development of a quite different discourse positioning cinema as an activity independent of politics, economics and any other art, the beginnings of which can be traced to the late 1970s. Interesting though that is, it is beyond the scope of this article.

14. *People's Daily* (Beijing), 12 January 1986. My translation.

15. *People's Daily* (Beijing), 25 January 1986. Films are usually released at different times by local distribution and exhibition corporations, and therefore most film advertisements appear in local newspapers.

16. Zhong Yibing, '"Appealing to Both Popular and Refined Tastes" is a High Artistic Standard' (*Ya Su Gong Shang Shi Yishu de Gao Biaozhun*), *Popular Cinema* (*Dazhong Dianying*; Beijing), 1986:3, p. 3.

17. All figures from an interview with Wu Xiaojin, deputy director of planning and research, China Film Corporation, 15 February 1988. Probably the most successful 'Fifth Generation' film to date has been *Secret Decree*, which sold 240 prints. *Black Cannon Incident*, which sold 99 prints, is its nearest competitor. *Red Sorghum* has also done very well, but no final figures were available at the time of the interview.

18. See translation.

19. See translation.

20. Interview, Hawaii International Film Festival, 28 November 1987.

21. A recent article by a Western sinologist represents Wu's piece as another conventional government attack on deviations from the traditional line. Although I do not disagree that the 'Fifth Generation' face considerable hostility, I think this representation is an over-simplification of a text that is both 'negotiated' and evidence of a new government line. See Geremie Barmé, 'Cultural commissars in the camera's eye', *Far Eastern Economic Review*, 10 March 1988, p. 42.

22. Ai Qi, 'Comedy – The Genre That Sells Most Seats Abroad' (*Xiju – Guowai Zui Mai Zuo de Leixingpian*), *Popular Cinema* (Beijing), 1987:7, p. 7.

124

23. See translation.
24. 'On the "Entertainment Film Fever"' (*Manyi Yulepian Re*), *Wen Hui News* (Shanghai), 26 June 1987.
25. To be fair, my interview with Wu Xiaojin did reveal that arthouse experiments had been attempted in both Shanghai and Guangzhou. However, they met with little success, not only because the fad wore off, but, ironically enough, because there was not enough art film supply to maintain the arthouse identities of the theatres involved.
26. Chris Berry, 'Out of the West – The Rise of the Xi'an Film Studio', *China Screen* (Beijing), 1986:4, p. 34.
27. Wu Xiaojin was completely candid with me on this, admitting: 'Not many reform films have been successful – I think that's because even when they're not just trying to flatter people, they're not realistic enough.'
28. Interviewed in Chris Berry, 'Hu Mei: Woman Film Director and PLA Officer', *China Reconstructs*, English edition (Beijing), XXXVII:4, April 1988, p. 55.
29. Interview, op. cit.

Translated Documents

A Reader's Letter That Will Make People Think*

MO ZHONG

To the editors of *Popular Cinema*

Hello!

I'm a ticket seller in a movie theatre. I love my work, because I give out admission passes to lots of people desperate for a little pleasure. However, over the last few years, I have found myself full of worry and confusion, sometimes to the point where I'm scared sick.

There's only one reason: our Chinese films (by which I mean mainland films) are getting the cold shoulder, and what's more, the indifference also contains a certain amount of scorn!

For work reasons, I often get in touch with factories, administrative organs and schools about selling blocks of tickets. As soon as I get through on the phone, the first thing they ask is: 'Is it a Chinese film? If so, we won't go!' When I'm selling tickets at the window, if it's an

---

* *Yifeng Qi Ren Shensi de Duzhe Lai Xin.*

average Chinese film, there aren't many takers. What's more, people are always asking me over and over again: 'Is it good? Is it really good?' The expression in their eyes and their tone of voice are full of vigilance, as if they are always on their guard against being cheated. They ask again and again; of course it undermines my self-respect and my enthusiasm.

Depressed, I set about investigating and comparing the releases of foreign and domestic films (by foreign films, I mean Hong Kong, Taiwan and films from abroad). I discovered that over the last few years box-office income from foreign and domestic films at our theatre has been more or less the same, but that we have screened four times as many domestic as foreign films.

Why do Chinese audiences (and especially urban audiences) not prefer our own Chinese films?

Some filmgoers are very sarcastic about it: 'When you go to see a foreign film, your chances of being taken for a ride are four to one against, but when it's a Chinese film, four times out of five you're duped. Who wants to pay money to be made a fool of?'

Many filmgoers are more reasonable about it: 'We have lots of things to do in our spare time, and it's not easy to get a chance to see a movie, so if seeing it ends up worse than not seeing it, what's the point of coming? All we can do is stay away.'

I remember the spring before last, our theatre was showing the Hong Kong film *Three Laughs* (*San Xiao*). The place was packed for several days from eight in the morning until ten at night. One night, a husband-and-wife directing team came specially to the theatre door. They asked the people, who were all wrapped up in cotton-padded clothes, waiting to buy the high-priced tickets: 'You've seen this film before, why do you want to see it again?' Back came the answer: 'I've seen it three times, and I still want to see it – I'm addicted!' The directing couple didn't know what to think as they walked off – they didn't think much of the film at all.

Comrade editors, today our theatre is showing another Chinese film which cost a million *yuan* to make. It's the first screening, there are only thirteen customers in the whole auditorium, and I'm scared to see the expressions on their faces when they come out. Caught between compulsion and confusion, I'm writing this letter to you. I really don't know if I should be mad at our audiences or mad at our film-makers.

Just what is the reason for all this?

Can you come up with an explanation that will convince me and the many other filmgoers?

I'm waiting!

Yours respectfully,

Mo Zhong, Shanghai

Originally published in *Popular Cinema*, 1987:8 (Beijing), p. 2.

A Director Who is Trying to Change the Audience*

A Chat with Young Director Tian Zhuangzhuang

YANG PING

Reporter: I hear you're not too willing to have exchanges with the audience.

Tian (looks dumbstruck, then expression suddenly clears): There's no way to exchange! I've never had exchanges with the audience.

Reporter: Lots of filmgoers can't take *Horse Thief* when it's screened; maybe that's proof of what you say.

Tian: I shot *Horse Thief* for audiences of the next century to watch. There are two aspects to any art: the popular and pure art. In music, for example, *bel canto* doesn't go down as well as popular music, but both of them are necessary. They influence each other. It's not a case of one or the other.

Reporter: But a film is made with state money, and a lot of money at that. If not even one print is sold, why should the state want you?

Tian: Yes, there are economic losses at the moment, but they're necessary. Wu Tianming once said, 'I'd rather a film didn't sell a single copy, just so long as the quality is good.'[1] I don't think one should fixate on one person's works, or on a group of people's works. Let's have less yelling and shouting just because one person's work is slightly different from the general run. If it hadn't been for *Yellow Earth*, there couldn't have been the whole debate about film aesthetics, and there couldn't have been the overall progress that cinema has made.

Reporter: But a director who is exploratory should keep the audience in mind, and try his or her best to get close to them.

Tian: I don't agree with that formulation. It should be a matter of getting close to each other. When the French New Wave movement began, it caused a lot of fuss too, and there were people attacking it from all sides. However, they stuck firm, and as a result attracted a large audience. The films at some festivals in France today are very dry, but the screenings are full to bursting point, and afterwards the audience debates and discusses with the director for hours. Why can audiences abroad accept both commercial and art films, but not in China? It shows how different their attitudes are. A French person once asked me, 'With all these debates [they meant the opinions being expressed about various exploratory films in China], is the problem with the audience or with you young directors?' I said I was afraid the main problem was the audience.

* *Yige Shitu Gaizao Guanzhong de Daoyan.*

127

Reporter: A German writer once fulminated: 'What the hell are readers and the people anyway?' You probably agree.

Tian (scratching his head, a little bit embarrassed): There's something to that. But it wouldn't be smooth sailing if there wasn't any audience, because you've got to think about how you're going to go on. If there wasn't an audience, you could curse the audience as much as you liked, but you wouldn't have any way of proving whether the direction of your explorations was correct or not. Van Gogh's paintings were the precursors of Fauvism, but at the time he himself didn't know, and there was no one who could prove that to him, so he lived a very hard life. In comparison, Picasso was a lot luckier. If it hadn't been for Van Gogh, it would have been very strange if he'd still had an easy time. That's what was lucky about *Yellow Earth*, too. It came at just the right time, and it has provided a cushion of support for us by making the sacrifice that a pioneer makes. Although it ran into a lot of criticism, most people recognise that it represents the future of Chinese cinema now.

Reporter: You're getting away from cinema. Let's talk about *Horse Thief* itself. Some people have said that it would be better to say *Horse Thief* is a documentary about customs than to say it is a feature film, that it is just one scene about local customs after another, that it's impossible to figure it out, and what on earth is the director trying to say? I feel that way myself.

Tian: How many times have you seen *Horse Thief*?

Reporter: Once.

Tian: I suggest you see it again. The theme of the film is very simple, in fact – the relationships between humanity and religion, and between humanity and nature. Its message is quite clear, too, otherwise how would we have been able to make sense of our fanaticism during the 'cultural revolution'? As for the customs being hard to understand, there's nothing strange about that. Tibet is very unfamiliar and distant to us. Zhang Xinxin, Zhang Chengzhi and Shi Tiesheng[2] had the same feeling after they saw the film. At first, all they could see were the customs and they tried to read all sorts of meanings into them, but the second time they saw the film they simply saw them as customs and that's all.

Reporter: But it's not as though the customs have nothing to do with the meaning of the film at all. In making a film, a director cannot select a lot of material that has nothing to do with the content of the film, nor should he or she select materials that the audience cannot understand at all. As for unfamiliarity, the usual demand is to use materials the audience can accept. Even if they only have a little knowledge about them, that's usually enough. The demand is that there be some explanation, whether through dialogue, narration or subtitles. Only if there's explanation is it O.K.

Tian: If I had to depend on explanation, I couldn't have made the film. There are five religion scenes in *Horse Thief* alone. Once I explained one of them, what could I do about the others? The Tibetans have tens of

Tian Zhuangzhuang's *Horse Thief*, set in Tibet

festivals every year, and each festival has its own distinct relationship to the existence of natural things. The significance of religion in their lives is far beyond what we can imagine or understand. Take the 'ghost dance' scene, for example. That's a story in its own right. Why are there so many evils in the world if not because there are so many ghosts and monsters? Therefore, Buddha's attendant warrior guardians must come to sweep away the ghosts and monsters, using ox heads as a symbolic protection. This scene occurs after the death of the son of the lead character, Rorbu (Luo'erbu), and it expresses his regret about horse-stealing. After that there's another dance, the second son is born, but the lead character can't support the child, and so is forced to return to his old ways and steal horses again. The audience does find it difficult to understand the significance of these customs for the lead character. It's an alien culture. You need to do a lot of preparation work and accumulate a lot of knowledge. But if you flick through a few books on Tibetan religion, lots of things will become clear quite easily. By the way, I want to tell you something interesting. One person's interest in Tibet rocketed after seeing the film, and now they're planning to go there and check it out at their own expense.

Reporter: But I don't understand the horse thief himself. At the beginning it says it take place in 1923, but no matter whether it's 1923 or 1983, horse-stealing is always wrong, so why does the film represent him the way it does?

Tian: Horse-stealing is very common in Tibet, to the point where it's almost a profession. For reasons of physical geography and lack of economic development, horses are a form of currency in Tibet, and so horse-stealing happens a lot. For me to become a horse thief would be the same as becoming a carpenter, and I wouldn't feel there was any difference.

Reporter: But the film itself doesn't make it clear why Rorbu steals horses. Just how poor is he? Is horse-stealing a hobby of his or is he forced into it? The film doesn't say, and so the audience is not in a position to exercise judgment.

Tian: I hadn't thought about that problem. Maybe I'm too used to going to minority nationality areas, and so it's very easy for me to understand what the author of the original work was trying to get at.

Reporter: Is anything we've said off limits? Will you mind if I just write this interview up as is?

Tian: Nothing's off limits. Do your worst!

Translator's notes

1. Wu Tianming was the head of Xi'an Film Studio, for whom Tian Zhuangzhuang made *Horse Thief* in 1986 on loan from his home studio, Beijing Film Studio.
2. All young, Beijing-based authors.

Originally published in *Popular Cinema*, 1986:9 (Beijing), p. 4.

A Changed Director*

Transcription of a Dialogue with Zhang Junzhao

GAO JUN

Gao: Many 'Fourth Generation'[1] directors, including Huang Jianzhong and Zhang Zi'en,[2] have said they fear the awakening of the 'Fifth Generation', because they think when the 'Fifth Generation' wakes up, it will form a powerful challenge to them.

Zhang: What does this 'awakening' mean?

Gao: To put it simply, it's a matter of getting close to the audience.

Zhang: That awakening should take place. Films are made for audiences

* *Yige bei Gaibianle de Daoyan.*

130

to see. If no one wants to see them, how can one begin to talk about social benefits?

Gao: As the director of *One and Eight*, how do you explain *Come On, China!* and *The Lonely Murderer*?[3]

Zhang (after a moment of silence): My first concern has to be surviving, right? If survival is threatened, talking about goals and ambitions is a waste of breath. To tell the truth, if I'd shot another film like *One and Eight*, I may well have been unable to continue as a director. Take Tian Zhuangzhuang, for example. *Horse Thief* and *On the Hunting Ground* lost tens of thousands of *yuan* between them, and no one went to see them. Do you think Xi'an Film Studio will dare to use him again?

Gao: Do you mean to say that you've been changed by the audience?

Zhang: In the relationship between artists and audiences, one can only talk of mutual change and harmony in an extremely normal creative atmosphere. That doesn't exist at the moment, or at least not completely. The current situation is that there are a few works which are different in too many ways, and so, once they're released, their original intentions are completely lost.

Gao: Some people feel there are clear divisions among 'Fifth Generation' directors, with Tian Zhuangzhuang the one whose explorations have gone furthest, and you as a typical example of someone who goes against the general tendency, the two of you forming two very distinctive extremes. What do you think of that?

Zhang: Divisions are very natural. No generation of directors are all the same. Everyone has a different understanding and different feelings about life and art – every person has their own begging bowl! As for extremes, I do in fact feel that formal experimentation is completely necessary. From quantitative change to qualitative change, one has to go through a process.

Gao: At the moment, some directors are searching desperately for an ideal point of overlap between artistic expression and being passed by the censors, between entertainment and art. Do you think this is of any significance?

Zhang: It's very necessary! I've wanted to go after that point of intersection for a long time, but it's very difficult. There are a lot of things in which chance plays too large a part. No one is willing to oppose already recognised norms. The cinematic art is wrapped in a layer of soft yet tough group consciousness. It will take a great many very individualistic artists to pierce it. In the film world, we should appeal for individuality.

Gao: Have you noticed that, generally speaking, the works of 'Fifth Generation' directors don't do too well at the box-office? Is this a strong point or a weakness? Are you in the habit of seeing the audience as gods or enemies?

Zhang: Two aspects of that have to be discussed. First, the film cultural level of the vast majority of moviegoers really is pathetically low. Too much pandering to that will unquestionably lower artistic standards, but

Zhang Junzhao's *One and Eight*

if you don't pander to it at all there's no way to survive. There's nothing that can be done. *The Lonely Murderer* is a cut below *One and Eight*, but it sold tens more prints. How do you explain that? Second, only a minority of people ever appreciate pure art. Take *Li Sao*[4] or *La Comédie Humaine*, for example. Whether in the past, the present or the future, only a minority of people have read them, are reading them or will read them. I wonder whether or not things could be like this from now on: you make a few top-grade entertainment films to get the right to go on, and then shoot some serious art films to do some exploration. It's a matter of swings and roundabouts.

Gao: I hear you've taken on a film called *Out on Parole* (*Jia Shi*). What are you aiming to do with that?

Zhang: I just want . . . to earn a little money for the studio.

Translator's notes

1. A periodisation current among Chinese critics divides Chinese film history into five generations of film directors. The 'Fourth Generation' consists of directors trained before the outbreak of the 'cultural revolution' in 1966, but who had little chance to practise their skills until after the fall of the 'gang of four' in 1976. The 'Fifth Generation' consists of the next group of students to graduate from the country's only film school, the Beijing Film Academy, i.e. the class of 1982, and also other young directors.
2. Huang Jianzhong is a fairly experimental director whose works include *As You Wish*, *A Good Woman*, *Questions for the Living* and *Chastity*. Zhang Zi'en is

known for stretching the limits of more commercially established genres, for example with the Anti-Japanese War movie *The Silent Little Li River*, and the *kung fu* film *Magic Braid*.

3. *One and Eight*, *Come On, China!* and *The Lonely Murderer* are all directed by Zhang Junzhao. The first, made in 1984, was shot by cinematographer Zhang Yimou in the dark, asymmetrical style he was to use again in *Yellow Earth*. Although *One and Eight* was made before *Yellow Earth*, and so qualifies as the first 'Fifth Generation' film, it has only ever been allowed abroad once, and so is not as famous outside China as *Yellow Earth*. Zhang Junzhao's follow-ups have all been more commercial films which, although they have helped to fill the studio coffers, have won him few critical plaudits in China.

4. *Li Sao* is the name of a famous poem by the fourth century B.C. Chinese poet Qu Yuan.

Originally published in *China Film News* (*Zhongguo Dianying Bao*) 56 (Beijing), 5 April 1987.

We Must Become Film Artists Who Deeply Love the People*

WU YIGONG[1]

What I want to say today is something that I have been bottling up for a long time. I hope you will all look upon it as the thoughts of a film director.

Beginning in the second half of last year, people started kicking up a fuss, levelling all sorts of criticisms at the so-called 'Xie Jin formula'.[2] I feel that in terms of objective results this is leading Chinese cinema down the wrong road. I have always felt that no matter whether an artist's creative pursuits, style, form and creative formulas are good, if they leave the people and the things the people care about, then even if they are held in the highest esteem the people will not recognise or accept them in the end. On the other hand, if an author or artist is able to synchronise their heart with the pulse of the times, get in touch with the tastes of the people, and also conscientiously pursue their own artistic ambitions, then no matter what sort of fuss a few people kick up, their works will always be approved of and liked by the great masses of the people. Their time will never be 'over', and their works will never be 'out of date'.

Tradition and innovation are interrelated, and one should not be over-emphasised at the expense of the other. An artist cannot be like Sun Wukong, the Monkey King, who sprang out of a crack in a rock.[3] The

* *Yao Zuo Yige Re'ai Renmin de Dianying Yishujia.*

133

development, individuation and formation of their thinking and the coming together of their art is a never-ending process. How can one possibly get rid of tradition altogether? Of course, without innovation and development, tradition may stagnate and become fossilised, too.

Some people are very hot on 'transcendentalism' at the moment (*chaoqianyishi*).[4] I believe this concept itself is utter nonsense. All of an artist's greatness lies in his capacity for sharp understanding of the present and profound exposition of the past. If someone sniffs at real life today, and just rushes madly after 'transcendence', then they'll be just like Lu Xun said, pulling their hair up in an effort to lift themselves off the earth.[5] What's the difference between that and idealist apriorism? Although the 'ego' cannot be absent in any artist's creative work, if you place the 'ego' above everything else, then neither the times nor the people will respect you.

There are also some people who say, 'That a film attracts an audience isn't necessarily a good thing.' I think that's extremely strange. Let's be upfront about this. Every artist has their own audience in mind, but what 'audience' means varies. If I say I make movies for myself, that's simply lying. What in fact is the starting point of creativity? Who you make your films for is, of course, not an issue that should be forced on people. However, history proves that if it is not the whole people, the people who nurtured them, that artists aim to serve, then although their works may be appreciated by some people and may even be very popular for a while, they won't survive, no matter what. If you take a look at the classics, which one of them has not withstood the test of time and the broad masses of the people?

Turning back to Xie Jin again, I feel the most valuable thing about his works is that he always bases them solidly in realism. He has put all his sincerity and passion into ardently creating a series of characters that embody the times, thus putting his feelings and thoughts about the times on the screen.

Some people say that film should chuck out the idea of appealing to both popular and refined tastes, and instead separate the artistic, the entertaining and the educational. They make it sound such a simple matter! The ancients in China praised the idea of appealing to both popular and refined tastes, and the high levels of attainment they achieved in this regard were extremely hard-won. It may be tough to make a film that has a limited audience and a high artistic level, but making a film that has a broad audience and achieves a certain artistic standard is even tougher. At the moment, the great majority of our film-making troops cannot satisfy either demand. Because of that, theory and criticism should not hold themselves apart too much or be too narrow-minded. Some people insist on going on about exploration, as though just mentioning exploration ups the value of their work a hundred-fold. In fact, if you analyse a few of those articles in detail, their level of theoretical preparation is very low.

Therefore, looking back now, I feel we should be a bit more self-confident.

How was last year's production at Shanghai Film Studio really? As far as art is concerned, in terms of variety of subject matters and styles, the development of new themes, the expression of directorial individuality and so on, there have been big changes. Taking variety of subject matters as an example, we had three young directors make films independently last year. They shot *The Last Sun*, a film about old age which encourages contact between young people and old people; *Me and My Classmates*, which explores subject matter about young people; and *Trapped on a Frozen River*, which is a eulogy to the Party. Urban films included *A Bible for Daughters*; children's films included *Kids Canteen*; *The Missing Girl Student* was a big breakthrough in films for teenagers; reform films included *T Province 1984–1985*; and epics included *President Extraordinary* and *Hibiscus Town*. In the production of these films, old, middle-aged and young film workers all displayed their talents. As far as the market is concerned, the average Shanghai film sold 156.9 copies in 1986, more than any other studio's films and well above the national average.

Just when Shanghai has been doing well both artistically and economically, one, two and even three waves of attack have been launched against it, and most of them have tried to sweep everyone aside, old, middle-aged and young alike. I can't believe this is just a coincidence.

Ever since 1982, I have had the vague feeling that some of the directions being taken by film theory are not too correct, but I didn't see it as clearly then as I do now. At the time, people used to complain about Shanghai, saying, 'You don't have any theory.' Yes, Shanghai had always placed more emphasis on practice, and theoretical work was very weak. Because of our shortcomings in theory, we often had to suffer in silence. That's why we've set up an art theory research office, and committed ourselves to making it a success.

The research that theorists have done into the essence of film started off very promisingly with the discussion on the 'divorce of film and theatre'. But since then some research has gradually been moving away from reality, abstracting and mystifying film art, taking it further and further away from its essential value as a medium for popularising things with the masses. One of the biggest problems in the theory world today is getting the value of film all upside down. Which comes first – its existential value or its essential value?[6] If an artist makes a film without taking the audience into account at all, then how can they see the film's essential value as a medium for popularising things with the masses? It's as though the act of making a film has become more important than what sort of film you make. I feel this is an inversion of values, and the existential value of the act itself has been elevated to an unsuitably high position. It cannot be denied that existential value has a certain use, but overvaluing it can lead to reversals.

In France, Italy and other countries, there has indeed been a sort of experimental cinema which specialises in exploring narrative methods and techniques. However, artistic experiments and artistic practice are not the same thing. We cannot take a few foreign experiments in film language as the yardstick by which to measure our own creative practice. The existential value of making a film itself is not so high, and we must still rely on its essential value. That's why, in the director's report on *My Memories of Old Beijing*, I wrote: 'What's important is what you narrate, not how you narrate.'[7] However, some people in the theory world have inverted the relationship between those two things now, so that 'how you narrate' has become the basic thing, and 'what you narrate' has been reduced to an afterthought. I think this runs counter to the laws of art.

Maybe some people would reply: 'Look what you're saying! Where does Griffith's greatness lie? Where does Eisenstein's greatness lie? They created the close-up, montage theory and so on.' Quite true, these things are the accumulated treasures of film theory. However, they were created under conditions according to the laws of synthetic art. Furthermore, only when it was blended into the content and thoughts that they wanted to express was the power of their theory produced and made clear.

I have always thought that theory and artistic practice should be separated, and that basic theory and film criticism should be separated. I once read a piece of criticism on *My Memories of Old Beijing*, in which there were many lines and dots, punctuated with red, blue and black. It said that the attacking power of the 270th shot was produced out of the 47th shot, and so on. I object very strongly to this sort of research. Of course, if people want to do that sort of thing, there's no reason why they shouldn't. However, I absolutely could not use that stuff to guide my art – I couldn't be taken in that far! It cannot be denied that theory has a very important guiding role to play in regard to practice, but fundamentally speaking, theory is born out of practice and not the other way around. The relationship between these two things cannot be inverted. How strange it would be if one could make a good film without real enthusiasm for life and artistic sensitivity and instead just a head jammed full of concepts and symbols.

This touches on the issue of an artist's attitude to life and their feelings of social responsibility. This seems to be a tired tune today, but in fact it is an irrefutable truth. All the outstanding artists in history sincerely had a warm love for life and a warm love for the people. However, some of our artists now are fixated on salon art, which only a few people appreciate.

At base, cinema is a popularising medium for the masses. Some people say my *Elder Sister* was a step forward from *My Memories of Old Beijing*, that *University in Exile* was a step back, and that *The Tribulations of a Chinese Gentleman* constitutes degeneration. I don't agree with these opinions. I made *The Tribulations of a Chinese Gentleman* with open eyes, of my own accord and clear-headedly, not in order to pander to anyone. I want to use my work to express my own outlook on life and on film. From *Our Tabby* to *Evening Rain, My Memories of Old Beijing, Elder Sister* and *University in Exile*, all the way through to *The Tribulations of a Chinese Gentleman*, I have only worked on one theme, and that is the discovery of self-worth. However, in making *The Tribulations of a Chinese Gentleman*, there was another consideration, too; to prove by making a comedy film that box-office value and the pursuit of the entertaining does not have to be seen as 'vulgar' and 'low'.

Of course, one of the reasons some young people today look down upon the Chinese cinema is that Chinese cinema has been disappointing in some ways. But it is also because the critics have evaluated certain films inappropriately. Maybe some people might say I'm a Narodnik, but I don't care.[8] I want to be a Chinese artist, and not a foreign artist or an artist enslaved to foreigners. Without Chinese national characteristics, how can something become international? If a film can't be understood by the Chinese people, how can it achieve international affirmation?

I feel that if Chinese film wants to go out into the world, there are two paths open to it. One is to rely on films like *Yellow Earth* and *My Memories of Old Beijing* to get a footing in foreign film salons. However, this is far from good enough. We must also take another path; obtaining the approval of Chinese audiences at the same time as winning the recognition of broad foreign audiences on the international market. Some of our comrades are too satisfied with salon success now, and I feel they set their sights too low.

Lots of people are discussing new cinematic concepts these days. So-called 'new concepts' are nothing more than one sort among many sorts of concepts. I have always emphasised that the essential thing about art is its ability to absorb all sorts of different things. The critics are trying to turn all directors into members of the 'Fifth Generation' at the moment. Xie Jin is Xie Jin and Zhao Huanzhang is Zhao Huanzhang; don't try to turn them into Chen Kaige.[9] Every director has their own socio-cultural background, and their own given character and talents. All this is created out of the infinity of life and history. If you criticise someone for making a stool badly, that's O.K. But if you say they shouldn't have made a stool, they should have made a modern sofa, then I'm afraid that's just empty talk. I have always felt that people who lack self-confidence can never make it as artists. The problem is not who says how your film is, but how your film really is. Quite a few artists have allowed their thinking to be all messed up by certain 'theories' these days. Maybe this is the inevitable mark of a still immature artist. If they were mature, it would not be possible for them to be deluded and controlled by these 'theories', and they would be able to persist in unwaveringly going their own way, no matter what comments and criticisms they face.

China's size, both in terms of population and territory, cannot be denied. However, since ancient times cultural figures have tended to look down on each other, and, tragically, this is still so today. I had hoped to avoid that, but in practice it has proved impossible to do so. People cannot live in a void. They are always positioned against a certain cultural background, and it is impossible for them to avoid being influenced by that. The whole of China is a big cultural background, the world is an even bigger cultural background, and Shanghai, Beijing and other places are all small cultural backgrounds. Therefore, I feel that at the same time as the call goes out to smash 'the Xie Jin formula', there is in fact another 'formula' in existence, and that is the desire to take the place of someone, but without openly having a contest of strength between their artistic works and yours! As it opposes one concept, in fact this also takes place against the background of affirming another concept. Therefore, my original hope not to see any two-way confrontations was naive. Therefore, I advocate being a little more self-confident, and not tolerating any interference. If history proves that I am an incompetent fool, I will fully accept the judgment of history.

Translator's notes

1. Wu Yigong is the head of the Shanghai Film Corporation, which includes China's largest feature film producer, Shanghai Film Studio. He is also a film director, best known for *My Memories of Old Beijing*, which won a prize at the Manila Film Festival in 1984.
2. In late 1986, a young critic named Zhu Dake attacked the hitherto untouchable Xie Jin, veteran director of invariably popular melodramas, as 'Confucian' (*Ruxue*). Xie Jin's studio is Shanghai. See Pei Kairui, 'Confucianist or Realist – The Xie Jin Debate', *China Screen* (Beijing), 1987:1, p. 12.
3. The Monkey King is a famous Chinese mythical figure from the tales *Journey to the West* (*Xi You Ji*).
4. 'Transcendentalism' is one of many Western terms imported into China and now bandied about at will regardless of their original meaning, presumably because they make the user sound educated and fashionable. The Chinese characters for 'transcendentalism' are 'overtaking the future', which helps explain why Wu places the term in contrast to the past and the present here. 'Ego', used later in this paragraph, comes of course from Freud, newly translated and available in mainland China.
5. Lu Xun was China's leading left-wing writer of the 1930s.
6. Ironically, given Wu Yigong's earlier complaints about other people bandying Western terms about loosely (see note 4), he himself starts using imported theory in a rather odd way here. If I were to translate literally, where I have now used 'essential', I would have to use 'ontological', and where I have now used 'existential', I would have to use 'behavioural'. I have substituted these different Western terms because I believe Wu's usage of 'ontological' and 'behavioural' is closer to the signification 'essential' and 'existential' would have for Western readers.
7. Where I have used 'director's report', the literal translation would be 'artistic summary'.
8. The late nineteenth-century Russian Narodnik party is known in China mostly through the article by Lenin attacking them: 'What the "Friends of the People" are and How They Fight the Social-Democrats'. Maybe Wu uses the term here for its connotations of a Pied Piper figure.

9. Xie Jin is introduced in note 1. Zhao Huanzhang is a middle-aged Shanghai Film Studio director, best known for his rural comedies like *The In-Laws*, *Our Niu Baisui* and *Our Demobbed Soldier*. Although very popular at the box-office in the countryside, they are not renowned for artistic innovation. Chen Kaige is possibly the most famous 'Fifth Generation' film director inside and outside China at the moment. His films to date are *Yellow Earth*, *The Big Parade* and *King of the Children*.

Originally published in *Shanghai Film Studio News*, 25 March 1987, and republished in abridged form in the national newspaper, *Guangming Daily* (Beijing), 30 April 1987. This translation is of the abridged version, on the grounds that this was the one issued for wide public consumption.

Filmography

NB: s = scenarist, d = director. This filmography includes mainland Chinese films mentioned in the translations that accompany the main article.

Evening Rain (*Bashan Yeyu*), s: Ye Nan, chief director: Wu Yonggang, d: Wu Yigong (Shanghai Studio, 1980).

Our Tabby (*Women de Xiao Huamao*), s: Jiang Tianyun, Zhang Youqiang, Wang Runsheng, Wu Yigong, d: Wu Yigong, Zhang Youqiang (Shanghai Studio, 1981).

As You Wish (*Ruyi*), s: Liu Xiaowu, Dai Zong'an, d: Huang Jianzhong (Beijing Studio, 1983).

My Memories of Old Beijing (*Chengnan Jiushi*), s: Yi Ming, d: Wu Yigong (Shanghai Studio, 1983).

Our Niu Baisui (*Zanmen de Niu Baisui*), s: Yuan Xueqiang, d: Zhao Huanzhang (Shanghai Studio, 1983).

Elder Sister (*Jiejie*), s: Ye Nan, d: Wu Yigong (Shanghai Studio, 1984).

One and Eight (*Yige he Bage*), s: Zhang Ziliang, Wang Jicheng, d: Zhang Junzhao (Guangxi Studio, 1984).

Secret Decree (*Diexue Heigu*), s: Cai Zaisheng, Lin Qingsheng, d: Wu Ziniu (Xiao-xiang Studio, 1984).

Yellow Earth (*Huang Tudi*), s: Zhang Ziliang, d: Chen Kaige (Guangxi Studio, 1984).

Army Nurse (*Nü'er Lou*), s: Kang Liwen, Ding Xiaoqi, d: Hu Mei (Beijing: August First Studio, 1985).

Black Cannon Incident (*Heipao Shijian*), s: Li Wei, d: Huang Jianxin (Xi'an Studio, 1985).

Come On, China! (*Jiayou, Zhongguodui*), d: Zhang Junzhao (Guangxi Studio, 1985).

Fascinating Musical Band (*Miren de Yuedui*), s: Fang Chunru, Yang Shuhui, d: Wang Haowei (Beijing Studio, 1985).

A Good Woman (*Liangjia Funü*), s: Li Kuanding, d: Huang Jianzhong (Beijing Studio, 1985).

Horse Thief (*Dao Ma Zei*), s: Zhang Rui, d: Tian Zhuangzhuang (Xi'an Studio, 1985).

On the Hunting Ground (*Liechang Zhasa*), s: Jiang Hao, d: Tian Zhuangzhuang (Inner Mongolia Studio, 1985).

The Silent Little Li River (*Momo de Xiao Li He*), s: Zhang Ziliang, d: Zhang Zi'en (Xi'an Studio, 1985).

Superstar (*Da Mingxing*), s: Teng Wenji, Ah Cheng, Xiao Mao, d: Teng Wenji (Xi'an Studio, 1985).

Swan Song (*Juexiang*), s/d: Zhang Zeming (Guangzhou: Pearl River Studio, 1985).

University in Exile (*Liuwang Daxue*), s: Tong Ting, Fang Zi, d: Wu Yigong (Shanghai Studio, 1985).

A Bible for Daughters (*Nü'er Jing*), s: Ye Dan, d: Bao Qicheng (Shanghai Studio, 1986).

The Big Parade (*Da Yuebing*), s: Gao Lili, d: Chen Kaige (Guangxi Studio, 1986).

Hibiscus Town (*Furongzhen*), s: Zhong Ahcheng, d: Xie Jin (Shanghai Studio, 1986).

Kids Canteen (*Wawa Canting*), s: He Guofu, Shi Meijun, d: Shi Xiaohua (Shanghai Studio, 1986).

The Last Sun (*Zuihou de Taiyang*), s: Fu Xiaoming, Jiang Haiyang, d: Jiang Haiyang (Shanghai Studio, 1986).

The Lonely Murderer (*Gudu de Moshazhe*), s: Ci Minghe, d: Zhang Junzhao (Guangxi Studio, 1986).

Magic Braid (*Shenbian*), s/d: Zhang Zi'en (Xi'an Studio, 1986).

Me and My Classmates (*Wo he Wo de Tongxue*), s: Xie Youchun, d: Peng Xiaolian (Shanghai Studio, 1986).

The Missing Girl Student (*Shizong de Nüzhongxuesheng*), s/d: Shi Shujun (Shanghai Studio, 1986).

Our Demobbed Soldier (*Zanmen de Tuiwubing*), s: Ma Feng, Sun Qian, d: Zhao Huanzhang (Shanghai Studio, 1986).

President Extraordinary (*Feichang Da Zongtong*), s: Sun Daolin, Ye Dan, d: Sun Daolin (Shanghai Studio, 1986).

Questions for the Living (*Yige Sizhe Xiang Shengzhe Fangwen*), s: Liu Shugang, d: Huang Jianzhong (Beijing Studio, 1986).

T Province 1984–1985 (*T Zhou de 84, 85 Nian*), s: Liu Guoqing, d: Yang Yanjin (Shanghai Studio, 1986).

Trapped on a Frozen River (*Binghe Siwang Xian*), s: Zheng Yi, d: Zhang Jianya (Shanghai Studio, 1986).

Chastity (*Zhennü*), s: Gu Hua, d: Huang Jianzhong (Beijing Studio, 1987).

Far from War (*Yuan Li Zhanzheng de Niandai*), s: Li Baolin, d: Hu Mei (Beijing: August First Studio, 1987).

Red Sorghum (*Hong Gaoliang*), s: Chen Jianyu, Zhu Wei, Mo Yan, d: Zhang Yimou (Xi'an Studio, 1987).

Travelling Players (*Gushu Yiren*), s/d: Tian Zhuangzhuang (Beijing Studio, 1987).

The Tribulations of a Chinese Gentleman (*Shaoye de Monan*), s: Yi Mingzhi, Qi Minsan, Hans Burger, chief director: Wu Yigong, d: Zhang Jianya (Shanghai Studio, 1987).

Problematising Cross-cultural Analysis
The Case of Women in the Recent Chinese Cinema

E. ANN KAPLAN

Preamble

The context for this paper is the recent, double-sided phenomenon of an American-Chinese film exchange. On the one hand (and actually initiating the exchange) is the new interest on the part of Chinese film workers of all kinds (not only film students and scholars, but also directors, actresses, critics, script-writers and translators), in contemporary American and European film and film theory, an interest that resulted in certain American scholars being invited to lecture in China; on the other hand (and partly as a result of the invitation) is the interest of American scholars in the recent Chinese film. Scholars visiting China were not only given a unique chance to see recent Chinese films, but also asked to pronounce judgments on them, which we tended to do in terms of our particular research interests.

So on the one hand, we have Chinese film scholars turning to American and European film theories to see what might be useful for them, in their writing on both the American film and their own cinema; on the other hand, we have some American scholars writing tentative essays on Chinese films. We have, then, a sort of informal film-culture exchange of a rather unusual kind, precisely because of its relative informality.

What is this exchange yielding so far? On the positive side, first, it is clear that some Chinese students can benefit from theoretical models they find in American and European theory; they may even benefit from paradigms Americans use in their tentative exploration of recent Chinese films. Second, American scholars have been made aware of a rich and diverse cinema they barely knew about before and stimulated to ask new kinds of questions about this cinema.

But the 'exchange' has its problematic sides as well. First, it is becoming clear that there are two distinct audiences for Chinese research: that of the American/European film community, and that of Chinese intellectuals in mainland China. That is, the critical-film discourse within China has certain expectations that do not prevail in the West. One wonders if Chinese scholars need to learn how to talk about film in one way for an American audience, in another way for a Chinese audience, and what the implications of that are. What exactly are the different critical paradigms?

141

Second, I am concerned when Chinese scholars assert that American film theorists are merely enacting a new kind of cultural imperialism when they undertake analyses of Chinese films. Is this true? In what senses? What can be done about it?

Third, Chinese scholars sometimes say (in response to an American reading of a Chinese film): 'This is not the *Chinese* way of thinking.' Or, 'Chinese do not think that way.' What does this mean? Does it mean that theories develop in very specific national/historical/intellectual contexts that are not readily transferable? Ought we to think of theory in terms of national/cultural issues? If not, how can we take care of questions like those above?

It is in the light of this recent, but burgeoning, American-Chinese film exchange (in which I have been personally involved) that the following essay, which touches on a few of the above problems, should be read.

Cross-cultural analysis, we know, is difficult – fraught with danger. We are forced to read works produced by the Other through the constraints of our own frameworks/theories/ideologies. If this is the case, we must then ask (as has, for example, Gayatri Spivak) what the point of such readings might be.[1] Are such analyses in danger of becoming 'a new form of cultural imperialism, when ... institutionalised in various college courses on Asian cinema'?[2] Or can we all learn something from them?

I will argue that cross-cultural film analyses can be illuminating, and, if clearly positioned, not necessarily 'erroneous'. (Indeed, this word is itself problematic, since it implies that there is a 'correct' reading [i.e. *one* correct reading], when the whole point of recent theory [especially Bakhtin and deconstruction] has been to show how texts themselves hide their multiple and shifting meanings.) Theorists outside the producing culture might uncover different strands of the multiple meanings than critics of the originating culture just because they bring different frameworks/ theories/ideologies to the texts. I will try to demonstrate a process of interweaving and overlapping cross-cultural readings in a special case study of Hu Mei's *Army Nurse* (1986).

But before doing this, let me note what I do not have time to do: this in turn permits me briefly to note different kinds and levels of cross-cultural readings that ideally would all be undertaken at the same time, as in Esther Yau's exemplary essay on *Yellow Earth* [see pp. 62–79]. In this analysis, Yau reads the 'interweaving and work of four structurally balanced strands on three levels: a diegetic level (for the construction of and enquiry about cultural and historical meanings), a critical level (for the disowning and fragmentation of the socialist discourses), and a discursive level (for the polyvocal articulations of and about Chinese aesthetics and feudalist patriarchy).'

While I will touch on some of these levels briefly, I will focus mainly and deliberately on questions of female desire, sexual difference, and subjectivity. First (and perhaps easiest), I will analyse some representations of women in films by and about Chinese women, from the self-conscious perspective of Western feminism, theories of subjectivity and desire, and finally of the modernism/postmodernism trajectory. Comparing and contrasting two recent Chinese films (*The Legend of Tianyun Mountain* and *Army Nurse*), one by a male, the other by a female director, will show what such frameworks are able to uncover about the films, while also setting the stage for the following discussions.

But second, I contest (or question) my own readings, which assume that the Chinese cinema arises from the same psychoanalytic desire for replacing the lost object, for introjection, displacement, projection, as we have theorised produces the desire for cinema in the West. I do this by comparing and contrasting my reading of *Army Nurse* with that of the director, whom I was lucky enough to interview.[3] In my final reading of *her* reading, I hope to raise (but not answer) the following questions: How do non-Western cultures think about representation? Are objectification and fascination with the specular regime part of a universal representational mode or one developed through Western philosophical/intellectual/aesthetic/political traditions? Do non-Western cultures use sound in relation to the image differently than does the dominant Hollywood cinema? Do other cultures, like China, use the cinema for other ends? Finally, I will tentatively set forth what I believe is the best hypothesis in relation to the Chinese cinema.

1. Comparison of *The Legend of Tianyun Mountain* and *Army Nurse*

Fredric Jameson's provocative recent statement that all Third World texts are 'necessarily allegorical' provides a useful framework for my discussion, since I want to argue that while Jameson's assertion might fit the first film, it must be qualified for the second. It is misleading to assert that 'even those texts invested with an apparently private or libidinal dynamic ... necessarily project a political dimension in the form of national allegory.'[4] It is also misleading to say that 'The story of the private individual is always an allegory of the embattled situation of the public third-world culture and society,' at least without adding that many Hollywood films are also blatant 'national allegories'. I will argue that new Chinese films attempt something different from (or in addition to) national allegory, which we find precisely around the issues of female desire and subjectivity.

The issue of 'national allegory' versus 'something else' is inevitably linked to the context within which Other World films are produced, although as is obvious from the case of America, it is not necessary for film studios to be state-controlled for them to be ideologically restricted; nor is it necessary that all state-produced films are mere 'propaganda'. All film production in China is organised through a series of state-run film studios and training academies, where directors, producers, actors/actresses etc. are employees of the state. The interesting questions here have to do with what film ideas arise, which are accepted for production, and which make it through the final review process. Interesting also is the fact that the various Chinese studios have all come to have their own special character: they range from the so-called 'experimental' (read 'resisting') Xi'an Studio to the more conservative Shanghai Studio which made *The Legend of Tianyun Mountain*. In order to get her film through the August First Studio, Hu Mei had to confront much opposition. Perhaps the fact that there is no opportunity in China for independent production (and therefore for explicit alternative cinematic practice in the Western sense) puts the most constraints on film-makers, and makes the most difference from America. In other words, it is not state control of the dominant production that ultimately matters: the state system still requires the concept of 'marketability', since the state needs people to fill the cinemas as much as does Hollywood, if for different reasons.

As Leo Ou-Fan Lee points out in his essay in this volume, there are two main legacies for the recent Chinese film as for recent Chinese literature, namely the humanist social-realist tradition of the 1940s, and second, the revolutionary propagandist tradition of the 'cultural revolution'. Made and set in 1980, *The Legend of Tianyun Mountain* represented a decisive break with the latter tradition, in which films still attacked the old, evil imperialist society and focused on decadence. The film offers a severe critique of both the 'cultural revolution' and of the earlier Anti-Rightist campaign. Its heroine is the new communist youth — energetic, hard-working and committed to correcting the Party's recent errors.

The film self-consciously derides the earlier romantic codes of the 50s generation in favour of the new communist heroine, who has no emotional problems because she has the new 'right' thinking. The older woman's story, narrated to the new heroine, is a standard melodrama, similar to many Hollywood films. The framing story thus comments upon the melodramatic one told by the old Party member and that involves the typical melodramatic conflict between ambition and love. The two main messages of the film are 1) that the Party must not commit the error of condemning good Party members because of a slight differ-ence over immediate strategy; and 2) that Party leaders must not allow personal revenge to affect their need to be just.

But there is another message, produced through the reactions of the new heroine to the older woman, which is that such melodramatic love relationships are messy and undesirable. The film thus retains a view of the subject as in the service of the state; problems between subject and state happened because the state made a wrong judgment, not because the *relationship between subject and state* was wrong. The film embodies the official voice in the figure of its ideal heroine, who is set off against her conflicted, unhappy and unsuccessful precursors, and in whom we find the film's 'happy ending'. *The Legend of Tianyun Mountain* insists that the 'happy' woman is the one who is committed to work for the state; or, to put it in psychoanalytic terms, the one who takes the state as

Individual desire versus duty to the state: *Sacrificed Youth*

her object of desire, or who displaces sexual desire into working for the state.

The newer films, especially those by women directors (and it is those I will concentrate on here), manifest a new self-conscious split between an evident but socially forbidden eroticism and romantic love, and the subject's interpellation by the state. The narratives foreground conflict between a sexual desire that is either socially impossible, and/or never spoken, or forever lost; and interpellation by the state, which insists on commitment to 'duty' over erotic, individual desire. (Cf. *Army Nurse, The Season for Love, Sacrificed Youth, Zhenzhen's Beauty Parlour*.)

In his essay in this volume Chris Berry has noted that classical Chinese films manifest what he calls 'an anti-individualistic aesthetic, contrary to the Western paradigm'. He argues, interestingly, that the viewing subject is only led (by the cinematic devices) to gender identification at negative points in the text – points of transgression, failure and collapse – which therefore take on a negative connotation. In a culture in which, as he notes, individual interest is negatively coded, so any focus on sexual difference (which implies individual interest) must be negative.

But it is precisely here that the films by women directors that I am looking at begin to violate the mandate. The films dare to insert female (and male) desire; and in the way they do this, they raise the problem of individual interest in a sympathetic manner. The viewing subject is made

145

to identify with the heroine whose desire is made 'impossible' by her obligations to the state. For example, in *Army Nurse*, there is a fantastic scene in which the heroine's desire for one of her male patients is graphically and unambiguously imaged: the camera cuts between the nurse's face – increasingly manifesting sexual arousal – and the man's shoulder with the wound she is dressing. The bandaging becomes eroticised to an almost unbearable point, as the camera also shows the man's increasing sexual arousal. (Hu Mei told me that this scene had originally been much longer, her studio leadership insisting it be cut.) The nurse and patient never consummate their love, and finally the soldier leaves the hospital. Although the couple have illegally exchanged addresses, the nurse never gets any replies to her letters. Finally, she moves to a better, city hospital; it is time to marry, so a 'suitable' match is found for her by her friends. At the last moment, the nurse refuses to engage in the loveless match, and finally she returns to her old remote army hospital position, where at least she has memories of her short happiness.

The entire focus of the film is on the heroine's conflict between love and duty: the filmic devices unambiguously position the spectator in sympathy with the heroine's erotic desire, which we want to be consummated. The film, that is, arguably exposes the constraints that contemporary Chinese culture imposes on sexual expression and fulfilment.

The heroine's personal emptiness is repeated in other films not ana-

Erotic desire: *Army Nurse* ...

146

... Girl from Hunan

lysed here: each of the films contains a key scene in which the heroine's erotic gaze is finally met by the male's returned desire. In each, the desire cannot be expressed or consummated; the heroines are left yearning to meet this 'gaze' again – a gaze that is the sign for romantic love and sexual union.

Let me note, briefly, that films by male directors are also preoccupied with the repression of sexual desire, and with the communal codes governing sexual relationships in Chinese life. However, most of the films I saw seemed less about the impossibility of a mutual desire (which is what preoccupies female directors) than about male fantasies of seduction or of revenge on women for men's cultural repression and passive position.[5] For instance, *Girl from Hunan*, read in psychoanalytic terms, embodies unconscious male desire for erotic union with the mother – except that one hesitates to label 'unconscious' a desire that is so overtly displayed on the text's surface. Set in a rural community in China, the film moves from 1910 up to the brink of the Liberation in 1949. It deals with the fate of a fifteen-year-old girl forced to marry a six-year-old boy. We see the little boy on the one hand sucking on his own mother's breast (the 'couple' live on the family farm belonging to the boy's mother), while at the same time parading his power as husband over his wife, and engaged in semi-erotic play with her. Since the 'wife' is really a kind of surrogate mother to the boy, the scenes are charged with an incestuous eroticism.

Even though the film does indicate the wife's sexual restlessness as she matures (that is, there is some inclusion of her own desire), the seduction scene is almost classically Hollywood in its voyeurism and rendering of the heroine as object of the male gaze. An itinerant farm-worker's lust for the heroine has been established earlier in the film; in each situation, however, the heroine has refused to return the gaze or become complicit with the man's desire. However, in the scene in question, the farmer peeks at her undressing when drenched in a rainstorm; gradually becoming aware of his gaze, the film shows the heroine's shy arousal and passive compliance in the intercourse that follows. The scene could be read again as a male fantasy of a female desire always awaiting arousal and happy to be satisfied by no matter whom. On the other hand, it could be read (from a Western feminist perspective) as essentially a rape scene.

On the one hand, then, the film acts out a male fantasy for regression to the infantile state, and for possession of the mother. But the film could also be addressing the contemporary male's unconscious desire for revenge on women for the new-found liberation in the communist state which insists on parity between the sexes in the public sphere. It is, after all, a parity that contrasts dramatically with the situation in pre-revolutionary China. The revenge is extracted by what amounts, indeed, from a Western feminist perspective, to a rape. (As Chris Berry has noted, a similar scene in the highly acclaimed *Red Sorghum* makes the rape much more clear: the new note of an insistence on male machismo in the Chinese film is a cause for concern.)[6]

In fairness to male directors, let me note that at least two films I saw did represent more mutuality in male-female desire: these are *In the Wild Mountains* and *The Old Well*. This latter film, although only seen in its partial, rough cut, had a remarkably erotic scene in which a married man and a single woman, usually extremely controlled about their adulterous fantasies, unleash their desire when they believe that they will not survive their entombment in the old well they are repairing.

Let me now summarise earlier discussions of eroticism in the films by female directors. Interpreted through the frameworks of Western feminisms, these films could be said to embody a new awareness of female subjectivity, along with a resistance of interpellation by the state (indeed, the two necessarily go hand in hand). While Western feminists might find the endings of the films retrogressive (that is, we have not been too pleased with narratives that set up desire for the male as the sole end of woman's life), the image of the single woman is itself (as others have pointed out) a new departure in a nation whose social codes translate 'woman' into 'married woman'. I understand that there is not only no social space for the single, professional woman, but also no word to describe her.

The underlying issue for women in China, then, from a Western point of view, would seem not to be entry into the public sphere – the right to work, to equal pay, to equal participation in the work force (issues that

In the Wild Mountains

preoccupied Western feminists in the 60s and 70s), but a new, as yet not fully articulated realisation about subjectivity. It is this new awareness that haunts the films mentioned in a visual/aural rather than verbal (and explicit) manner. The old concept of self as a construction for/by the state is now pitted against a new ideology of individualism, perhaps learned partly from exposure to Western cultural products like the Hollywood film. Indeed, part of the popularity of the Hollywood films in China may be precisely the resonances they evoke for the Chinese spectator through the representation of a subjectivity he/she is interested in.

Missing from the films (again from a Western feminist perspective) are images of female-female bonding of the kind that would rival hetero-sexual priorities, and representations of the mother (whether in the form of hypostasisation, denigration, or exposure of the mother's positioning): the figure was simply not there in most of the films we saw, and when present represented an unquestioned mother-function position, marginal to the narrative.[7] (A striking exception to this was the representation of Guilan in *In the Wild Mountains*, who, in the wake of her husband's desertion, manages the farm alone, despite having a young baby to care for, and whose love affair with her husband's brother represents a daring violation of cultural codes.)

It has been said (for example by Judith Stacey) that Chinese commun-ism grafted its repression of subjectivity on to the new state,[8] and that it was able to do this because of the prior centuries of Confucianism. This

149

general repression of subjectivity (male subjectivity was, and is, also repressed) in part accounts for the repression of sexuality in modern China, or its channelling into perverse forms (female foot-binding) in Confucian society. This raises fascinating questions from a Western theoretical standpoint about what a 'feminism' in China might look like, and about links between Western feminisms and a modernism that arguably has still not taken place (and perhaps never should or will take place) in China. In the USA, feminisms got under way in the 60s through turning bourgeois capitalism's own values on itself. Since Chinese ideology demands the submission of the subject to the state, 'duty' over personal desire, the idea of feminism as an oppositional practice is hard to insert. One could argue that China is, from a Western point of view, still a premodern state. In this case, the idea of a new subjectivity that is linked to new questions about sexual desire and sexual difference could signal the start of the modernism that in the West ushered in bourgeois capitalism.

This, if true, would be ironic for Western feminists whose 70s and 80s efforts were aimed ultimately at moving beyond the subjectivities offered in bourgeois capitalism, and who have in any case begun to witness the transmutation of that bourgeois capitalism into its postmodern forms. Western feminisms, in this analysis, confront the challenges (and perhaps possibilities) offered by postmodernism at the very moment that Other world nations, like China, begin to move through a modernist feminism.

2: Contesting the above analysis: Hu Mei and *Army Nurse*

On one level, the above analysis assumes that the desire for cinema is a desire either to represent what the *state* desires (i.e. the repression of individuality and its accompanying sexual difference/sexual desire) or to represent directly what the state represses (i.e. sexual difference/sexual desire). The analysis assumes a cultural or political unconscious that finds expression, or in the second case release, in state films. It also assumes that human subjectivity is constituted through sexual difference; that, as Juliet Mitchell puts it, 'human subjectivity cannot ultimately exist outside a division between the sexes – one cannot be no sex.'[9] Since this is the case, a nation that does not evidence preoccupation with sexual difference must then be 'repressing' this difference. The fact that the mother is not represented or much discussed anywhere also points to repression of a psychoanalytically central figure in the subject's developing into a 'subject'.

On another level, the analysis attempts to understand Chinese representations in relation to Western feminist readings of Western texts, which in turn rely on certain formulations of what Western feminisms were about.

Finally, the analysis proposes links between certain societal, aesthetic and psychic modes; and sees these constellations as indicating different phases/periods in a nation's history (i.e. premodern, modern, post-modern).

I do not have space to contest all these assumptions; and would merely suggest that they need careful examination as to their cross-cultural validity. Two small examples will make the point. First, the absence of mother-images has an obvious practical, social level to it, outside of any possible psychoanalytic ones, namely the need of the state severely to limit births due to drastic overpopulation; second, cross-cultural readings are especially problematic in relation to sexuality: would a Chinese audience read the sex scene in *Girl from Hunan* as a rape? How is rape conceptualised in China? Does the definition of rape vary from culture to culture? Is rape acceptable as a representation but not socially? Are we driven to an undesirable relativism in such cross-cultural comparisons?

Since these questions take me too far afield, let me end by noting and commenting on some interesting discrepancies between my above reading of *Army Nurse* and the director's own comments on the film. Hu Mei first talked about her wish in the film to describe what she felt were specifically female ways of thinking: she noted that women had a less linear way of thinking than men, that women are split, disoriented by the many demands that have always been made on them. Women for her were characterised by a fragmentation and disorientation – a shorter attention span than men – all of which she attributed to conflicting demands.

Now these statements at first seemed to fit into standard Western feminist analyses about the need for women constantly to attend to men – to their husbands at home and then to their bosses at work. But in retrospect, I think Hu Mei was talking about a much older historical situation of women in China as always being only for the Other, only constructed from the place of the Other, unable ever to experience their own desire. She had wanted to convey this sense of her heroine's fragmented, dispersed thinking in a voice-over that would have consisted of unfinished sentences, meaningless phrases, disjointed series of sentences, etc. But the studio leadership would not permit a soundtrack that did not accord with their notion of realist conventions.

I thought these comments were surprisingly in accord with ideas that we associate particularly with French feminisms, and I was struck by that. But Hu Mei went on to provide a completely alternative analysis of what she was trying to do – one which turned the film into a 'national allegory' of the kind Jameson was talking about. She reasoned that there were so many Chinese films, including her own, dealing with female issues and having central female characters, because the female situation could act as an emblem for *all* Chinese peoples' frustrations; for men too the pressure of 'consensus' ideology is heavy, but this would be too threatening to deal with directly. The issue of sacrifice and the conflict between individual desire and the demands of the state are dealt with quite safely when put in terms of female love situations. For Hu Mei, it seemed, these narratives embody everyone's frustrations – the impossibility for both men and women to function as individuals – rather than being specifically about sexual difference or female erotic desire. I will comment on this reading in my first 'ending' that follows.

3: The endings

It is only fitting that there should be two endings to this paper – one providing the 'ending' as produced through the Western frameworks I began with; the other an ending that addresses the difficulties of cross-cultural textual reading. The first ending might go something like the following.

It seems that there is a new moment in China, and that this is reflected in recent films. It is not by accident that female directors and writers are central in dealing with the change: since women's situation is the more extreme, they are the ones making the strongest demands for subjectivity – for articulation of female desire. In addition, it is clear that the younger women directors, like Hu Mei, relate differently to the state than do the older generation, who lived through the 'cultural revolution'. Far more than the older group, this new one is fascinated with America, which they know about primarily through Hollywood films and contact with Hong Kong. Cynical about the revolution, and with no memories of Imperialist China and its horrors, they want modernity, Western goods, and a chance to visit America.

From some Western feminist perspectives, much of this is problematic: we worked hard in the 60s and 70s to rid ourselves of bourgeois subjectivities. Ironically, many of us at the height of things (May 1968) looked to the Chinese Revolution as the model of what could be done – namely, of how a tyrannical order could be overcome and a utopian equality apparently achieved. Kristeva's book *About Chinese Women* embodies some of these idealisations.[10] We responded then to the Chinese revolutionary ideal of commitment to the community, the submersion of self in the collective.

In the 80s, however, Chinese women educated precisely in such values sensed something lacking: they wanted a subjectivity we had identified as linked to bourgeois capitalism and to a modernism that we were attempting to move beyond. From this perspective, one could see Chinese women as working their way through a modernist phase in their assertion of subjectivity. But there seems to be some guilt about the assertion of a specifically *female* subjectivity, *female* desire: this I read from Hu Mei's rather abrupt outlining of an allegorical reading for her and other female directors' films about female desire. We see in operation, again, the difficulty for the Chinese of confronting difference (here specifically sexual difference) head on. Hu Mei got concerned about an analysis that seemed to separate males from females – to emphasise specifically *female* frustrations and repressions – and she resorted to an analysis that would apply to *all* the Chinese, that would reassert the collective.

Meanwhile, those of us in America who went through the 60s confront a paradigm shift variously called postmodernism, post-industrialism or New Age Consciousness. Having long ago abandoned the utopian ideal of submersion of self in the collective, we now seem on the brink of a postmodern crisis presaging the impossibility of subjectivity in the old senses. Here then we find a big distance between women in China and in America today.

The second ending might go as follows. Cross-cultural readings are fraught with dangers, as I noted to begin with. Some of those dangers are clear in the assumptions of my readings that I outlined. But how are we to arrive at a method, a theory, for reading texts from Other worlds until we have first answered some of the questions about how different cultures think about representation in the first place? And second, until we know more about the unconscious of different cultures as it might pertain to the level of the imaginary and to the terrain of the visual artistic text? And finally, whether or not the very construction of social 'phases' (feudalism, modernism, postmodernism) is intricately linked to traditions of Western thought, and not relevant to the Chinese situation?

To take but one example from the questions listed here, it seems that gender representations signify on a whole series of levels. For one thing, the gaze is often more mutual than in American films – men's desire imaged as equally frustrated and impossible as that of women; but, further, the entire signifying of sexual relations may stand in as a metaphor (or analogue) for the broader political/social/intellectual frustration of both genders. In other words, as Hu Mei indicated, representing woman's unhappiness in film may mask the impossibility for everyone in modern China to give rein to a whole series of desires beyond the sexual.

But we could take the reading even further. If men also suffer from the need to submit to the demands of the state, they are arguably emasculated by their situation. Given the prior phallic order, and given classical Oedipal rivalry with the Father, they may be harmed even more than women. State communism, in demanding male submission to the Law of the Father with little possibility for obtaining at least some parity with the Father position (as in free-enterprise capitalism), may produce men psychically damaged in deeper ways even than women. In addition, the inability to consummate love hurts them, too, as some recent films stress (cf. Chen Kaige's *King of the Children*).

It is, however, hard to be certain about such readings that rely on a perhaps culturally specific concept of the psyche, or about their worth, as I noted at the beginning. The uncertainty exposes the need for more research. If cross-cultural analysis lays bare this need, if it has at least opened up the questions we need to answer, then it will have created the space for beginning a dialogue that may benefit us all.

153

Notes

1. Gayatri Spivak, *In Other Worlds: Essays in Cultural Politics* (New York and London: Routledge, 1988).
2. Cf. Ma Ming, 'The Textual and Critical Difference of Being Radical: Reconstructing the Chinese Leftist Films of the 1930's', *Wide Angle* 11:2, pp. 22–31.
3. Thanks to the kind auspices of Chris Berry, I interviewed Hu Mei when visiting Beijing in Summer 1987.
4. Fredric Jameson, 'Third World Literature in the Era of Multinational Capitalism', *Social Text* 15, Fall 1986.
5. Informal discussion with Berry at the Asian Cinema Studies Conference, Athens, Ohio, 1988.
6. Berry, ibid.
7. Cf. Tao Chun in *Country Couple*; Xiu Chen in *Garlands at the Foot of the Mountain*; and Qiao Zhen in *Life*.
8. Judith Stacey, *Patriarchy and Socialist Revolution in China* (Berkeley: University of California Press, 1983).
9. Juliet Mitchell, 'The Question of Femininity', in *The British School of Psychoanalysis: The Independent Tradition* (New Haven and London: Yale University Press, 1986)
10. Julia Kristeva, *About Chinese Women*, trans. Marion Boyars Publishers (New York: Urizen Books, 1977).

Filmography

NB: s = scenarist, d = director.

The Legend of Tianyun Mountain (Tianyunshan Chuanqi), s: Lu Yanzhou, d: Xie Jin (Shanghai Studio, 1980).

Country Couple (Xiang Qing), s: Wang Yimin, d: Hu Bingliu (Guangzhou: Pearl River Studio, 1983).

Garlands at the Foot of the Mountain (Gaoshanxia de Huahuan), s: Li Zhun, Li Cunbao, d: Xie Jin (Shanghai Studio, 1984).

Life (Rensheng), s: Lu Yao, d: Wu Tianming (Xi'an Studio, 1984).

Army Nurse (Nü'er Lou), s: Kang Liwen, Ding Xiaoqi, d: Hu Mei (Beijing: August First Studio, 1985).

Girl from Hunan (Xiangnü Xiaoxiao), s: Zhang Xian, d: Xie Fei, Ulan (Wu Lan) (Youth Studio, 1985).

In the Wild Mountains (Yeshan), s: Yan Xueshu, Zhu Zi, d: Yan Xueshu (Xi'an Studio, 1985).

Sacrificed Youth (Qingchun Ji), s/d: Zhang Nuanxin (Youth Studio, 1985).

Old Well (Laojing), s: Zheng Yi, d: Wu Tianming (Xi'an Studio, 1986).

The Season for Love (Lian'ai Jijie), s: Wen Xiaoyu, d: Urshana (Wu'er Shana) (Inner Mongolia Studio, 1986).

Zhenzhen's Beauty Parlour (Zhenzhen de Fawu), s: Xia Lan, d: Xu Tongjun (Youth Studio, 1986).

King of the Children (Haizi Wang), s: Chen Kaige, Wan Zhi, d: Chen Kaige (Xi'an Studio, 1987).

Red Sorghum (Hong Gaoliang), s: Chen Jianyu, Zhu Wei, Mo Yan, d: Zhang Yimou (Xi'an Studio, 1987).

The Distinct Taiwanese and Hong Kong Cinemas

CHIAO HSIUNG-PING

As I write, the 1987 nominations for the annual Golden Horse Awards have only just closed, but let's forget about all the controversy they've generated for the moment. Looking at the forty-odd Taiwanese and Hong Kong films entered, they show that in many ways Taiwanese and Hong Kong films are completely opposite. This article will attempt to explore these differences from a number of angles, and through them shed some light on the patterns of film culture today's audiences are receiving.

The differences between Hong Kong and Taiwanese films go back to the very beginnings of the two industries. The Hong Kong industry grew up around the right-wing and commercial film-makers who retreated there after the establishment of the People's Republic in mainland China in 1949, but the roots of the Taiwanese feature film industry lie in the documentarists and newsreel film-makers who worked with the KMT Nationalist government in Chungking (Chongqing) during the Second World War and accompanied the KMT to Taiwan. Despite the many links that have been established since then, these different origins still make themselves felt, and other divergences have also appeared.

There was almost no feature film industry in Taiwan at first. Film-making was dominated by three government-owned studios (The Agricultural Education Motion Picture Corporation, China Film Studio and Taiwan Film Studio), all of which specialised in non-fiction films. Although they churned out pseudo-feature films, these were barely disguised propaganda and educational films with such limited appeal that by 1954 fully 76 per cent of box-office revenue was taken by imports.

To combat this phenomenon, the Taiwanese studios used the American funds made available to them in 1955 to work with the Hong Kong industry. The resulting features were modelled along the lines of Hong Kong family melodramas, with female roles given special emphasis as carriers of traditional values. A burst of Amoy (Taiwanese) dialect films that ran the gamut from opera to horror by way of detectives and slapstick won working-class audiences in the late 50s, but was soon eclipsed by more technically sophisticated Mandarin-language films.

In 1963, the independent Central Motion Picture Corporation launched the Mandarin feature film industry down the road of 'whole-

155

some realism', a concept adapted from Socialist Realism. Set against proletarian backgrounds, these melodramas of everyday life were optimistic and positive in outlook, combining entertainment and political simplicity. They succeeded in gaining a wide export market in Southeast Asia, and helped boost annual production to 230 features in 1968.

While female roles and everyday realism continued to be prominent in these Taiwanese films, Hong Kong established a range of thoroughly commercial macho swordplay and *kung fu* genres in the late 60s. In contrast, female-dominated films continued in Taiwan, eventually leading to escapist romantic fantasies in the 1970s.

These differences in Hong Kong and Taiwanese films helped establish demographic differentiation among film audiences, with the swordplay films of Hong Kong appealing to men, and the Taiwanese weepies appealing to women. This tendency to demographic differentiation continued with the economic boom of the 1980s, during which the developing cultural awareness of intellectuals and the expanding size of the newly formed bourgeoisie laid the foundations for a filmgoing public ready for change. The Hong Kong and Taiwanese new cinemas, created by young directors and critics, mostly in their thirties and often educated in Western film schools, have been the result.

However, despite these recent parallels, a history of difference continues to make itself felt today. In their choice of subjects and genres, Taiwanese films tend toward rural topics (or perhaps I should say topics which inherit the spirit of old rural novels). In other words, Taiwanese film-makers are rather more concerned about everyday reality; they have a respect for the people and the soil; they are sensitive to the problems of everyday life; and they are willing to put time and energy into exploring issues in the world around us.

To take some examples from the 1987 Golden Horse nominations. *Strawman* is about the preposterous situation the countryside found itself in, stuck between the two superpowers, America and Japan, during the Japanese occupation of Taiwan. *Love is Grown With Flowers* investigates the transformation of the Taiwanese countryside. In an almost farcical manner, it presents such phenomena as the improvement of the Taiwanese economic situation, the over-production of rice and the change from agriculture to horticulture as the people became able to afford more luxuries, and is full of nostalgia and idealism about the countryside and farmers. *Auntie Chin-Shui* is a direct adaptation of a novel by Wang To (Wang Tuo), and records the changing face of Taiwan's fishing villages following urban progress and transformation, and the impact of this on ordinary people. This includes the gradual replacement of pedlars by the Taipei (Taibei) Chingkuang (Qingguang) market, the migration of young people to the cities, protection rackets, and so on.

As well as their sensitivity to everyday life, Taiwanese films also seem to delight in socio-political phenomena. For example, *Daughter of the*

Made in Taiwan: *Strawman*

Nile and *After Midnight* both touch on the 'midnight cowboy' problem (i.e. male prostitution). *Missing People* takes prostitution as its main theme, and *My Father is Not a Thief* draws its materials directly from the newspaper (to protest against unfair court verdicts). *We Went to See the Snow That Year* takes the break in diplomatic relations between Taiwan and the USA as a pretext for tracing the decade of transformation, including anxiety about such social phenomena as strip joints, and nostalgia for rural clan halls.

The condemnation of the city is in complete contrast to the important themes that have come out of life in the countryside. *Auntie Chin-Shui* and *Missing People* both make a simplistic, one-sided attack on the city (the city creates prostitutes, and the city also makes young people ungrateful, disobedient to their parents and only interested in pursuing their own pleasures). *White Teeth and Black Skin* and *We Went to See the Snow That Year* even parallel urbanisation with the growing creation of an underworld (crime, gambling, call girls), the splitting up of good friends, prostitution, and other aspects of exploitation.

All this reflects an interesting creative attitude. Altogether, Taiwan entered twenty-one films into the Golden Horse competition, and more than half the film-makers (by which I mean screenwriters, directors and others who influence the direction of the film) are educated people in their thirties and forties. Hou Hsiao-Hsien (Hou Xiaoxian), Hsiao Yeh (Xiao Ye), Wu Nien-Jen (Wu Nianzhen), Wang Tung (Wang Tong), Wang Hsiao-Di (Wang Xiaodi), Chen Kun-Hou (Chen Kunhou), Ting

157

Ya-Min (Ding Yamin), Liao Chin-Sung (Liao Qingsong), Lin Ching-Cheh (Lin Qingjie), Chiu Ming-Shen (Qiu Mingcheng), Chang Yi (Zhang Yi), Wang Hsia-Chun (Wang Xiajun), Li Yao-Ning (Li Youning) and others are all examples.

Their age shows that their own development has been more or less contemporaneous with Taiwan's rapid transformation. As a result, their collective character tends towards reflection and nostalgia for the old life, and they also have a certain dissatisfaction with contemporary life and modernisation. Previous criticisms have placed them in the context of debates about nostalgia for the past and childhood, but have not considered how the main themes this group of young and middle-aged artists have worked to present are also the most important in their own lives. Following their own loss of innocence, these artists have begun to cherish the rural values of their own childhoods.

Only by understanding this creative obsession can we appreciate why so many films pursue the past and memory, even films about contemporary society. In this regard, voice-over narration often brings on subjective memory, and since *Growing Up* it has become almost an indispensable technique. *Strawman*, *We Went to See the Snow That Year*, and *White Teeth and Black Skin* all adopt this mode, and even *Daughter of the Nile* and *My Father is not a Thief* use voice-over to turn contemporary life into memories. The only exception is *Auntie Chin-Shui*, which applies dramatic (even inflammatory) techniques, insistently sticking a documentary-style subtitle with the year, month and day on every scene, creating an unbalanced embarassment.

The dominance of rural subjects and everyday reality has also enabled Taiwanese film to free itself from the escapism and entertainment of the past, and the star system has evaporated. The faces that appear in these new films really do have a certain bumpkin-like look. Only a couple of real stars have come out of the rural wave, and they stick out like sore thumbs in films with rural topics. Wang Tsu-Hsien (Wang Zuxian) gives the audience quite a shock in her short shorts and revealing blouse among the fields of *Love is Grown with Flowers*.

However, some of these films still lurch towards entertainment, compromising their own creative integrity. For example, *White Teeth and Black Skin* throws itself into the exaggerated violence of Hong Kong action films, and *Love is Grown with Flowers* works by adopting traditional popular farce.

Only a few Taiwanese films have stuck to escapism and fantasy. *The Flag is Flying* is a spy film along the lines of the legend of Yoshiko Kawashima, the famous spy during the Sino-Japanese War of the 1930s and 1940s. *The Legend of Dr Sun Yatsen* turns an epic poem into a studio-bound drama without substance, and even includes *kung fu* scenes. In *Split of the Spirit*, even though director Fred Tan (Dan Hanzhang) tries using optical printing special effects to package a very cheap wronged-ghost-seeks-revenge story, and even though the film does have some significance because of its formal innovation, its contents are moribund.

These escapist fantasy films have not been successful commercially, which shows that Taiwan's entertainment films are still a long way behind Hong Kong's. Media reports often accuse the new cinema of damaging the vitality of Taiwan's film industry, but this is wrong-headed. If the Taiwanese film market appears lost to Hong Kong films, that is because Taiwanese commercial films are made with tacky, unprofessional methods that put audiences off. There is no overlap between the audience for commercial films and that for the new cinema. The audience for Hong Kong commercial films is a new mass audience. They are not part of the audience that has grown up for the new cinema, and they are even less interested in Taiwan's so-called commercial films.

In contrast, the only special characteristics of Hong Kong cinema are precisely entertainment and commerce. Hong Kong cinema belongs to a young audience, and its creativity tends towards the high spirits and unrestrained fantasies of the young. In this system, stars are a box-office guarantee that is still required. Chow Yun-Fat (Zhou Runfa), Jacky Chan (Cheng Long), Yuan Bao (Yuan Biao), Samo Hung (Hong Jinbao), Alex Wan (Wan Ziliang), Li Hsiu-Hsien (Li Xiuxian), Pat Ha (Xia Wenxi) and Leslie Cheung (Zhang Guorong) almost monopolise the entire output.

Because they are young, the Hong Kong audience is especially attracted by speed, novelty and fantasy. If one can say Taiwanese films are the products of reflection and nostalgia by intellectuals in their thirties and forties, then Hong Kong films represent the dynamism of people in their early twenties. Because they emphasise introspection and restraint, Taiwanese films have developed a lyrical style based on long takes and a slow rhythm. In contrast, Hong Kong films are a synthesis of chaos and energy, and techniques such as fragmenting extreme close-ups of the body, rapid montage and spatial and temporal disorder are used frequently and indiscriminately. For example, *A Chinese Ghost Story*, *Project A: II*, *Eastern Condors* and even the so-called 'hero films' (*Yingxiong Pian*) and 'wetback gang films' (*Da Quan Cun Pian*), which are about illegal immigrants from the mainland, all have these characteristics, reflecting the dominance and vigour of young people's tastes produced under the influence of television and computers.

Also because their audiences are young, Hong Kong films have none of the slow retrospection and entanglement of Taiwanese films. They all look ahead, and never turn back. Taiwanese films like the past and use voice-over to enter the memory, but Hong Kong films are entirely contemporary. As a result, when *Fifty Years of Sunrise and Sunset*, which models itself on *Back to the Future*, heads back into the past, it is certainly not a display of nostalgia for the 1950s. On the contrary, the film pursues the past by going down a time tunnel from a future point 'after the year 2000', and the 'past' it chases after is in fact the 1980s. Even though *Project A: II* takes the colony of Hong Kong during the late

Made in Hong Kong: *Rouge*

Qing dynasty rebellion as its setting, in all sorts of ways it is really given over to addressing the contradictory situation whereby Hong Kong now fears the 1997 return to the mainland and would rather remain colonised. Although *A Chinese Ghost Story* is set in the ancient world, its techniques and dialogue are 'young' and 'modern', including the dazzlingly modern optical techniques of Hollywood science-fiction and the modern cynical philosophy of the famous Hong Kong director Tsui Hark (Xu Ke). *The Legend of Wisely* is an even more obvious example. The film is full of the ancient and the exotic, but takes a very modern approach to ancient Chinese traditions, explaining the dragon that the people of long ago saw in the skies as a super-intelligent extraterrestrial. The lingering over history and memories that one finds in the Taiwanese cinema holds no interest at all for Hong Kong people.

Rouge is a relatively complex instance. This film tells the story of a seductive prostitute during the 1930s, who sacrifices herself for love but cannot make her lover die with her. All alone on the road to the spirit world, she returns to the 1980s in search of her old lover. The story cuts back and forth between 1930 and 1980, using outstanding artistry and cinematography to draw us into a glamorous world with an atmosphere of old Chinese decadence, worldliness and despair, and the seduction, luxurious clothes and flirtation of the brothel. However, although this

160

creates a yearning for the passions of that world, *Rouge* still wants to address contemporary problems. The film's contemporary world centres on a couple with new thinking. Their love clearly represents emotional inhibition, increased independence, growing estrangement and the discovery that living together and sex are overriding emotional commitment; all things that many people are experiencing today. This pair of lovers manage to break through their emotional inhibitions because of the power of their infatuation with the 1930s, but *Rouge* remains a film with contemporary problems at its core.

If Taiwanese rural themes extend to a critique of urban industrial and commercial society, Hong Kong films are full of condemnation and hatred of wealth. Wealth is the main reason why people degenerate and go wrong. The porno magazine boss and his dissolute son in *Road Warriors* spend every day committing outrageous acts with women, corrupting policemen and persuading lawyers to win over the courts for them, thus becoming the main villains of the film. In *Lady in Black* the hero daydreams of making money, and to this end steals, gambles, and kills his wife, becoming a guilt-ridden man. Thus his dreams of becoming rich destroy his little family completely. *The Story of Hay Bo*, which examines wealth and crime, takes fashionable ideas about material wealth and sex to criticise abnormal and twisted relationships among members of rich families. Original author Yi Shu has an especially deep understanding of this philosophy, whose ideology follows American family dramas prevalent in the 1950s, such as the stories of incestuous relationships in a society that only cares for fortune and fame found in *Home from the Hill*, *Written in the Wind* and *Imitation of Life*. But the self-pitying and self-indulgent writing style of Yi Shu erases the strong social self-criticism of these originals.

The 'hero film' genre also grows out of the condemnation of wealth, and has been the mainstream of Hong Kong commercial cinema in recent years. The focus of scripts about underworld gangs has been the conflict between wealth and power. *Underworld Friendship*, *City of Fire*, *A Hearty Response*, *Road Warriors*, *Flaming Brothers*, *Brothers* and *Long Arm of the Law: II* are all products of this genre. Their main characteristics are a conflict over money and territory, accompanied by much violence, and a crisis that threatens anarchy, combined with a feeling that one cannot escape defeat and death.

Apart from contradictory love-hate narratives about a money-minded society, the rise of these 'hero films' is also due in no small part to a certain fatalism and fear of chaos that hovers over the critical juncture of 1997. Recurrent factionalism may reflect contemporary China's disunited political situation in a certain way. A strong sense of crisis and a refusal to compromise by any party can be seen in certain scenes that appear again and again, which can be decoded as follows:

1. Enemies and friends cannot be clearly distinguished, and can change over at any time. Blood brothers can become bent on mutual revenge and

161

husband and wife can start to abuse each other. This represents thorough disillusion with blood brotherhood in human relations in Hong Kong. Many 'hero films' are cop movies, using a feud to motivate a tragedy involving great violence and cruelty.

2. Because of the above-mentioned chaos and degenerate morality, 'hero films' compensate by putting special stress on the heroism of brotherhood, mutual support and eternal loyalty. Precisely because of the lack of social justice, and because there is a lot of opportunistic behaviour in Hong Kong, people yearn for heroes. 'Hero films' draw the line between good and bad characters very simply on the basis of brotherhood. Whether it is drug smuggling, murder or even overthrowing other gang leaders, all you have to do is talk about brotherhood and you're still a definitive 'hero'. Chow Yun-Fat is a typical example of this sort of character.

3. The lack of any clear distinction between friends and enemies is also reflected in the frequent transformation of characters from good to bad. For example, in *Brothers*, Alex Wan starts out as a CID cop, but resigns to become a criminal. Li Hsiu-Hsien starts out as a good policeman assisting his brother, Alex Wan, but he is mistaken for a criminal and shot. On the one hand, this shows that the line between cops and criminals is a very thin one, but it also explains Hong Kong people's deep disappointment about friendship and human relationships. *Underworld Friendship* is the most striking example of this. Sworn brothers kill each other, a father executes his own son with a machine-gun, and this collapse of the regular feudal order leaves the viewer terrified. The impossibility of telling whether Li Hsiu-Hsien and Alex Wan are good or bad characters is also symbolic.

4. This blurring of status is often a metaphor for the political situation. The Chinese, British and Hong Kong complications of *Project A: II* are an example. The roles in *Long Arm of the Law: II* are most ambiguous. As far as the Hong Kong people are concerned, the mainlanders are illegal immigrants who can be repatriated at any time, but the lead character thinks of himself as an ex-police officer who is assisting the Hong Kong police force to 'attack bad elements'.

5. Imagery is often used to express China's deadlocked disunity of the last forty years. In these films, three or four lead characters often threaten their opponents with guns or other weapons. A stand-off develops, with no one daring to move an inch. *Eastern Condors*, *Flaming Brothers* and *Long Arm of the Law: II* all have these deadlocks. *A Chinese Ghost Story* also has a critical juncture where Leslie Cheung is caught between Wu Ma and Lin Wei's swords when they are fighting each other.

The rise of the 'hero film' also has direct roots in the violent tradition of martial arts and *kung fu* films: lots of shots flowing with blood, lengthy detailing of deadly battles, and lonely loyal heroes. It is just a matter of changing real martial arts skills into machine-guns and bullets. Completely different from the works of the middle-class creative temperament of Taiwanese film artists, 'hero films', like martial arts and *kung fu* films, are low-class cinema. Gang loyalty, the laws of the underworld and the activities of street trash form the world of the hero film. Many films even go straight for a macho/gay feel, as for example in *Flaming Brothers*, where Chow Yun-Fat finally dumps his wife, whose religious background requires her to dress in white, and fights side by side with Dung Kong-Yung (Deng Guangrong). When the two of them fire and rush toward their opponents in slow motion, the shot is full of gay overtones (guns, sexual consummation, and the fact that in Taiwanese films slow-motion shots of people running towards each other always used to mean love).

'Hero films' often appear as cop movies (*Long Arm of the Law: II, Underworld Friendship, A Hearty Response, Road Warriors, City on Fire* and *Project A: II*). Villains and blood are both essential elements, and the villains are often indistinguishable from the cops. Although most Hong Kong films turn to escape and entertainment, cop films represent a different sort of thinking: they are concentrated symbols of Hong Kong's government and bureaucrats. Plots about collusion between cops and criminals, cops taking bribes, and the oppression and exploitation of ordinary people – from *Project A: II* and *Underworld Friendship* to *Long Arm of the Law: II* – appear again and again. If these films allude to Hong Kong people's resentment of officials, they also reflect the depression of the urban petty bourgeoisie in the face of their inability to change reality.

For the lifestyles of street criminals, Hong Kong films also use special aesthetic techniques. Steadicam camera movements create sharp visuals for street gang warfare, chases, murder and robbery. Hong Kong cinema is always keen to try out new technology (for example the models and optical printing in *A Chinese Ghost Story*). *Eastern Condors* went to the Philippine locations used in *The Killing Fields*, *The Legend of Wisely* used Nepal and Egypt, and *Easy Money* went to Paris for its car chases. This film also features helicopters, gliders, the latest racing bikes and all sorts of computer equipment. Locations in Cambridge feature in *The Story of Hay Bo*, New York in *An Autumn Fairytale*, Thailand in *Lady in Black*, and Malacca in *Underworld Friendship*. The world of these films tries hard to break out of the tiny territory of Hong Kong and use new technology to develop new visual experiences.

Because of differences in regional environment, the films of Taiwan and Hong Kong are completely different in form, content and direction. Not only are Taiwanese and Hong Kong films different, but compared with each of them mainland films are a world apart.

Originally published in October 1987 in *Wenxing* (*Literary Star*) magazine no. 112. Republished in *The New Taiwanese Cinema* (*Taiwan Xin Dianying*), ed. Chiao Hsiung-Ping (Jiao Xiongping) (Taibei: Times Publishing House [Shibao Chuban

Gongsi], 1988). Translated and adapted by Chris Berry, with additional material supplied by Chiao Hsiung-Ping.

Filmography

NB: s = scenarist, d = director.

Growing Up (*Xiao Bi de Gushi*), s: Hou Hsiaohsien, d: Chen Kun-Hou (Chen Kun-hou) (Taiwan: Central Motion Picture Company, 1982).

After Midnight (*Wuye Guohou*), s/d: Wang Hsiao-Hai (Wang Xiaohai) (Taiwan: Scholar Company, 1987).

An Autumn Fairytale (*Liumang Daheng*), s: Alex Lau (Luo Qirui), d: Zhang Wanting (Hong Kong: D & B, 1987).

Auntie Chin-Shui (*Jinshui Sao*), s/d: Lin Ching-Chieh (Lin Qingjie) (Taiwan: Lung-Cheh Company, 1987).

Brothers (*Xiongdi*), s/d: Hsien Si-Ren (Xian Siran) (Hong Kong: D & B, 1987).

A Chinese Ghost Story (*Qiannü Youhun*), s: Ran Chih-Che (Yuan Jizhi), d: Chen Hsiao-Tong (Cheng Xiaodong), producer: Tsui Hark (Xu Ke) (Hong Kong: Film Workshop, 1987).

City on Fire (*Longhu Fengyun*), s: Shen Shi-Chen (Shen Xicheng), d: Lin Ling-Tung (Lin Lingdong) (Hong Kong: Cinema City, 1987).

Daughter of the Nile (*Niluo He Nü'er*), s: Chu Tien-Wen (Zhu Tianwen), d: Hou Hsiao-Hsien (Taiwan: Chun-I Company, 1987).

Eastern Condors (*Dongfang Tuying*), s: Huang Bin-Yao (Huang Bingyao), d: Samo Hung (Hong Kong: D & B, 1987).

Easy Money (*Tongtian Dadao*), s: Yeh Kuan-Jen (Ye Guangjian), Peng Chi-Chie (Peng Jicai), Wei Chia-Huei (Wei Jiahui), d: Hsien Si-Ren (Hong Kong: D & B, 1987).

Fifty Years of Sunrise and Sunset (*Richu Riluo Wushi Nian*), s: Hu Shen (Hu Shan), d: Ho Chia-Chui (He Jiaju) (Hong Kong: Hsin-Hui Company, 1987).

The Flag is Flying (*Qi Zheng Piaopiao*), s/d: Ting Shen-Shi (Ding Shanxi) (Taiwan: Central Motion Picture Company, Thomson and Golden Harvest, 1987).

Flaming Brothers (*Jianghu Longhudou*), s/d: Chang Tung-Tsu (Zhang Tongzu) (Hong Kong: Mak Production Company, 1987).

A Hearty Response (*Yi Gai Yuntian*), s: Li Wen-Chow (Li Wenzhuo), d: Lo Wen (Luo Wen) (Hong Kong: Dai-Yun, 1987).

Lady in Black (*Duoming Jiaren*), s: Shao Huei-Hsiung (Xiao Huixiong), d: Sun Chun (Sun Zhong) (Hong Kong: D & B, 1987).

The Legend of Wisely (*Weisili Chuanqi*), s: Cheng Chong-Tai (Zheng Chongtai), Pan Yuan-Lian (Pan Yuanliang), d: Chang Kuo-Ming (Zhang Guoming) (Hong Kong: Cinema City, 1987).

The Legend of Dr Sun Yat-Sen (*Guofu Zhuan*), s/d: Ting Shen-Shi (Ding Shanxi) (Taiwan: The First Film Company, 1987).

Long Arm of the Law: II (*Shenggang Qibing Xuji*), s: Chen Hsin-Chen (Chen Xinjian), d: Johnny Mak (Mai Dangxiong) (Hong Kong: Mak Production Company, 1987).

Love is Grown with Flowers (Fangcao Biliantian), s: Wu Nien-Jen, d: Tsai Yang-Ming (Cai Yangming) (Taiwan Film Production Company, 1987).

Missing People (Shizong Renkou), s: Lin Huang-Kun (Lin Huangkun), d: Lin Ching-chieh (Taiwan: Jin-Ge Company, 1987).

My Father is not a Thief (Wo de Baba Bu Shi Zei), s/d: Wang Chun-Kuan (Wang Chongguang) (Taiwan, 1987).

Project A: II (A Jihua Xuji), s/d: Jacky Chan (Hong Kong: Golden Harvest, 1987).

Road Warriors (Tiexue Jingqi), s: Feng Rei-Hsiung (Feng Ruixiong), d: Li Hsiu-Hsien (Hong Kong: Wang Non, 1987).

Rouge (Yanzhi Kou), s: Chiu Kon-Chien (Qiu Gangjian), d: Stanley Kwan (Guan Jinpeng) (Hong Kong: Golden Harvest, 1987).

Split of the Spirit (Lihun), s/d: Fred Tan (Taiwan: Lo Wei Film Company, 1987).

The Story of Hay Bo (Xi Bao), s/d: Fong Lin-Chen (Fang Lingzheng) (Hong Kong: Silver-Metro Company, 1987).

Strawman (Daocaoren), s: Wang Hsiao-Di, Sung Hung (Song Hong), d: Wang Tung (Wang Tong) (Taiwan: Central Motion Picture Company, 1987).

Underworld Friendship (Jianghu Qing), s: Shao Rau-Yuan (Xiao Ruoyuan), d: Huang Tai-Lie (Huang Tailai) (Hong Kong: Yun-Shun Company, 1987).

We Went to See the Snow That Year (Nayinian Women Qu Kan Xue), s: Hsiao Yeh, d: Li Yao-Ning (Taiwan: Central Motion Picture Company, 1987).

White Teeth and Black Skin (Heipi yu Baiya), s: Yu Li-Jen (Yu Liren), d: Yang Li-Kuo (Yang Liguo) (Taiwan: Hun-Tai Company, 1987).

A Cultural Interpretation of the Popular Cinema of China and Hong Kong

JENNY KWOK WAH LOH

1. On cultural interpretation

The task of relating cinematic expression and national culture has been central to the study of national cinema for a long time. The major difficulty is that there are many different views on what 'culture' is and what 'national' means. To help solve this problem, I have drawn on ideas from the field of anthropology, where the subject of culture is discussed most intensively.

Interpretive anthropologists, such as Clifford Geertz, argue that in order to understand the cultures and cultural products of different societies we have to grasp the native systems of signification.[1] To interpret a gesture or an event or a symbol within its cultural context, we have to think in terms of the system of meanings by which a given group of people perceive, interpret and act or react with respect to different phenomena. To use one of Geertz's favourite examples – 'winking' – it is pointed out that to identify 'winking' is not to see it simply as eyelid contraction but to understand the conspiratorial meaning, or whatever meaning is assigned to such an eyelid movement by a group of people. Culture therefore consists of socially established structures of meanings in terms of which people do things, such as winking, interpret things, such as taking winking as a conspiracy, and formulate their actions in response to their comprehension of reality, such as punishing a conspiracy.[2]

When this concept is used in the study of Chinese films the same kind of knowledge is required of the systems of meanings associated with what is visually and aurally presented in the context of Chinese culture. In order to read Chinese films in the native way, one has to know what phenomena (scenes, shots, actions, or any filmic elements) one has to look for and know what is the Chinese way of relating these different phenomena. Otherwise, it is easy for an observer to fail to record the things depicted in the films only because he/she does not recognise their cultural significance, or to impose interpretation which may not be appropriate. This first step of apprehension and interpretation must be well taken and practised before one can explain Chinese films in ways that are closer to the Chinese perception of reality. When this step is ignored, the result could be like playing Chinese Chess with foreign rules. The game might still be interesting but it is not Chinese Chess. This paper is an attempt to relate Chinese films and their interpretation to the cultural context, i.e. their system of meanings, in terms of which they are produced and perceived.

Although studies of Chinese culture in general have not followed the Geertzian approach, works that are helpful in providing a cultural framework for the contextual reading of Chinese cultural products are still available. The work of the young Chinese scholar Sun Longji is such a resource.[3] Sun's description of Chinese culture shares similarities with some psycho-cultural studies done on Chinese personality by other scholars.[4] The present study employs Sun's model because unlike most methods, which concentrate on single individual aspects of some cultural traits, Sun's theory is a broad-based description of Chinese culture as a whole.

In his book *The Deep Structure of Chinese Culture*, Sun uses the notion of 'personhood' as the major defining theme found in the Chinese ethos.[5] He suggests that the Chinese have developed a 'system' according to which persons are perceived and social actions are formulated.[6] This 'system' is basic to the Chinese interpretation of reality. According to Sun, the Chinese view of a person can be dichotomised into the 'body' (*shen*) and the 'heart' (*xin*).[7] The physical body is what contributes to the physical life of a person, while the relationship with fellow human beings defines the spiritual realm of existence. The task of a person in the context of Chinese culture is to preserve his/her body and to keep the spiritual alive by maintaining proper relations with associates.

The Chinese think of a person as being defined by social relationships, which are shaped by the activities of the person's 'heart'. The 'heart' generates an emotion called '*qing*' (emotive feeling). When this is directed towards another person, it should result in empathy and concern. This is called 'having heart'. The dynamic of '*qing*' manifests itself in a variety of ways, such as the rules of conduct and the precedence of '*qing*' over '*li*' (reason). In contrast, the concern for the preservation of the body results in pragmatic survivalism of which the attitude of '*jing*' (cleverness) is an example. A '*jing*' person calculates his/her tactics to gain advantages, which may result in his/her refusal to 'have heart' for others. The survival of the body and the domination of the 'heart' form the two dialectical themes according to which the Chinese organise their systems of meaning and interpretation.

With these cultural concepts as my frame of reference, I will analyse the three most popular films made in two major Chinese societies, the People's Republic of China and Hong Kong, during the period of 1981–85. My analysis will concentrate on the characterisation of fictional figures as they relate to the themes of the films. I shall identify the primary similarities and differences between the films from China and Hong Kong, by uncovering the cultural assumptions according to which they are made and perceived. I shall thus attempt to isolate several important characteristics of the two cinemas in a comparative context. By comparing the two cinemas in this way, one can see that certain differences and similarities are only superficial and that there are deeper differences and similarities that define the idiosyncrasies of each.

2. Films from China

In 1977, a year after the Chinese 'cultural revolution' when film production had come to almost a complete halt, Chinese cinema regained its productivity and produced twenty-eight feature films.[8] The production rate quickly increased and by the early 1980s the annual rate reached well over a hundred.[9] Traditionally, Chinese cinema has been progressive and revolutionary. During the 'cultural revolution', this ideological consciousness was pushed to the extreme. But from the late 1970s onwards, the movement of ideological liberation severely criticised the formula approach. The new era of the 1980s was marked by a rejection of the dogmatism of the 70s in both form and content. The desire to use film to explore reality now takes priority over the previous fabrication of ideals. Some of these films gained enormous popularity for their attempt to explore new subjects for filmic presentation. This question of the recent progressivism of the Chinese films is also a concern of the present paper.

The three prize-winning films from China I have chosen to discuss attracted a great deal of attention when they were first released.[10] *The Legend of Tianyun Mountain* is considered to be one of the most important films since the 'cultural revolution', and deals directly with the adverse effects of the political struggle of the 1950s–1970s in China.[11] Luo Qun is an honest, hard-working engineer, sent to Tianyun Mountain for a development project in the 1950s. He falls in love with one of his teammates, Song Wei. Later, in a political movement, Luo Qun is falsely accused and purged. Song Wei leaves Luo Qun while her girlfriend, Feng Qinglan, sees that Luo Qun is only being bad-mouthed by cadres. She decides to help the bedridden Luo Qun by marrying him. Critics judged the film to be a success for its realistic and convincing depiction of the lives of the three people who represent three kinds of real-life people in China.[12] Because of their different personal values, these three characters respond disparately to the political situation in the country and hence follow totally different paths in life.

At Middle Age depicts the problems of middle-aged professionals, who continue to suffer after the 'cultural revolution'. The heroine, Lu, is a doctor, who works quietly in her overloaded and underpaid job.

According to the magazine *Popular Cinema*, the third film, *The In-Laws* scored the highest audience record of 2.7 million viewers for the first twelve days screening in Beijing.[13] Qiangying, the antagonist, is a jealous and gossipy woman, who creates problems in the Chen family which are later solved by the 'good-hearted' Shuilian.

Although the themes of the three films are very different, many reviewers believe that these films appeal to their Chinese audience chiefly for their 'untraditional realism'. 'Realism' here means that the audience takes the stories, though fictional, to be a faithful description and interpretation of reality. The films are also championed because they celebrate personal virtues, and portray heroes or heroines who represent the 'ideal new socialist person'.[14]

However, it is important to recognise that both the film-makers and the audience use cultural assumptions which are only implicit. First, neither the audience in general nor the critics in particular seem to be aware that the films embrace a highly hierarchical social order, and accept it as a 'normal' way of life. In *The Legend of Tianyun Mountain*, although the film-maker is aware of the problems created by bureaucracy, which cause Luo Qun to suffer, he is unwilling to criticise such a system. Luo Qun is first purged because the cadres discredit him. But he is also raised from disgrace because of another cadre – the first secretary, who sees his 'merits'. Luo Qun's problem is finally solved by manoeuvring within the same hierarchical system. A similar hierarchy is taken for granted in both *At Middle Age* and *The In-Laws*.

Second, it is obvious that the film and its audience value highly the use of '*qing*' (emotional feeling) rather than '*li*' (reasoning, principles) in dealing with problems. Song Wei abandons Luo Qun. The montage sequence, which consists of close-ups of different friends and authorities urging her to leave Luo Qun and the flashbacks of the romantic moment when she first met him, shows that her choice is not a question of logical reasoning about the correctness of the accusation against Luo Qun but a question of compliance, whether she should succumb to her '*qing*' towards Luo Qun or that towards her social associates. Although the film explicitly condemns her lack of a rational response to the situation, the logical criticism of society expressed by other characters in the film is not taken positively. In both *At Middle Age* and *The In-Laws*, the logical arguments of friends and family members are also ignored. The audience praises the use of '*qing*' in all these films, and admires those characters who use their 'heart' to accept unfair treatment without complaint.

The third traditional assumption is that the definition of a person's worth is based on (a) good relations with others or affirmation by the group, (b) usefulness in society, and (c) self-effacement.

In both *At Middle Age* and *The Legend of Tianyun Mountain*, the tension in the stories comes from the fact that their protagonists are 'good' people whose sufferings are unjustified. Luo Qun is 'good' because his geological theory is correct while Lu is 'good' for her outstanding medical skill. A link is made between their professional competence and their integrity. In terms of their social relationships, Lu is the wife of a good husband, and Luo Qun is the son of a revolutionary martyr. Their merits are affirmed by good cadres, fellow workers and their social associates. The films strongly relate the heroes' positive images to group affirmation.

A self-effacing person is one who does not advocate himself/herself. Luo Qun never defends his own expertise. Lu is never arrogant about her professional competence. Nor does Shuilian admit that she is good at anything. Further, they refuse to fight for their 'rights'. Just as Luo Qun never fights for his rehabilitation, both Lu and Shuilian do not ask to be treated better. In all these characters, self-denial prevents them from pursuing anything for themselves.

According to their critics, these three films are viewed as rather 'un-traditional', which basically means abandoning the previous policy of portraying only the positive side of communist society. But if 'untraditionality' is taken more fundamentally, to mean adopting a critical attitude towards established systems of norms, values, meanings and organisations, then the films are clearly very 'traditional' in their use of old and conventional ways of interpreting reality and assigning meanings. Although there may be some minor deviation from convention, such as slightly different roles for women, or comments on government policy, each film as a whole basically abides by traditions.

3. Films from Hong Kong

Hong Kong is also a major film production centre in Asia. About 90–100 films are produced each year for local audiences.[15] The business of exporting Hong Kong films, or their videotape versions, for commercial distribution overseas is only a very minor source of revenue in most cases, except for the few films that have starred such international movie idols as Bruce Lee and Jacky Chan. Moreover, during the five years from 1981 to 1985 the box-office record of locally produced films has far surpassed that of imported films, even those that have come from Hollywood. For example, of the twenty-two most successful films in 1984, twenty were produced in Hong Kong.[16] The Hollywood hit of that year, *Raiders of the Lost Ark*, which was also the year's best-selling foreign film in Hong Kong, occupied only sixth place on the overall popularity chart.[17] While a James Bond film, *Never Say Never Again*, which was the second most successful foreign film, was fourteenth.[18] It is therefore accurate to say that the Hong Kong audience prefers Hong Kong films, and that Hong Kong films are basically aimed at the local audience, thus reflecting a close cultural relationship between the two.

The three box-office hits from Hong Kong which I shall review here are *Modern Security Guard*, *Aces Go Places (III)* and *Paragon*. *Modern Security Guard* is about a nasty security guard captain, Chow (Zhou), who is demoted and has to learn to cooperate with his colleagues and work responsibly. *Aces Go Places (III)* is representative of the overall style of the whimsical detective comedy of the *Aces Go Places* series, which were the best-selling films from 1982 to 1984. It is a story of a skilful burglar, King Kong, who ends up helping his police friend Baldy to catch a group of mafiosi who deliver false orders from a fake Queen of England. *Paragon* starred the well-known local *kung fu* star Hung (named Cheng [Zheng] in the film) who, together with his four close friends, is forced by the police to catch a group of Japanese gangsters. These three films express norms and values that are both similar to and different from those found in the films from China.

The attitude of 'jing', as a pragmatic position of taking advantage of people and situations, is strongly present in the major characters of all three Hong Kong films. Chow's assistant Sam, who always helps his boss to solve problems in *Modern Security Guard*, King Kong in *Aces Go Places (III)* and Cheng in *Paragon* are all 'clever' people who take advantage of every situation to get what they want. They avoid emotional or metaphysical questions, which they consider a hindrance in their struggle for survival. The burglar King Kong has only one concern: to 'do the right thing to survive'. The opening chase sequence is a good metaphor, whose pattern is often repeated in the film. In this scene, King Kong is chased by the mafiosi on the streets of Paris. He takes different routes and ends up climbing the Eiffel Tower. He tries to fight with his pursuers. But seeing that he is physically not strong enough to win he uses different tactics, including the use of a fire extinguisher, a parachute, cutting the strings of the parachute of his enemy, jumping into the sea, using his sports shoes to help him swim, and so on. When these efforts fail, he alters his principles without hesitation. Theoretical or moral questions, such as his so-called 'personal principle' of not working for any group, are alterable. He is 'flexible' enough to give in to the mafiosi's request and cooperate with them. Similarly, Cheng in *Paragon*, asked by the police to leave the jail and participate in a crime-solving operation, does not argue for his rights to refuse the proposal; and Sam in *Modern Security Guard* lies to the ghetto residents in order to capture the crime suspect.

The Chinese notion of human relationships is dramatised in the Hong Kong films by the acute distinction between the 'insiders' and the 'outsiders'. The presence of foreign figures, such as Westerners or Japanese, the English Queen or the US President in *Aces Go Places (III)*, is only a superficial instance. In most cases, the line between the two groups of people is more subtle. *Paragon* uses a complicated hierarchical system centred round the major character, Cheng. This system determines what will happen in the action of the story. For example, the film does not explain why Cheng turns to his four friends for assistance. They are not particularly skilful or wise; in fact, they create a lot of problems for Cheng. He chooses them only because they are his 'buddies'. On the other hand, the police are 'outsiders' whom Cheng and his friends would not defend. In *Aces Go Places (III)*, King Kong and Baldy are the 'core'. Even Baldy's wife and King Kong's girlfriend are only secondary. The bondedness and 'blind' loyalty among the core-group members is much glorified, especially in *Paragon*.

Although the attitudes found in the Hong Kong films – the notion of 'jing', and 'insiders and outsiders' – are not alien to the Chinese, the Hong Kong films have pushed these practices to an extreme. By doing so,

171

they create an imbalance with the other side of traditional Chinese culture, which is a culture of the 'heart', and constitute a unique deviation from their Chinese origin.

4. Comparing films from Hong Kong and China

The most obvious similarity between the films from Hong Kong and China is the definition of and emphasis on a 'good' person. All three Hong Kong films emphasise good interpersonal relationships between the heroes and their peers. In *Modern Security Guard*, Chow is a negative figure because he antagonises everybody, whereas Sam is liked by all his colleagues. This film thus shares a characteristic with the Chinese film *The In-Laws*, where Qiangying is shown to be negative because of her negative relationships with everyone, and Shuilian is the 'good' person loved by every family member. The affirmation of the group goes hand in hand with good relationships. In both *Paragon* and *Aces Go Places (III)*, the major characters are rewarded by the police for their achievements.

On the question of 'usefulness' and 'self-effacement', the Hong Kong and Chinese protagonists are very similar. They demonstrate professional competence while never advocating their abilities. Like Luo Qun in *The Legend of Tianyun Mountain*, the Hong Kong characters contribute to society and share their merits with their colleagues.

Despite these similarities, there are differences in emphasis in the two sets of films. While establishing the image of a 'good' person is the major concern of the films from China, the Hong Kong films suggest that practicality is of greater interest. The stories are about people who know how to survive, rather than about those who are traditionally 'good'.

Another similarity is the secondary position given to rationality in the films. In all the films from China, '*qing*' (emotion) is a much greater concern than '*li*' (principle, reason). Problems are solved by 'good heart' rather than good reasoning. Hong Kong films show almost a negative attitude towards the role of the intellectual. Rationality, however, is not replaced by '*qing*', as in the Chinese cases, but by pure pragmatism.

Finally, although both groups of films basically abide by the Chinese tradition, the Hong Kong films are more capable of being satirical, if not critical, towards older traditions. For example, authority figures, such as the police, the Queen, or even parents, which are greatly revered in traditional practice, are frequently joked about in the three Hong Kong films. Similarly, the Hong Kong emphasis on '*jing*' can also be viewed as a reaction against the over-domination of '*qing*'. In *Modern Security Guard*, Chow's penchant for inflicting physical pain on others is ridiculed by Ying, one of Chow's newly recruited assistants, with extreme self-effacement which almost turns into an act of masochism. This form of self-effacement, which is ironically taken as a major point for humour, is an example of the overall contradictory, love/hate position with respect to traditional ways of assigning values which is characteristic of the Hong Kong films.

5. Conclusion

The films from China abide by traditional Chinese cultural norms, especially the notion of (a) hierarchical social relationships, (b) the domination of '*qing*', and (c) the definition of a person by group affirmation, usefulness and self-effacement. These films reflect the traditional culture of the 'heart', and are not as untraditional as they first seem.

The films from Hong Kong also abide by traditional Chinese cultural values, especially in the definition of a 'good' person, where they display attitudes similar to those expressed in the films from China. Yet the Hong Kong films are also different in that they are dominated not by the 'heart', but by the notion of the survival of the physical body, which entails the practice of (a) '*jing*', and (b) a strong distinction between 'insiders' and 'outsiders'. Although the Hong Kong films are satirical towards tradition and are apparently Westernised, they are still fundamentally Chinese.[19] Like the films from China, they are bounded by and are not critical of their own form of Chinese culture.

Notes

1. Clifford Geertz, *The Interpretation of Cultures* (New York: Basic Books, 1973), pp. 7–10.
2. Ibid., p. 12.
3. Sun Longji's major theory of Chinese culture is developed in his book *Zhongguo Wenhua de Shenceng Jiegou* (*The Deep Structure of Chinese Culture*), which has not been translated into English. However, a few essays written in English by the author himself, expressing some of his major themes, can be found in the book *Seeds of Fire*, ed. Geremie Barmé and John Minford (Far Eastern Economic Review, 1986).
4. Sun's description of Chinese culture shares similarities with other works such as those found in the anthology *The Psychology of the Chinese People*, ed. Michael Harris Bond (Oxford University Press, 1986).
5. Sun Longji, 'The Long March to Man', in *Seeds of Fire*, p. 163.
6. Sun uses the term 'system of consciousness', which he regards as the basis of a culture. But one must note that his notion of culture as a structure of mind is being replaced here by Geertz's definition of culture as structures of meaning.
7. *Zhongguo Wenhua de Shenceng Jiegou*, pp. 11–81 passim.
8. John Howkins, *Mass Communication in China* (New York: Longman, 1982), p. 67.
9. Filmography of each year is published in each issue of the *China Film Year Book* (*Zhongguo Dianying Nianjian*) from 1981–85 (Beijing: *Zhongguo Dianying Chubanshe*).
10. The 'Hundred Flowers Awards', organised by the film magazine *Popular Cinema* (*Dazhong Dianying*), is voted for by the general audience and is an indication of the popularity of the films.
11. *Film Biweekly* (Hong Kong), 77 (7 Jan. 1982), p. 23. See also *Film Art* (*Dianying Yishu*), 104 (Feb. 1981), p. 24.
12. *Film Art*, 104 (Feb. 1981), pp. 24–33, and 106 (April 1981), p. 36.

173

13. *Popular Cinema*, 338 (August 1981), p. 11.
14. For *The Legend of Tianyun Mountain*, see *Film Art*, 104 (Feb. 1981), pp. 24–33, 106 (April 1981), pp. 32–6, and *Popular Cinema*, 330 (Dec. 1980), pp. 2–3, 333 (March 1981), p. 9. For *At Middle Age*, see *Popular Cinema* 356 (Feb. 1983), pp. 2–4, *Film Biweekly*, 140 (5 July 1984), p. 25, 148 (Nov. 1984), p. 16, and *Film Art*, 362 (Oct. 1983), pp. 18–20. For *The In-Laws*, see *Popular Cinema*, 334 (April 1981), pp. 3, 10–11, and 348 (June 1982), p. 3.
15. For filmography of each year, see December issue of *Film Biweekly* of respective year.
16. *Film Biweekly*, 153 (3 Jan. 1985), p. 22.
17. Ibid.
18. Ibid.
19. The Hong Kong films could be considered as Westernised only in terms of their outlook, which basically imitates contemporary American movies. But as this study indicates, Hong Kong films should not be taken as a fundamentally Westernised group, as viewed by some critics in China. See *China Film Year Book* (Beijing: *Zhongguo Dianying Chubanshe*, 1983), p. 792.

Filmography

NB: s = scenarist, d = director.

The Legend of Tianyun Mountain (*Tianyun shan chuanqi*), s: Luo Yanzhou, d: Xie Jin (China: Shanghai Studio, 1980).

The In-Laws (*Xi ying men*), s: Xin Xianling, d: Zhao Huanzhang (China: Shanghai Studio, 1981).

At Middle Age (*Ren dao Zhongnian*), s: Chen Rong, d: Wang Qimin (China: Changchun Studio, 1983).

Modern Security Guard (*Modeng bao biao*), s/d: Michael Hui (Hong Kong: Hui Brothers, 1981).

Aces Go Places (III) (*Zui jia paidang III*), s: Huang Bioming (Huang Baiming), d: Tsui Hark (Xu Ke) (Hong Kong: Cinema City, 1984).

Paragon (*Fu xiang gaozui*), s: Huang Bingyau (Huang Bingyao), d: Samo Hung (Hong Jinbao) (Hong Kong: Golden Harvest, 1985).

The Wan Brothers and Sixty Years of Animated Film in China

MARIE-CLAIRE QUIQUEMELLE

The Chinese animation cinema, appreciated by the entire world today for its original national style and its high artistic level, is over sixty years old, for it was in 1927 in Shanghai that the Wan brothers, after years of research and fruitless trials, produced their first cartoon, *Turmoil in a Workshop*. The events that led to this first production and the professional struggles that followed it form a remarkable story. It is not only a tale of the Wan brothers' personal struggles, but also one that highlights, informs and in various respects characterises the development of a distinctively Chinese animation cinema.

At Nanking (Nanjing), in the first few years of the twentieth century, there were four brothers: Wan Laiming, the eldest, his twin brother Guchan, and the two youngest, Dihuan and Chaochen. They all loved to draw and swore that one day they would find a way to confer the motion of life on to their pictures. This idea arose out of the depths of Chinese tradition, as Wan Laiming explained: 'I remember how we loved to play with the shadows of our hands from the weak light given off by an oil lamp when we were children.[1] When we were a little older, we happened to see a shadow theatre performance, and were very taken with it. After that we spent all our evenings cutting out cardboard figures, which we fixed on sticks. Then, illuminating them with the oil lamp, we made their shadows move along the wall. It was a marvellous game ... I recall another time, when seeing the shadow of trees glide along a wall at the mercy of the wind and become lifelike, we thought it very beautiful and decided that our cardboard silhouettes should become animated in the same manner as the tree branches when swept by the wind. From that moment on, the expression animated picture rooted itself in our childhood imaginations, but we were far from realising that we had found our calling.'[2]

Wan Laiming was very gifted at art and, at the age of eighteen, when he had to look for work to support his family, he had the idea of sending a letter accompanied by a few sketches to the Commercial Press, the big publishing house in Shanghai. He was hired in the illustration section. Later, he called for his brothers and helped them attend art school in Shanghai.

Together again, they started to dream about animated pictures once more. They began examining various apparatuses which allow for the

175

artificial animation of pictures, in particular the 'lamp of the galloping horse', a kind of magic lantern which had been traditional in China for centuries and was turned by convection caused by the heat of an oil lamp. One day, when visiting the Great World Amusement Centre, they discovered an extraordinary machine, imported from the West. According to Wan Laiming's description, when a coin was inserted the light turned on, the motor began, and then one could watch Charlie Chaplin appear, spinning his hat, and performing his famous duckwalk. The motion was perfectly recreated.[3] The scene was lifelike. Back at home, Wan Laiming took a notepad on which he drew, page after page, a succession of scenes representing a cat chasing a mouse. When he flipped the pages between thumb and forefinger, the sequence became animated. He called his brothers and they were all overwhelmed with joy: they had finally discovered the secret of animation. But at this stage they were still totally ignorant of the new technology of the cinema, and could not foresee that this new art would give them the possibility of bringing about their dream.

Shanghai in the early 1920s was a big cosmopolitan centre, up to date on all the recent inventions, where the cinema appealed to a large audience. However, Chinese cinema itself was still very young and the majority of films available were foreign, especially American. The day when the Wan brothers saw their first cartoon was a big moment.[4] They were instantly overwhelmed. From then on they became fervent admirers of the cartoon, decided that they would solve its mystery, and, in the words of Wan Laiming, swore that 'one day they would produce a cartoon, in the Chinese style, to rival the Americans'. This was an extravagant project on the part of the four penniless brothers who knew nothing of the cinema and would never find anyone in Shanghai to teach them. But they could rely on their natural talent, their persistence, and luck, which always rewards those who are daring enough.

Let us listen to Wan Laiming relate the evolution of this grand project: 'In 1922, my brothers received their degree from the School of Fine Arts and entered the cinema section of the Commercial Press. For my part, I was illustrating children's books. It was our persistent desire to produce a cartoon one day that led us to pursue our research. In the daytime we worked, but at night we carried out our experiments at home. At the time, it was difficult because we lacked not only money but also materials. In the one and only little room we had, we owned nothing but a few lamps, some pencils, and an old camera. We had to do everything ourselves: write the scenario, think up the characters, draw the pictures, take care of shooting, developing, editing. ... Day after day, night after night, our research absorbed us totally, leading us to forget all about meals, sleep, our families, our children, life. All the rest was secondary. I have no idea how many times we failed, until one evening, on a white wall in our room, the drawings began to appear lifelike. They were animated. We were overcome with happiness. This occurred maybe fifty

176

years ago, but I can still remember it very vividly. .... The cinema section of the Commercial Press, hearing of our success, asked us to produce, as non-professionals, an advertising cartoon: *The Typewriter for Chinese by Shu Zhendong*. Today that film would seem simplistic and a trifle ridiculous, but it does not alter the fact that it was the original model upon which we built all our following movies and that it gave us first-hand experience in the art of the production of a cartoon. Then my brothers and I were hired by the Great Wall Studio as set makers. But we were asked to produce an animated film in our spare time, as well. It was in 1927, in our small room, that we finished making the first Chinese cartoon.'

This was *Turmoil in a Workshop*, which, as was also common in American cartoons of the time, was a combination of real-life and cartoon figures. It is the story of an artist. He has a piece of paper in front of him and is busy drawing a little man, but suddenly the little figure comes to life, gets down from the drawing-board and sets about creating havoc in the room. Eventually the artist gets hold of him and fixes him back on the drawing-board with a pin. This film was of course strongly influenced by Max and Dave Fleischer, whom the Wan brothers admired very much. 'After such a promising start,' Wan Laiming continues, 'we had to wait several years before we could make another cartoon, because the Shanghai producers regarded animation as too costly both in material and in personnel.'[5]

None the less, in 1930, the Wan brothers produced *The Rebellion of the Paper Man* for the Great China Studio. This film was based on a scenario very similar to *Turmoil in a Workshop*, which might explain the frequent confusion between the two films. In 1932, the brothers were asked to work at the Lianhua company, at the time the most successful film studio in Shanghai and well known for the high artistic level of its productions. This took place in the wake of the Japanese attack on Shanghai of 28 January 1932, and the Wan brothers produced six 'educative' and 'patriotic' cartoons, including *Citizen, Wake Up!* and *The Price of Blood*. Then, in 1933, they were hired by the Mingxing company where they remained until the declaration of war in 1937, living for the first time in comparative comfort and security and able to devote themselves to their art at last. During this period they produced nine short films, many with a strong patriotic message. Among the titles: *The Painful Story of the Nation*, *The Year of Chinese Goods*, and *The Motherland is Saved by Aviation*. In 1935, they produced their first talkie, *The Camel Dance*, and during the same period they produced animation sections for two feature-length films: *The Beautiful Cigarette Girl*, a progressive film in which the animation section showed golden dollars assaulting Chinese factories, and *Scenes of Urban Life*, the famous film by Yuan Muzhi.

At the beginning their creations, which also appeared as comic strips in newspapers and in artistic or satirical reviews, were much influenced by the American style – for example, 'The Father of Miss Lu', a short man

177

with a strong jaw and dressed in the Western style, or 'The Smiling Monkey', a copy of Mickey Mouse.[6] In an article published in July 1936 in the periodical issued by the Mingxing company, the Wan brothers stressed the importance of American cartoons and recognised that they themselves had been influenced by Max and Dave Fleischer. Then, after discussing Felix the Cat and Mickey Mouse, with which they were very familiar, they insisted that the American cartoons were not the only ones. German and Russian cartoons were very good too. As for the Chinese, they themselves had already produced about twenty short films (approximately 1,000 feet each) and they were very conscious that in future characters should be more authentically Chinese, just as American, German and Russian cartoons bore the character of their own countries. 'In a Chinese film,' they argued, 'one ought to have a story based purely on real Chinese traditions and stories, consistent with our sensibility and sense of humour.... Also, our films must not only bring pleasure, but also be educational.'[7]

Unfortunately, there remains nothing of the earliest masterpieces by the Wan brothers, but the oldest film which has survived, dating back to 1938, illustrates these theories. It is based on a poem by Yue Fei, the famous patriotic general of the Song dynasty, called *The River is Red With Blood*. Sung by the Wuhan Chorus, it becomes a vehement criticism of the aggressive war fought by Japan against China. The representation of Yue Fei draws inspiration from ancient statues, but the style of the pictures is direct and caricatural, reminding one of the etchings made by contemporary Chinese artists.

On 7 July 1937, China, which had in fact been in conflict with Japan since the occupation of Manchuria in 1931, finally declared war. On 13 August that year the Japanese occupied Shanghai. The Wan brothers left for Wuhan where they set out to produce two series of patriotic shorts for the China Film Studio: *The Posters of the Anti-Japanese War* and *The Songs of the Anti-Japanese War*. When Wuhan was also occupied by the enemy, the employees of the company were transferred to Chongqing. There, the Wan brothers learned that no more cartoons would be produced, and so they returned to Shanghai where their families were waiting for them.

In Shanghai, the foreign concessions remained sheltered from the Japanese invasion until 7 December 1941, when Japan attacked Pearl Harbor and declared war on Britain and the United States, and so it was on this 'orphan island' that the free Chinese cinema survived from 1937 to the end of 1941. 'In 1940–1941,' Wan Laiming continues, 'I opened an animation section for the United China company with my brother Guchan. At the time, the first American feature-length cartoon, *Snow White*, was a big success in Shanghai, receiving great acclaim. This made Chinese capitalists greedy, and so they proposed that we make a full-length Chinese cartoon. Inspired by a chapter from the ancient novel *Journey to the West*, called "Lending the Fan Three Times", we pro-

Sun Wukong transforms himself in the Wan brothers' *Princess Iron Fan*

duced *Princess Iron Fan*. It was clear to us that we had to arouse the national spirit of the public by stressing the need for resistance. The end of the shooting occurred just at the time of the invasion of the foreign concessions by the Japanese, so, when the prints came out, we had to cut in a song for Zhu Bajie, the pig, with the lyric "People Rise and Fight Until Victory". 7,000 feet long, it was the first feature-length Chinese cartoon. It played for a month and a half without a break in three cinemas in Shanghai. It was also shown in Singapore and Indonesia, and was warmly received everywhere.'[8]

The hero of the film, Sun Wukong, the Monkey King, is escorting the holy Monk San Zang on his trip to the West, accompanied by Zhu Bajie, the pig, and Sha Seng, the monk. Aided by his quick-wittedness and far-reaching powers, the Monkey King is strong enough to fight with monsters on the pilgrims' path and always manages to triumph over evil.

179

This production on the 'orphan island' of the French Concession in the middle of the war was a real feat not only on the artistic level but also on the technical level. Seventy artists, in two teams, worked without a break for a year and four months, all in the same room, in limited space, in the cold of the winter, and in the atrocious heat of the summer. To assure the accuracy of the movement, certain scenes were filmed with actors to serve as a guide to the artists. This film, with its many inventions, sparkles with humour, fantasy and poetry. It is a delight to the spectator. But it suits adults and older children better than very young children, who might be frightened by the violence in the fight scenes, underscored as it is by brutal music. Even if, at times, the influence of Disney is still noticeable, we are far from his sweetness and prettiness, far from America and its prosperity. *Princess Iron Fan* bears witness in its own way to the brutal reality of the daily violence in a country crippled by war, where it would have been impossible for any aware film-maker to produce a film designed purely to amuse.

When it came out, *Princess Iron Fan* benefited from huge curiosity on the part of the Shanghai public. It was an immediate success. Only two years after *Snow White*, the audience appreciated this Chinese production which flattered national pride. In addition, the public picked up on the satire of the film, which ridiculed the Japanese enemy indirectly. Japan was personified as the Buffalo King, a dangerous monster, riding a sort of dinosaur to a heavy march reminiscent of the Japanese tanks. Finally, Sun Wukong succeeds in defeating the monster, but only after having mobilised the people against it.

After this big success, the Wan brothers hurried back to work. They wished to produce a second feature-length film, *The World of Insects*, which was also a disguised condemnation of Japanese aggression. The preparatory work was almost completed when the foreign concessions in Shanghai were invaded by the enemy and the production had to be abandoned. The Wan brothers then became involved in a new project dear to them: to portray another story from *Journey to the West*, 'The Monkey King Disturbs the Celestial Palace', in a cartoon. After months of effort during which they ran into countless problems, they managed to find a producer and had already established the form of the artistic project when, Wan Laiming explains, 'our boss suddenly ordered us to stop everything. At the time the cost of the film and the chemicals were increasing so much that the capitalist figured that selling the materials would bring him more money than our producing the film! Six months of effort were reduced to nothing, and the hopes of several years dashed. For my part, I put away my paint brushes. Our Sun Wukong was over. Apart from our own grief, what saddened us most was to send away our team of specialists which we had spent several years training. Each had to manage on his own, and it was with sad hearts that we ourselves also had to face up to changing jobs. At that time I was close to fifty and I told myself that never again would I be able to work on this project.'[9]

The Wan brothers then abandoned the cinema for a long time. They still have sad memories of those years of misery when they had to work at any job they could find. They were happy when they were able to use their artistic gifts in advertising jobs. At the time, in order to earn a little money, Wan Laiming sometimes cut out silhouettes in the streets of Shanghai. His pride was deeply hurt by this, and so he usually offered his skills to foreigners. In less than a minute, the black paper profile would be finished.

However, by the early 1940s the Wan brothers were no longer the only ones interested in cartoons, as had been the case for the last twenty years. In August 1941 in Hong Kong, nineteen young artists founded the Chinese Cartoon Association, which produced *The Hunger of the Old, Stupid Dog* as well as short cartoons by Qian Jiajun.[10] These were the first attempts of young people full of enthusiasm, but circumstances were rather difficult.

Furthermore, even before the liberation of 1949, animation proved to be an important preoccupation for the Communist Chinese cinema workers. In 1946 the Communist Party took the initiative in establishing the North-east Studios at Xingshan, Manchuria, which produced documentaries and two animation films: *The Dream of the Emperor* (1947), a puppet film, and *Catch the Turtle in a Jar* (1948), a cartoon. *The Dream of the Emperor* was inspired by a caricature of Chiang Kaishek by Hua Junwu. The script and direction were by Chen Bo'er. Thirty minutes long, it was integrated in the fourth section of a newsreel serial, *The Democratic North-east. Catch the Turtle in a Jar* was a ten-minute long caricature cartoon ridiculing Chiang Kaishek's policies. The script was by the artist Zhu Dan, and the direction by Fang Ming. These two films were screened in Communist areas, mainly to soldiers, and were welcomed warmly.

As early as October 1949, an Animation Film Section was established at the Changchun Studio, involving twenty-two people, including the cartoonist Te Wei, the author of children's books Jin Jin, and the 'artistic cadre' (*wenyi ganbu*) Jin Xi. In the month of October 1949, Te Wei became Director and Jin Xi Vice-Director of the Section. In February 1950, the group was transferred to Shanghai and integrated with the Shangying Studio. There, the initial team was strengthened by the addition of personalities such as Qian Jiajun (mentioned above), puppeteer Yu Zheguang, writer Ma Guoliang, film-maker Chang Chaoqun, painter Lei Yu, and last but not least the Wan brothers: Wan Chaochen from 1950; Wan Laiming and Wan Guchan in the middle of the 50s.

During the civil war, in 1949, the twins Wan Laiming and Wan Guchan had emigrated to Hong Kong where, taking up their old project once again, they started work on the full-length colour cartoon *The World of Insects* for the Great Wall company. Although well under way, the film was dropped some months later due to lack of capital and qualified personnel. The Wan brothers only found employment as set designers and special effects experts in Hong Kong, and they were never again involved in cartoon-making. But during a trip to Shanghai in 1954, the studio asked Wan Laiming for his collaboration, and also that of Guchan. One can imagine their happiness at the idea of finally making another animation film. They accepted.

By this time the importance of the Animation Studios had greatly increased. Young students fresh out of art institutes or film schools had been hired, and added to the original team. From twenty-two members in 1950, the personnel had grown to two hundred in 1956.

In the early 50s there was an effort to think out the aims of Chinese cartoons, as stated in an article published by Jin Xi in 1959.[11] I will give a few of the significant points. It is interesting to observe how these aims echo many of those the Wan brothers had already set for themselves back in 1936. Firstly animation films, destined primarily for children, must not only amuse but also educate. The second point emphasises the importance of technical issues, in particular those concerning photography and the use of colour. It was in 1953 that the studio's first colour film was produced. A puppet film entitled *The Little Heroes*, it was directed by Wan Chaochen, with Chang Chaoqun responsible for cinematography.

The third point deals with characters, which need to be embodied with certain human traits to be successful. For example, when a film depicts animals, it is through them that children have to be able to find their own interests and aspirations: 'They have the same habits that animals have, but at the same time human characters and even movements must be naturally melded into the animals.'[12] Also, the utmost attention has to be devoted to the aesthetic quality of the work: 'the audience, while appreciating the artistic construction of the story, will also appreciate the beauty of the picture.'[13] This point is particularly noteworthy because Chinese cartoons aimed at being artistic films from the start, and this is probably what allowed them to reach a high level at a very early stage, rendering them far more competitive on the international market than feature films or documentaries.

The fourth point is that animation films must express what the Chinese call 'national character'; that is, they must show the originality of Chinese culture, a demand which, one will remember, had already been stressed by Wan Laiming in 1936. This is an understandable reaction to the excessive influence of American cartoons before 1949 and of Soviet cartoons in the early 50s. *The Magic Paintbrush*, a puppet film produced in 1955 by Jin Xi, and *The Conceited General* (1956), a cartoon by Te Wei, are good examples of Chinese animated films with authentic Chinese flavour. This success encouraged research and allowed new techniques to be discovered, inspired by popular arts and traditions: the articulated cut-outs, the folded paper figures, and the ink and wash paintings.

The fifth and final point concerns the great variety of subjects which are dealt with in animated films. This gives them a certain advantage over feature films, which are often imprisoned in the narrow restraints of socialist realism. It is this comparative freedom that enables animators to search for their inspiration in classical literature, mythology, national legends, fairy tales and folk songs, as well as political caricatures, comic strips and so on.

After the first few years of establishment and development, the Chinese animated film made rapid progress in the pursuit of these goals. It is clear that the policies of the 'Hundred Flowers' period (1956–7) favoured the spirit of creation and encouraged innovations both on the artistic and the technical levels. On the whole, even though there were difficulties due to political campaigns which today are labelled 'leftist', it is clear that studio potential and activity were increased (even just on the personnel level, where it grew from two to three hundred in the early 60s), and the productions improved both qualitatively and quantitatively (ninety-one animated films appeared between 1949 and 1959). Furthermore, some remarkable work led to the invention and development of new, distinctively Chinese forms of animation.

The first new form, the Chinese articulated cut-outs, had been thought up by Wan Guchan as early as 1950. To that end, in 1956, after his return to the mainland, he went to the province of Shanxi to study the shadow theatre and the traditional decorative arts that used paper-cuts. Then, in collaboration with Qian Jiajun and young men such as Hu Jingqing, Liu Fenzhan and Chen Zhenghong, he proposed a new type of animation which was not only a major aesthetic success but also allowed for great economies of labour relative to traditional cartoons. In fact, it was adequate to make one cut-out for all the scenery, then cut-outs for each character front on, profile and three-quarter, with close-ups, medium shots and long shots. Because they were articulated, all that was required after that was to move their position slightly between each shot, as in puppet films, except that in this case the cut-outs were placed flat to be photographed from above, as with cartoons.

The first paper-cut film was *Zhu Bajie Eats the Watermelon* (1958). The colours were gay, the cut-outs simple and harmonious, the story full of humour and well worked out. The opera music went perfectly with a style of animation still close to that of traditional shadow theatre. After this first success, Wan Guchan specialised in articulated cut-outs and, with his team, he produced *The Fisherboy* (1959), *The Spirit of Ginseng* (1962), which was to be the winning film at Leipzig that year and at Alexandria in 1979, and *The Golden Conch* (1963).

Another remarkable innovation is due to Te Wei and Qian Jiajun. With the collaboration of Xu Jinda, Duan Xiaoxuan and Tang Cheng, they produced the animated ink and wash film (*shuimo donghuapian*), inspired by traditional Chinese painting. *Where is Mama?* was produced in 1960. It was a faithful homage to the work of the old master Qi Baishi, and both a lesson on the life in a pond and a means of rendering accessible to children the art of a great artist. The story is very simple: under the

183

gaze of goldfish and chicks, black pearls at the bottom of a pond become little tadpoles which happily move off in search of their mother. Since they do not know what she looks like, there follows a series of amusing mistakes. This film is a real pleasure for both old and young, captivating in the mastery of the paint brush, the freshness of the colours and liveliness of movements. It was just as much praised in China as abroad, and won first prize at several festivals.

In 1963, Te Wei and Qian Jiajun produced a second animated ink and wash film, *The Flute of the Cowherd*, a homage to another great contemporary artist, Li Keran, famous for his paintings of the Chinese countryside to the south of the Yangzi river. It is a masterpiece of charm and poetry, and received a gold medal in Denmark in 1979. Unfortunately, the Shanghai animation studio produced no more ink and wash, a type of film requiring particularly lengthy and difficult work. But the result is so marvellous that we cannot help but hope that one day Te Wei will take his paintbrushes once more and allow the public to discover another great Chinese painter via the medium of animated film.

The third innovation was the development of animated folded paper films. Paper folding is a traditional popular art that the Chinese (as well as the Japanese) learn to do from their early childhood. Starting with a simple page of paper folded in a thousand ways and occasionally cut out and coloured, they create all sorts of decorative patterns as well as little characters and animals. Animated with skill in front of the camera, these folded papers tell pretty tales to children, who are delighted to watch them move just as if by magic. The first film of this sort, *The Intelligent Little Duckling*, was produced in 1960 by Yu Zheguang. In addition, animated puppet films experienced remarkable growth, but during that decade the cartoon section was still the most active, with many talented young artists joining the veterans Te Wei, Wan Laiming and Qian Jiajun.

In addition to participating in these developments after his return to mainland China in 1956, Wan Laiming finally got the chance to realise the dream which had haunted him for nearly twenty years. He was at last able to produce *Uproar in Heaven* (1961 and 1964). The first part of the film, 1,223 metres long, was finished in 1961, after a year of intensive work. It involved no less than 70,000 drawings. Wan Laiming was given all the resources he needed, but the groundwork was long, demanding much effort. The adaptation of the script, the development of the characters, the scenery, the costumes (based on the magnificent drawings of Zhang Guangyu), and the animation itself, created many problems. For example, how was one to represent the character Sun Wukong, who is at one and the same time a monkey and a god whose powers are great, while all along behaving with human reactions? The 'mountain of flowers and fruit', home of Sun Wukong, is full of life, breathing happiness; it is the residence of an immortal, a simple but magnificent garden contrasting with the Celestial Palaces which are impressive but cold.

184

Uproar in Heaven

The hero of the film is Sun Wukong again, the famous monkey who, after having taken possession of the pillar holding the sky vault in the palace of the Dragon King, uses it as a powerful weapon to defy the Jade Emperor. Having become a celestial mandarin, he steals the peaches of longevity, gets hold of the elixir of immortality and stands against the hundred thousand warriors sent by the Jade Emperor to capture him. The living symbol of intelligence and courage, he fears neither Heaven nor Earth.

When seeing this film one is first overwhelmed by the beauty of the drawings and the vividness of the colours, both in accordance with the tradition of popular imagery and of the opera. 'The colour must embody the popular tradition, while still full of originality and imagination. The scenery must not be too naturalistic, so as to maintain the fairy-tale atmosphere.' Because of these considerations, the settings are sumptuous and the scenery fantastic, all in a style which has managed to include certain Occidental influence within an art strongly marked by Chinese tradition. The frescoes of Dunhuang were the source for the representation of the seven fairies, sisters of the buddhist apsara. Other characters, such as Nezha or the Jade Emperor, seem to originate more from popular sources. The Peking opera served as a source of ideas for the costumes with their vivid colours, and for the make-up full of nuances both strong and delicate. The palaces imitate the old architectural models; the mountains, the waterfalls, the waves and the flames are influenced by classical painting. The music, which uses a lot of percussion, is reminiscent of Peking opera.

185

The second part of the film was finished in 1964, and the two parts were made into one film, almost two hours long. But at that time it was the eve of the 'cultural revolution', and so the film was not screened. Wan Laiming was criticised for his representation of the Jade Emperor, which was said to resemble Chairman Mao too closely. However, in 1977 *Uproar in Heaven* was rediscovered and gained attention in China and abroad. In 1978 it won a best film award at the London festival. It was shown on British television, and on French television in a French dubbed version. At the same time, Chinese animation as a whole has experienced a remarkable revival. The Shanghai animation studios are in full growth again. With a staff of five hundred, and buildings recently enlarged, their activity is ever increasing and they have resumed their prestigious place on the world scene. With the final triumph of *Uproar in Heaven*, the Wan brothers have played a central role in this latest achievement as they have in the whole history of the Chinese animation cinema.

Translated by Claire Béliard

Notes

1. This game, still very popular in China, became fashionable in Europe at the end of the 19th century, and was performed in public shows of the period.
2. Wan Laiming, 'Fifty-five Years of Activity in the Art of Animation' ('*Donghua yishu shengya wushiwu nian*'), in *Yingju meishu*, 1981, no. 1.
3. Yao Fangzao, 'The Wan brothers and *Uproar in Heaven*', in *Yishu shijie*, 1979, no. 1.
4. Wan Laiming, op. cit. This first cartoon was an episode from the serial *Out of the Inkwell* by the Fleischer brothers.
5. Shi Cu, 'About Cartoons' ('*Donghua manhua*'), in *Dazhong dianying* (*Popular Film*), 1962, no. 5–6.
6. Ibid. Other characters included a little black cat, a little black dog, and a little white rabbit.
7. Wan Laiming, Wan Guchan, Wan Chaochen, 'Talking about Cartoons', in *Mingxing huabao*, 1936.
8. Wan Laiming, op. cit.
9. Ibid.
10. Shi Cu, op. cit., and Cheng Jihua, *History of the Development of Chinese Cinema* (*Zhongguo dianying fazhanshi*; Beijing: China Film Press, 1963), vol 2, p. 93. The only thing we know about this film is that it was a satire against the Japanese enemy.
11. Jin Xi, 'The Development of Chinese Animation Film', *Dianying yishu* (*Film Art*), 1959, nos. 4, 5.
12. Ibid.
13. Ibid.

Appendix 1

Major Directors

CHRIS BERRY AND PAUL CLARK

This appendix includes directors chosen not so much on the basis of some judgment of merit as on their prominence in this volume. There are no doubt many other major directors who could have been included, but if discussion in the various articles has been limited they have been omitted. The filmographies are for feature films only.

Although we have included pinyin to aid those interested in further research, the Chinese words found only in this appendix are not included in the glossary of Chinese characters. Further Chinese-language sources of information on directors and films might include: Cheng Jihua's *A History of the Development of Chinese Cinema* (*Zhongguo Dianying Fazhanshi*, Beijing: China Film Press [*Zhongguo Dianying Chubanshe*], 2nd ed., 1981) for the pre-1949 period; the ongoing multi-volume series *Chinese Film-Makers' Biographies* (*Zhongguo Dianyingjia Liezhuan*, Beijing: China Film Press) for all periods, but excluding Hong Kong and Taiwan; and the *China Filmography* (*Zhongguo Yishu Yingpian Bianmu*, Beijing: Culture and Art Press [*Wenhua Yishu Chubanshe*]) for the 1949 to 1979 period on the mainland.

(CB)

CAI CHUSHENG

Born into a poor Guangdong family in 1906, Cai Chusheng taught himself painting and play-writing before joining the film industry in Shanghai in 1927. Working first with Zheng Zhengqiu at the Mingxing Studio and then for the Lianhua Studio after 1930, he emerged as one of the most prolific and successful of the leftist directors of the 1930s and 1940s. In 1935 his *Song of the Fishermen* won an award at the Moscow Film Festival, the first major international prize for a Chinese film.

Cai spent the war years in Hong Kong, where he worked on patriotic films with another veteran director, Situ Huimin. After the war, he returned to Shanghai and helped to establish the openly leftist Kunlun Film Studio, which worked against the Nationalist Guomindang government. In 1947, he co-directed the cathartic epic *A Spring River Flows East* together with Zheng Junli. Telling the story of a couple separated and finally tragically reunited during the war years, it remains one of the most popular films of the period.

After the 1949 Liberation, Cai took part in the reorganisation of the film industry, but ceased to work as a director, producing only one film before his death in 1968, a victim of the 'cultural revolution'.

Everyone Aids the Nation (*Gong Fu Guo Nan*; co-directed with Sun Yu, Wang Cilong and Shi Dongshan), Lianhua Studio, 1932.

Spring in the South (*Nanguo Zhi Chun*), Lianhua Studio, 1932.

Pink Dream (*Fenhongse de Meng*), Lianhua Studio, 1932.

Dawn in the City (*Duhui de Zaochen*), Lianhua Studio, 1933.

Song of the Fishermen (*Yuguang Qu*), Lianhua Studio, 1934.

New Women (*Xin Nüxing*), Lianhua Studio, 1934.

Stray Kid Goats (*Milu de Gaoyang*), Lianhua Studio, 1936.

Little Wu (*Xiao Wuyi*), (episode in *The Lianhua Symphony* [*Lianhua Jiaoxiangqu*]), Lianhua Studio, 1937.

Old Wang (*Wang Laowu*), Lianhua Studio, 1937.

Blood-Splattered Baoshan (*Xuejian Baoshancheng*), New Era Film Company (*Xin Shidai Yingpian Gongsi*), Hong Kong, 1938.

The March of the Guerrillas (*Youji Jinxingqu*), Qiming Company, Hong Kong, 1938.

Paradise on the Orphan Island (*Gudao Tiantang*), Dadi Film Studio, Hong Kong, 1939.

A Brilliant Future (*Qiancheng Wanli*), New Life Film Company (*Xin Sheng Yingpian Gongsi*), Hong Kong, 1939.

A Spring River Flows East (*Yijiang Chunshui Xiang Dong Liu*) (directed with Zheng Junli), Kunlun Studio, 1947.

Waves on the Southern Sea (*Nanhai Chao*), Pearl River Film Studio (*Zhujiang Dianying Zhipianchang*), 1963.

(CB)

CHEN KAIGE

Chen Kaige, the Fifth Generation director with the largest international reputation, was born into a film family. Chen Huaikai, his father, made his name at the Beijing Film Studio as a director of Chinese opera films. His mother worked as a script editor. Chen's high-schooling ended in 1966, with the start of the 'cultural revolution'. Two years later, Chen was sent with a group of schoolmates to Yunnan province in the far southwest. He worked there on a rubber plantation, until his basketball talents earned him a place in the army. He made his way back to Beijing five years later and worked in a factory. At the Beijing Film Academy (1978–82) Chen was something of a loner, spending time in provincial television studios gaining experience. He was assigned to his father's Beijing Film Studio upon graduation.

Opportunity came at a small studio, when Zhang Yimou encouraged Chen to join the 'Youth Film Group' at the Guangxi studio. There, with Zhang as cinematographer, Chen made his reputation. *Yellow Earth*

(1984) put the Fifth Generation and China on the world film map. Its minimal dialogue and action, combined with stunning images, served as a profoundly ambiguous and multi-layered contemplation on China's revolution and Chinese civilisation. *Big Parade* (1985, released 1987) examined relations between the individual and the collective in an air-force unit arduously preparing for fleeting participation in the 1985 National Day parade in Tiananmen Square.

Chen made his third feature at Xi'an Film Studio, encouraged by studio head Wu Tianming. *King of the Children* drew on Chen's experiences in Yunnan province during the 'cultural revolution'. But, as in his other films, his focus was much wider than the setting at hand. *King of the Children* was the most philosophical of Chen's films to date. In it he raised heavy questions on how children become part of a culture and what education does to their nature.

In 1988, Chen took up a fellowship at New York University. He remained there through 1989, making a Duran Duran music video to raise funds for future projects, including one about Red Guards during the 'cultural revolution'.

Yellow Earth (*Huang Tudi*), Guangxi Film Studio, 1984.

Big Parade (*Da Yuebing*), Guangxi Film Studio, 1985.

King of the Children (*Haizi Wang*), Xi'an Film Studio, 1987.

(PC)

HOU HSIAO-HSIEN (Hou Xiaoxian)

Hou Hsiao-hsien is one of the two major talents in the 'new Taiwan Cinema' that emerged in the 1980s to challenge the nostalgia and dated formulas of the established, transplanted cinema on the island. His films come close to being cinematic equivalents of the 'roots literature' (*xiangtu wenxue*) that emerged a decade earlier in Taiwan as an expression of 'nativist' sentiment.

Hou himself is a transplant. Born in Guangdong province in 1947, his Hakka family moved to Taiwan in 1949, settling near Kaohsiung (Gaoxiong). After graduating from the film department of the Taiwan national Academy of the Arts in 1972, Hou entered the industry the following year. He worked as a production assistant, and then as an assistant director for several established directors, for whom he wrote scripts.

Hou drew attention to his directing talents through one episode in the portmanteau film *Sandwich Man*. His earlier *Green Green Grass of Home* had established much of his cinematic concerns. The rural setting and emphasis on children growing up continued in *The Boys from Fengkuei*, in which several young men from the countryside try to make it in the big city, and *A Summer at Grandpa's*. With *A Time to Live and a Time to Die*, Hou reached international attention. A highly autobiographical work, the film chronicles a mainland family in Taiwan exile through the 1950s. Hou's restraint and tact with this material is remark-

189

able. *Dust in the Wind* was another story of rural people moving to the city and young people maturing, in this case with help from the military draft. *Daughter of the Nile* was something of a departure, with a strictly contemporary, urban setting for its story of youth, petty crime and gambling. In 1989, Hou completed a project he had planned for many years. *A City of Sadness* examined the different responses of four sons to the replacement of the Japanese by the Nationalist regime in the 1940s.

Cute Girl (*Jiu Shi Liuliude Ta*), 1981.

Cheerful Wind (*Feng'er Ti Ta Cai*), 1982.

Green Green Grass of Home (*Zai Nei Hepan Qingcao Qing*), 1982.

The Son's Big Doll (*Erzi de Da Wan'ou*), episode in *Sandwich Man* (*Erzi de Da Wan'ou*), 1983.

The Boys from Fengkuei (*Fenggui Laide Ren*), 1983.

Summer at Grandpa's (*Dongdong de Jiaqi*), 1984.

A Time to Live and a Time to Die (*Tongnian Wangshi*), 1985.

Dust in the Wind (*Lianlian Fengchen*), 1987.

Daughter of the Nile (*Niluohe Nü'er*), 1987.

A City of Sadness (*Beiqing Chengshi*), 1989.

(PC)

HU MEI

One of the leading female talents of the Fifth Generation grew up in an army family and spent much of her professional life until the end of the 1980s in the army. Her father rose to the rank of conductor of the central symphony orchestra of the People's Liberation Army after 1949, until his degradation at the hands of the Red Guards in 1966. Sent to live with her grandmother in 1967 when she was ten, Hu Mei grew up on the outskirts of Beijing. She developed a talent in performing and entered an army dance troupe after graduating from high school. She passed the Beijing Film Academy entrance exams four years later in 1978.

Upon graduation in 1982, Hu returned to army ranks when she was assigned to the People's Liberation Army August First Film Studio in Beijing. In this unlikely context she proceeded to direct two unusually nuanced psychological studies. *Army Nurse* (1985), co-directed with an Academy classmate, is a highly subjective film. A nurse examines her life and career, in which duty has often taken precedence over emotional fulfilment. In *Far from War* (1987), a complex series of flashbacks connects an army family in contemporary Beijing, suffering from vaguely urban ennui, with an episode during the War of Resistance against Japan which still troubles the grandfather of the family. *Far from War* won a silver award for young directors at the Tashkent International Film Festival in 1988.

After making a more commercial film for August First called *The Gunslinger Without a Gun*, Hu Mei managed to end her association with the army studio in 1989. She hoped to freelance.

190

Army Nurse (*Nü'er Lou*), August First Film Studio, 1985 (co-directed with Li Xiaojun).

Far from War (*Yuan Li Zhanzheng de Niandai*), August First Film Studio, 1987.

The Gunslinger Without a Gun (*Wuqiang de Qiangshou*), August First Film Studio, 1988.

(PC)

LÜ BAN

Lü Ban's career in film spanned the transition from 1930s 'progressive' film-making in Shanghai to the consolidation of socialist cinema in the late 1950s. For the last eighteen years of his life, his talents were wasted.

Born in 1913, Lü Ban worked as an apprentice and miner before passing entrance examinations for a Beijing (then Beiping) acting school in 1930. Upon graduation, he worked as continuity assistant on the first production of the Beiping branch of the Lianhua Film Company. Moving to Shanghai in 1931, he joined a leftist drama company as an actor. In 1937, he made his on-screen debut in *Crossroads* (*Shizi Jietou*) and soon afterwards appeared in *The March of Youth*, two important 'progressive' films from the pre-war decade.

During the War of Resistance against Japan, Lü Ban studied in Yan'an, the Communist headquarters, and served in drama troupes there and in other Communist base areas. In 1948, he returned to film at the newly established Northeast (later Changchun) Film Studio. He starred in Communist China's first feature film, *The Bridge*. From 1950 onwards, Lü Ban worked as a director.

In 1956, his *Before the New Director Arrives* was one of the first satirical comedies from the new film industry. Responding to the relative liberalisation of the 1956 Hundred Flowers period, Lü Ban made two more satires at Changchun: *The Man Unconcerned With Details* and *Unfinished Comedy*. The latter, perhaps the most accomplished film made in the seventeen years between 1949 and the 'cultural revolution', was never released. Lü Ban was labelled a 'rightist' in the backlash against the openness of the Hundred Flowers period. He did not make another film before his death in November 1976.

The Invisible Front-line (*Wuxing Zhanxian*), Northeast Film Studio, 1949 (assistant director).

Heroes Lü and Liang (*Lü Liang Yingxiong*), Beijing Film Studio, 1950 (co-directed with Yi Lin).

Heroic New Sons and Daughters (*Xin Ernü Yingxiong Zhuan*), Beijing Film Studio, 1951 (co-directed with Shi Dongshan).

Gate No. 6 (*Liuhao Men*), Northeast Film Studio, 1952.

Heroic Drivers (*Yingxiong Siji*), Northeast Film Studio, 1954.

Yellow River Cantata (*Huanghe Dahechang*), documentary, Central Newsreel and Documentary Film Studio, 1955.

Before the New Director Arrives (*Xin Juzhang Daolai Zhiqian*), Changchun Film Studio, 1956.

The Man Unconcerned with Details (*Buyu Xiaojie de Ren*), Changchun Film Studio, 1956.

Unfinished Comedy (*Wei Wancheng de Xiju*), Changchun Film Studio, 1957.

(PC)

SHI DONGSHAN

Shi Dongshan was born in Hangzhou, up river from Shanghai, in 1902. He started working in the film industry in the chaotic 1920s, turning out martial arts films, and although none of his films from this period are known to have survived, he is one of the few film-makers to have established a name for himself during this period. After a break from film during which he concentrated on painting at the end of the decade, in the 1930s he joined the leftist film movement, and during the war he followed the Nationalist government as it retreated first to Wuhan and then to Chongqing, making patriotic documentaries and newsreels for the common cause. After the war, he returned to Shanghai and helped to establish the leftist Kunlun Studio, for which he directed *Eight Thousand Li of Cloud and Moon* in 1948. He died in 1955.

Catkin (*Yanghua Hen*), Shanghai Film Company, 1925.

Roommates Romance (*Tongju Zhi Ai*), Dazhonghua Baihe Studio, 1926.

Blessed with Children (*Ersun Fu*), Dazhonghua Baihe Studio, 1926.

Beauty Plan (*Meiren Ji*; co-directed with Lu Jie, Zhu Shoutao, and Wang Yuanlong), Dazhonghua Baihe Studio, 1927.

The Four Heroes of the Wang Family (*Wang Shi Si Xia*), Dazhonghua Baihe Studio, 1927.

Two Stars in the Milky Way (*Yinhan Shuangxing*), Lianhua Studio, 1931.

The Constant Woman (*Heng Niang*), Lianhua Studio, 1931.

Everyone Aids the Nation (*Gong Fu Guo Nan*; co-directed with Sun Yu, Wang Cilong and Cai Chusheng), Lianhua Studio, 1932.

Struggle (*Fendou*), Lianhua Studio, 1932.

Women (*Nüren*), Yihua Studio, 1933.

Birth (*Ren Zhi Chu*), Yihua Studio, 1935.

Song of Hate (*Changhen Ge*), Xinhua Studio, 1936.

Carnival Night (*Kuanghuan Zhi Ye*), Xinhua Studio, 1936.

March of Youth (*Qingnian Jinxingqu*), Xinhua Studio, 1937.

Defend Our Territory (*Baowei Women de Tudi*), China Film Studio, 1938.

The Good Husband (*Hao Zhangfu*), China Film Studio, 1939.

March of Victory (*Shengli Jinxingqu*), China Film Studio, 1940.

Give Back My Homeland (*Huan Wo Guxiang*), China Film Studio, 1945.

Eight Thousand Li of Cloud and Moon (*Baqian Lilu Yun he Yue*), Kunlun Film Studio, 1947.

A Young Woman's Anger (*Xingui Yuan*), Kunlun Film Studio, 1948.

Tale of the New Heroes (*Xin Ernü Yingxiong Zhuan*), Beijing Film Studio, 1951.

(CB)

SHUI HUA

Born in 1916, Shui Hua was active in the leftist drama movement during the 1930s and the war years. In the Communist mountain fastness of Yan'an, he taught drama at the Lu Xun Academy, and then travelled to the newly liberated Northeast before entering the Beijing Film Studio soon after Liberation in 1949.

He is most associated with the period of liberalisation that followed the collapse of the Maoist Great Leap Forward in the early 1960s, during which more complex 'middle characters' were allowed in films. The heroes of his *The Lin Family Shop* (1959) and *A Revolutionary Family* (1961) were both classic examples. Persecuted during the 'cultural revolution', he has since returned to work but has not produced any particularly distinguished films.

The White-Haired Girl (*Baimao Nü*; co-directed with Wang Bin), Northeast Film Studio, 1950.

Earth (*Tudi*), Changchun Film Studio, 1954.

The Lin Family Shop (*Linjia Puzi*), Beijing Film Studio, 1959.

A Revolutionary Family (*Geming Jiating*), Beijing Film Studio, 1960.

Immortals in the Flames (*Liehuozhong Yongsheng*), Beijing Film Studio, 1965.

Regret for the Past (*Shangshi*), Beijing Film Studio, 1981.

The Blue Flower (*Lanse de Hua*), Beijing Film Studio, 1984.

(CB)

SUN YU

Like Lü Ban, Sun Yu's career spanned both the pre- and post-revolutionary years, and also like Lü Ban he suffered in the second part of his career.

Born in Chongqing, Sun was trained in literature in Tianjin and later at famous Qinghua University in Beijing. In 1923, he went to study literature and theatre at the University of Wisconsin and film in New York, returning to China in 1926. He made his first film as director in 1928, and was most active in the 1930s.

Sun's films combined popular subject matter with sophisticated and polished techniques such as dream sequences and complex trick cinematography. As a result, they drew a more cultured audience into the cinemas. He was also a committed and prolific member of the leftist film movement. Among his famous films from this period are *Spring Dream in the Old Capital* (1930) and *Big Road* (1934).

During the wartime years, Sun followed the Nationalist government to Wuhan and then to Chongqing, involved in patriotic front activities. In the years immediately following the war, he fell ill, and retired from filmmaking until 1951, when he made *The Life of Wu Xun*. Ironically enough, this film caused him to enter a second period of enforced retirement. It was condemned for not being revolutionary enough, and a campaign around it provided the pretext the government needed to close the last of the private film studios. With the exception of a brief return to directing at the end of the 50s, Sun Yu directed no more films before his recent death.

The Spider Gang (*Zhizhu Dang*), Great Wall Studio, 1928.

The Angling Martial Arts Hero (*Yudiao Guaixia*), Great Wall Studio, 1928.

Ace Swordsman (*Fengliu Jianke*), Minxin Studio, 1929.

Spring Dream of the Old Capital (*Gudu Chunmeng*), Lianhua Studio, 1930.

Wild Grasses and Flowers (*Yecao Xianhua*), Lianhua Studio, 1930.

The Spirit of Freedom (*Ziyou Gui*), Lianhua Studio, 1931.

Ghost of the Wild Rose (*Yemei Gui*), Lianhua Studio, 1932.

Everyone Aids the Nation (*Gong Fu Guo Nan*; co-directed with Wang Cilong, Shi Dongshan and Cai Chusheng), Lianhua Studio, 1932.

Blood on the Volcano (*Huoshan Qingxie*), Lianhua Studio, 1932.

Daybreak (*Tianming*), Lianhua Studio, 1933.

Little Toy (*Xiao Wanyi*), Lianhua Studio, 1933.

Queen of Sport (*Tiyu Huanghou*), Lianhua Studio, 1934.

Big Road (*Da Lu*), Lianhua Studio, 1934.

Back to Nature (*Dao Ziran Qu*), Lianhua Studio, 1936.

Madman's Rhapsody (*Fengren Kuangxiangqu*; section seven of *The Lianhua Symphony* [*Lianhua Jiaoxiangqu*]), Lianhua Studio, 1937.

Spring Comes to Humanity (*Chun Dao Renjian*), Lianhua Studio, 1937.

Baptism of Fire (*Huo de Xianli*), China Film Studio, 1940.

The Broad Skies (*Changkong Wanli*), China Film Studio, 1940.

The Life of Wu Xun (*Wu Xun Zhuan*), Kunlun Studio, 1950.

Brave the Storm (*Chengfeng Polang*), Jiangnan Film Studio, 1957.

The Story of Lü Ban (*Lü Ban de Zhuanshuo*), Jiangnan Film Studio, 1958.

Qin Niangmei, Haiyan Film Studio, 1960.

(CB)

TIAN ZHUANGZHUANG

Among the most famous of China's Fifth Generation of young directors, Tian Zhuangzhuang was born into a prominent mainland Chinese film family in 1952. His mother, Yu Lan, was a major star, and is now head of the Beijing Children's Film Studio. His father, Tian Fang, now deceased, was also an actor and at one time Vice-Head of the Ministry of Culture's Film Bureau.

Although he went along to censorship board screenings with his father, by his own account Tian avoided movies from around the age of twelve after vomiting because he sat too close to the screen during a Soviet epic. However, after joining the army during the 'cultural revolution' (1969–1976), he trained as a still photographer, and then as a cinematographer at the Beijing Agricultural Film Studio after returning to civilian life in

Tian Zhuangzhuang's *On the Hunting Ground*

1975. He was admitted to the director's class at the Beijing Film Academy when it reopened after the 'cultural revolution' in 1978.

Tian first achieved fame as early as 1980, with a television play entitled *Our Corner*. At a time when Chinese film was moving away from dramatic conventions, the naturalism and minimal dialogue in this piece about a young girl and a group of handicapped men was seen as very advanced. These qualities have continued to characterise the films he is best known for, *On the Hunting Ground* and *Horse Thief*. Almost non-narrative, these spectacular films about the Mongolian and Tibetan national minorities have been debated and discussed by far more people than have seen them in China. Indeed, their difficulty and strangeness has alienated the Chinese audience while winning plaudits abroad, and gained Tian a reputation as the most formally radical of the current generation of Chinese film-makers.

Less well known is Tian's virtuosity. He has also directed a children's film (*The Red Elephant*), a character study about a middle-aged woman (*September*), a literary adaptation (*Travelling Players*), and, most recently, a breakdance musical (*Rock'n'Roll Kids*). Although outside China at the time of the Tiananmen massacre of 4 June 1989, he has since returned to Beijing.

Our Corner (*Women de Jiaoluo*), Beijing Film Academy, 1980.

The Red Elephant (*Hong Xiang*), Children's Film Studio, 1982 (co-directed with Zhang Jianya).

September (*Jiuyue*), Kunming Film Studio, 1984.

195

On the Hunting Ground (*Liechang Zhasa*), Inner Mongolia Film Studio, 1985.

Horse Thief (*Daoma Zei*), Xi'an Film Studio, 1985.

Travelling Players (*Gushu Yiren*), Beijing Film Studio, 1986.

Rock'n'Roll Kids (*Yaoke Qingnian*), Youth Film Studio, 1988.

(CB)

WU TIANMING

The most prominent member of China's Fourth Generation of film-makers, Wu did more than any other person to encourage the Fifth Generation in his capacity as head of the Xi'an Film Studio.

Wu's father, a Communist Party veteran, was a county administrator before becoming a banking official in Xi'an. Born in 1939 in Shaanxi province north of Xi'an, Wu began his career as an actor in 1960 by joining a class of the Xi'an Film Studio's Drama Troupe. He played a country youth in *Red Wave at Bashan* in 1961. Wu soon developed an interest in directing. In 1974–5, he served on veteran director Cui Wei's production team for *The New Doctor*, made at the Beijing Film Studio. Returning to Xi'an, in 1976 and 1977 he was production assistant on *New Song of the Wei River* and *Raging Tide on Fisherman's Island*.

In 1979, as the Xi'an studio resumed production, Wu co-directed with Teng Wenji *Reverberations of Life*, a late 'cultural revolution' story of intellectual resistance to the 'gang of four'. The next year, the two directors worked together again on *Kith and Kin*, a film on family connections between the mainland and Taiwan. In 1983, Wu made his independent directing debut with *River Without Buoys*, a 'cultural revolution' story of the social and emotional disruption of those years. At the 1984 Hawaii International Film Festival it won the first international prize for a Xi'an Film Studio production.

Wu became head of the Xi'an studio in October 1983, as he began work on *Life*, a contemporary study of urban-village conflict in north-west China. As studio head, Wu encouraged younger, active film-makers, causing resentment from less resourceful staff at the Xi'an facility. *Old Well* (1987) followed, again set in a northwestern village. These two films represented Wu's effort to have the studio produce Chinese 'Westerns', set in the rural northwest.

A parallel effort was Wu's crucial encouragement of Fifth Generation film-makers. Tian Zhuangzhuang made *Horse Thief*, Huang Jianxin directed *Black Cannon Incident*, Chen Kaige made *King of the Children*, and Zhang Yimou directed *Red Sorghum* at the Xi'an studio under Wu Tianming's leadership. When his term came to an end in 1988, Wu reluctantly agreed to stay on as studio head, even though the financial condition of the film industry made production of further non-commercial films less likely in the future. Wu was in New York on a visiting fellowship at New York University when the 4 June 1989 Tiananmen Massacre occurred. He now lives in Los Angeles.

196

Reverberations of Life (*Shenghuo de Chanyin*), Xi'an Film Studio, 1979 (co-directed with Teng Wenji).

Kith and Kin (*Qin Lü*), Xi'an Film Studio, 1980 (co-directed with Teng Wenji).

River Without Buoys (*Meiyou Hangbiao de Heliu*), Xi'an Film Studio, 1983.

Life (*Rensheng*), Xi'an Film Studio, 1984.

Old Well (*Lao Jing*), Xi'an Film Studio, 1987.

(PC)

WU YIGONG

A representative product of the Shanghai Film Studio of the 1970s, Wu Yigong now heads the Shanghai Film Corporation. In the 1980s he positioned himself as a more orthodox studio head than Wu Tianming, his Xi'an Film Studio counterpart. Both are now regarded as Fourth Generation film-makers.

Wu was born in 1938 and entered the directing department of the newly established Beijing Film Academy in 1956. Upon graduation in 1960, he was assigned as a director's assistant to the Haiyan Film Studio, one of the three feature film studios and an animation film studio into which the Shanghai Film Studio had been split in 1957. The Shanghai Film Studio was recombined in the early 1970s as production resumed after 'cultural revolution' disruption. In 1979, Wu served as assistant director on *In a Silent Place*, an adaptation of an anti-'gang of four' play. At this time also, he wrote and directed a short fiction film, *Our Tabby*. In 1980, he directed *Evening Rain*, under the general direction of Wu Yonggang, a veteran director active in the 1930s. An account of popular, muted resistance during the 'cultural revolution', the film won several domestic awards.

Wu's 1982 film, *My Memories of Old Beijing*, an adaptation of a Taiwan writer's memoir of life in the city in the 1930s, also won awards. His *Elder Sister* (1983) was something of a departure for Wu. Its setting in the arid northwest and a visual style occasionally suggestive of Fifth Generation work matched its wartime story of soldiers in retreat. The film attracted little attention. *University in Exile* (1985) was a more orthodox Shanghai production, with a melodramatic story of noble intellectuals during the War of Resistance with Japan.

Having become head of the Shanghai Film Corporation in 1983, Wu turned his attention to new ventures. He served as general director (supervising Fifth Generation director Zhang Jianya) on a West German-funded adaptation of the Jules Verne comic story, *Tribulations of a Chinese Gentleman* (1986). It was neither a commercial nor an artistic success. Wu turned his attention to management of the studio.

In a Silent Place (*Yu Wusheng Chu*), Shanghai Film Studio, 1978 (assistant director).

Our Tabby (*Women de Xiao Huamao*), Shanghai Film Studio, 1979.

Evening Rain (*Bashan Yeyu*), Shanghai Film Studio, 1980.

My Memories of Old Beijing (Chengnan Jiushi), Shanghai Film Studio, 1982.

Elder Sister (Jiejie), Shanghai Film Studio, 1983.

University in Exile (Liuwang Daxue), Shanghai Film Studio, 1985.

Tribulations of a Chinese Gentleman (Shaoye de Monan), Shanghai Film Studio, 1986 (general director).

(PC)

XIE JIN

With the much younger Zhang Yimou, perhaps the best known film director in China, Xie Jin has managed to attract large audiences for his often epic films. His career, spanning from the 1940s to the 1980s, illustrates the continuities in much of Chinese film-making.

Born in 1923, Xie worked in a theatre in Chongqing from 1943 to 1948. In that year he started work in the Shanghai film industry, serving as assistant director on such productions as *The Silent Wife* and *Martyrs of the Pear Orchard*. He also acted on screen. Xie has worked in the Shanghai Film Studio since 1951. He was assistant director on *The Letter with Feathers* (1954), and co-directed his first feature, *An Incident*, in the same year. Before the start of the 'cultural revolution' he established himself with a string of popular hits: *Woman Basketball Player No. 5*, *The Red Detachment of Women*, *Big Li, Little Li and Old Li* and *Stage Sisters*. Three of these four titles focused on women, and this has remained a feature of Xie's films. Xie was attacked as a bourgeois artist at the start of the 'cultural revolution'. In 1972 he co-directed an opera film with a strong female lead, *On the Docks*, one of the 'revolutionary model operas'. His 1977 *Youth*, featuring a deaf telephone operator, was followed in 1979 by *Ah! Cradle*, about orphans in the wartime Communist capital at Yan'an.

Xie Jin seemed exceptionally bold in his criticism of Party bureaucratism and abuses of power in *The Legend of Tianyun Mountain*. *The Herdsman* addressed questions of China's relations with the rest of the world. In 1983 the boldness of *Tianyun Mountain* was replaced by a sturdy patriotism (despite naturalistic battle scenes) in *Wreaths at the Foot of the Mountains*, set during the 1979 Chinese invasion of Vietnam. *Hibiscus Town* was a huge box-office success in 1987, with its epic chronicling of political abuse from the Anti-Rightist campaign of 1958 to the start of reform in the 1980s. In 1989 Xie completed an adaptation of a story by the Taiwan writer Pai Hsian-yung (Bai Xianyong). *The Last Aristocrats* was set in the 1940s in Shanghai, New York and Venice, and told the story of three wealthy sisters.

The Silent Wife (Yaqi), Datong Film Company, 1948 (assistant director).

Martyrs of the Pear Orchard (Liyuan Yinglie), Datong Film Company, 1949 (assistant director).

Letter with Feathers (Jimao Xin), Shanghai Film Studio, 1953 (assistant director).

Women's Representative (Funü Daibiao), Shanghai Film Studio, 1954 (assistant director).

An Incident (Yichang Fengpo), Shanghai Film Studio, 1954 (co-directed with Lin Nong).

Rendezvous at Orchid Bridge (Lanqiao Hui), Shanghai Film Studio, 1954.

Spring Over the Irrigated Land (Shuixiang de Chuntian), Shanghai Film Studio, 1955.

Woman Basketball Player No. 5 (Nülan Wuhao), Tianma Film Studio, 1957.

Short Stories of the Storm (Da Fenglangli de Xiao Gushi), Tianma Film Studio, 1958 (one episode entitled *The Force of the Wind Tests the Grass [Jifeng Jingcao]*).

Little Masters of the Great Leap Forward (Dayuejin Zhong de Xiao Zhuren), Tianma Film Studio, 1958 (one episode entitled *Service [Fuwu]*).

Huang Baomei (Huang Baomei), Tianma Film Studio, 1958.

The Red Detachment of Women (Hongse Niangzijun), Tianma Film Studio, 1961.

Big Li, Little Li and Old Li (Da Li, Xiao Li, he Lao Li), Tianma Film Studio, 1962.

Two Stage Sisters (Wutai Jiemei), Tianma Film Studio, 1965.

On the Docks (Haigang), Beijing and Shanghai Film Studios (two versions, 1972 and 1973; co-directed with Xie Tieli).

Youth (Qingchun), Shanghai Film Studio, 1977.

Ah! Cradle (A! Yaolan), Shanghai Film Studio, 1979.

The Legend of Tianyun Mountain (Tianyunshan Chuanqi), Shanghai Film Studio, 1980.

The Herdsman (Muma Ren), Shanghai Film Studio, 1982.

Wreaths at the Foot of the Mountains (Gaoshan xia de Huahuan), Shanghai Film Studio, 1983.

Hibiscus Town (Furongzhen), Shanghai Film Studio, 1986.

The Last Aristocrats (Zuihou de Guizu), Shanghai Film Studio, 1989.

(PC)

EDWARD YANG (Yang Dechang)

Together with Hou Hsiao-hsien, Edward Yang is the major figure in the 'New Taiwan Cinema'. In contrast to Hou, however, Yang has specialised in urbane city dramas with a look sometimes compared with Antonioni's.

Yang's family was from the same Guangdong county (Meixian) as Hou, and Yang was also born in 1947, but in Shanghai. His family moved to Taiwan in 1949. He graduated in engineering in Taiwan in 1969 and gained an MA in computer science in 1972 at the University of Florida. In 1974 he enrolled at the University of Southern California to study film, but left after a year. He remained in the United States working in the computer industry before returning to Taiwan in 1981.

Like his Hong Kong 'New Wave' counterparts in the 1970s, Edward Yang made his directorial debut in television. He directed an episode called 'Floating Leaf' in a television series titled *Eleven Women*. His first work in cinema was in an omnibus film, *In Our Time*, designed to span Taiwan's postwar history showing social and economic changes. Yang's part, called 'Desires', like Hou Hsiao-hsien's episode in *Sandwich Man*, was the best in the film. Yang's *That Day, On the Beach* (1983) was a cool contemplation of the breakdown of a marriage told with great psychological insight from the wife's point of view. *Taipei Story* (1985) deals with the lives of several characters from different social classes, centring on their success or failure in adjusting to modern urban life. Yang continued in this vein of urban alienation in *The Terroriser*. A bored young woman makes a random phone call that brings ruin to the life of a novelist married to a medical researcher. The film won the Jury Prize at the 1987 Locarno Film Festival.

'Floating Leaf', episode in television series *Eleven Women*, 1981.

Desires, second of four parts in *In Our Time* (*Guangyin de Gushi*), 1982.

That Day, On the Beach (*Haitan de Yitian*), 1983.

Taipei Story (*Qingmei Zhuma*), 1984.

The Terroriser (*Kongbu Fenzi*), Central Motion Picture Corporation, 1986.

(PC)

ZHANG JUNZHAO

Born in 1952 in Henan and raised in the Central Asian province of Xinjiang in China's far Northwest, Zhang Junzhao is now the most commercial of China's Fifth Generation of young directors. Unable to continue his education after the outbreak of the 'cultural revolution' in 1966, Zhang joined the army as an ordinary soldier. His career in the arts began when he joined the Urumchi People's Theatre in the publicity area after returning to civilian life in 1974, and in 1978 he was admitted to the directors' class at the Beijing Film Academy.

After graduation, Zhang was sent to Guangxi Film Studio in the far Southwest together with the cinematographer Zhang Yimou and the art director He Qun. Small, understaffed and desperate for product to put on the market, Guangxi gave the young film-makers a free rein, and as a result Zhang and his colleagues were able to produce the first Fifth Generation film, *One and Eight*, in 1984. A slow, visual film about the hitherto taboo subject of prisoners and suspected traitors in the ranks of the revolutionary army in the 1930s and 1940s, *One and Eight* was a critical success but a box-office failure. While his colleagues have persisted with their alternative films, Zhang has pioneered another type of film-making, namely fully commercial, box-office oriented films. Since *One and Eight*, he has produced the football film *Come On, China!*, the bandit movie *The Lonely Murderer*, and a psycho-thriller, *Arc Light*, as well as various TV dramas.

One and Eight (*Yige he Bage*), Guangxi Film Studio, 1984.

Come On, China! (*Jiayou, Zhongguodui!*), Guangxi Film Studio, 1984.

The Lonely Murderer (*Gudu de Moshazhe*), Guangxi Film Studio, 1985.

Arc Light (*Huguang*), Guangxi Film Studio, 1988.

(CB)

200

ZHANG YIMOU

The most versatile talent of the Fifth Generation film-makers, Zhang Yimou was born near Xi'an in 1952 into a professional family. His mother was a dermatologist. His father had no regular work because of his political background: he had been an officer in the Nationalist KMT army before the Communist takeover in 1949. During the 'cultural revolution', Zhang was sent in 1969 to a village north of Xi'an. Later transferred to a cotton mill in a city 40 kilometers northwest of Xi'an, Zhang took up still photography. His application to the Beijing Film Academy in 1978 was thwarted because he was over the age limit for enrolment. Zhang entered after special pleas to the school authorities and the Minister of Culture.

Lacking the political connections of his Beijing classmates, Zhang was one of those sent upon graduation in 1982 to the new, tiny Guangxi Film Studio in the far southwest. There he was a major figure in the launching of the Fifth Generation, serving as cinematographer on *One and Eight*, *Yellow Earth* and *Big Parade*. On loan to Xi'an Film Studio in his home town from 1986, Zhang proved his versatility by taking the lead role in Wu Tianming's *Old Well*, on which he also shared the job of cinematographer. He won the best actor award at the second Tokyo International Film Festival in 1987 for his performance.

Zhang's first film as director made him the most successful Chinese director ever, when his *Red Sorghum* won the Golden Bear best picture award at the 1988 Berlin Festival. The film was also a big hit in China. But the box-office pressures on the industry meant Zhang's next work was in a strictly commercial vein. The action film *Code Name Puma* included a political message, with mainland and Taiwan officials becoming involved in resolving a plane hijacking. Acting assignments in several Hong Kong-financed productions, including a role as an ancient terracotta tomb soldier come to life, kept Zhang busy between directing more action films.

Zhang's typical style – frequent immobile camera and striking framing of natural scenes – reflects his beginnings as a still photographer. In *Red Sorghum*, Zhang brought out a physical, earthy treatment, the spontaneity and raunchiness of which had great popular appeal.

Red Elephant (*Hong Xiang*), Children's Film Studio, 1982 (assistant cinematographer).

One and Eight (*Yige he Bage*), Guangxi Film Studio, 1984 (co-cinematographer with Xiao Feng).

Yellow Earth (*Huang Tudi*), Guangxi Film Studio, 1984 (cinematographer).

Big Parade (*Da Yuebing*), Guangxi Film Studio, 1985 (cinematographer).

Old Well (*Lao Jing*), Xi'an Film Studio, 1987 (cinematographer, lead actor).

Red Sorghum (*Hong Gaoliang*), Xi'an Film Studio, 1987.

Code Name Puma (*Daihao Meizhoubao*), Xi'an Film Studio, 1988.

Mourning (*Judou*), Xi'an Film Studio, 1989 (co-directed with Yang Fengliang).

(PC)

201

ZHENG JUNLI

Born into a poor family in Guangdong in 1911, Zheng Junli finished his formal education after the second year of high school. In 1928 he entered the South China Academy of Fine Arts, and from there became involved in leftist drama. In 1932 he joined the Lianhua Studio, and rapidly established himself as one of the leading leftist actors of the 1930s.

During the war, Zheng took part in the patriotic drama movement, following the Nationalist government upriver to Chongqing. He also made his directing debut on documentaries at this time. Based at the leftist Kunlun Studio in Shanghai after the war, he co-directed the cathartic war epic *A Spring River Flows East* in 1947 and the famous social satire *Crows and Sparrows* in 1949.

After Liberation, Zheng remained active. As well as documentaries, his best known features include the biography of the leftist composer Nie Er in 1959, and in the same year *Lin Zexu*, a film about the Opium Wars of the previous century. A victim of the 'cultural revolution', Zheng died in jail in 1969.

A Spring River Flows East (*Yijiang Chunshui Xiang Dong Liu*; co-directed with Cai Chusheng), Kunlun Studio, 1947.

Crows and Sparrows (*Wuya yu Maque*), Kunlun Studio, 1949.

Among Us Women (*Women Funü Zhijian*), Kunlun Studio, 1951.

Song Jingshi, Shanghai Film Studio, 1955.

Lin Zexu, Haiyan Film Studio, 1959.

Nie Er, Haiyan Film Studio, 1959.

The Withered Tree Revives (*Kumu Fengchun*), Haiyan Film Studio, 1961.

Li Shanzi, Haiyan Film Studio, 1964.

(CB)

Appendix 2

Chronology

CHRIS BERRY

In the period after 1949, this chronology concentrates on mainland China. Chinese terms that appear only in this chronology and not in the main text are not included in the character glossary at the end of the book.

Date	General History	Cinema History
1894	Sun Yat-sen sets up his anti-imperial society for the 'regeneration of China'.	
1895	China admits defeat by Japan and signs the first of a series of 'unequal' treaties with the foreign powers, which lead the carve-up of China.	
1896		First recorded film screening, 11 August, Shanghai; a foreign projectionist screens Lumière films.
1900	Boxer Rebellion suppressed by foreign powers, who then extract heavy indemnities from China.	
1903		China enters film industry when Liu Zhushan brings projector and films to Peking.
1905	Abolition of examination system of access to imperial positions marks erosion of traditional system.	China starts making films when Feng Tai Photography Shop films Peking opera *Dingjun Mountain* in Peking.
1911	1911 Revolution overthrows Qing dynasty and establishes a republic, with the head of the Northern Army, Yuan Shikai, as president.	
1913		First independent screenplay filmed in Shanghai: *The Difficult Couple* directed by Zheng Zhengqiu and Zhang Shichuan. World War I disrupts supplies of film stock.

203

1916	Death of Yuan Shikai leads to loss of central authority and the warlord era.	Zhang Shichuan establishes first Chinese-owned film production company when film stocks are renewed.
1919	May Fourth Movement to modernise and revitalise China launched in protest against the Versailles Treaty, which gives Japan Shandong Province. This becomes a long-lived cultural reform movement.	
1921	Chinese Communist Party established.	First feature-length film, *Yan Ruisheng*. Its success stimulates imitators.
1923	Sun Yat-sen and Chiang Kai-shek's Nationalists establish links with Moscow, leading to a series of united front operations with the Chinese Communists.	
1925	Death of Sun Yat-sen.	Film industry is dominated by martial arts films and romances during this period. Almost none of these has survived.
1927	Chiang Kai-shek seizes Shanghai and massacres the Communists.	Soviet documentarist Bliokh films Chiang's massacre of the Chinese Communists.
1928	Warlord era ends with establishment of KMT Nationalist government, led by Chiang Kai-shek.	
1929		KMT film censorship rules introduced.
1930	Urban revolts led by Communists are a failure, which lays the foundation for Mao's later rural-based policies.	Luo Mingyou sets up the Lianhua Company, which becomes committed to the production of less commercial, more high-minded films. It also becomes the centre for leftist film production.
1931	Japan annexes Manchuria.	Mingxing Company premieres first sound film: *Singsong Girl Red Peony*. League of Left-wing Dramatists established, including film-makers affiliated to the CPC. First feature completed using stock produced entirely in China.
1932	On the pretext of anti-Communist demonstrations, the Japanese bomb Shanghai. The Communists declare war on the	Temporary disruption of the Shanghai-based film industry by the bombing.

Japanese, but the KMT government prefers appeasement.

1933	Further Japanese territorial encroachments in the north.	Large numbers of leftist films begin to appear, including *Spring Silkworms*.
1934	The Long March begins in response to Chiang Kai-shek's efforts to eliminate the Communists.	Major leftist films include *Big Road*, *The Goddess* and *Song of the Fishermen*.
1935	Mao Zedong takes control of the Chinese Communist Party and begins to assert independence from Comintern.	Cai Chusheng's *Song of the Fishermen* wins China's first international film award at the Moscow Film Festival.
1936	The Xi'an Incident. The warlord Zhang Xueliang imprisons Chiang Kai-shek, effectively forcing him to focus his energies less on destroying the Communists and more on the Japanese.	
1937	Anti-Japanese War of Resistance begins. Japan takes over Shanghai, and at the end of the year carries out the Nanjing Massacre.	The Chinese film industry is dispersed. Some follow the Nationalist government upriver to Wuhan and then Chongqing. Some flee to Hong Kong. Some join the Communists in Yan'an. Some stay on the 'orphan island' of the foreign concessions in Shanghai, and some work with the Japanese.
1938	Nationalist government sets up government upriver in Chongqing.	Film-makers with the KMT start producing patriotic war films.
1939	World War II begins in Europe.	The Japanese set up a film industry in Manchuria and take over the Shanghai film industry, producing films for their own troops and for the local population. Joris Ivens gives the Communist 8th Route Army their first 35mm camera. The first documentaries from the Communist mountain stronghold of Yan'an follow.
1941	America enters the war in the wake of the Japanese attack on Pearl Harbor.	
1942	Mao's *Talks on Literature and Art at the Yan'an Forum* set cultural policy for the	

205

	Communists, based on the idea of the subordination of art to politics.	
1945	End of Anti-Japanese War of Resistance.	
1946	Civil War between the KMT and the CPC begins.	Progressive film-makers return to Shanghai, take over Lianhua again, and determine to resist the KMT, later setting up the new Kunlun Studio as their base of operations.
1947	The Russians retreat from Manchuria, allowing the Communists to take it over and shift their attack to the north.	Communists set up Northeast Film Studio at Xingshan. Cathartic war epic *A Spring River Flows East* directed by Cai Chusheng and Zheng Junli in Shanghai.
1949	Establishment of the People's Republic in October. Chiang Kai-shek and the KMT retreat to Taiwan.	Northeast Film Studio moves to Changchun and work begins on first feature: *Bridge*. Taiwanese film industry based around documentary film-makers who retreat to Taiwan with the KMT.
1950	Beginning of the Korean War.	Remaining American films withdrawn from circulation.
1951	Crackdown against counter-revolutionaries.	Campaign against *The Life of Wu Xun*.
1953	Launch of the first 5-year plan. End of the Korean War.	Complete nationalisation of the film industry achieved, and efforts made to extend film distribution beyond the major cities using mobile projection teams.
1956	Hungarian Uprising.	The Hundred Flowers Campaign, liberalisation in literature and the arts, resulting in production of satirical film comedies, and articles criticising previous films for their unpopularity at the box-office.
1957	The Anti-Rightist Campaign launched to check the 'excesses' of the Hundred Flowers. Many prominent intellectual and cultural figures are condemned.	Satires banned and succeeded by Maoist orthodoxy.
1958	Sino-Soviet split, precipitated by Khruschev's 'revisionist' Anti-Stalin stance.	Soviet Socialist Realism replaced by the supposedly more Chinese 'combination of revolutionary

		realism and revolutionary romanticism' as the model in film-making.
1959	The Great Leap Forward is launched with the aim of forcing rapid modernisation by sheer human effort.	Film production is also increased massively, with large numbers of crude revolutionary documentaries.
1960–1	The excesses of the Great Leap Forward lead to famine and then a reduction in Mao's power.	Relaxation of Maoist line in literature and art leads to the replacement of pure proletarian heroes with more ambiguous 'middle characters' in films.
1963	Jiang Qing (Mme Mao) advances 'reform' of the theatre, gradually replacing classical productions with revolutionary operas.	
1965	Press discussion of 'capitalist roaders' and the need to resort to force mark the beginnings of Mao's efforts to reassert power.	
1966	The 'cultural revolution' is launched.	Feature film production ceases, and the film industry becomes a particular target for Jiang Qing, an ex-starlet with many scores to settle. Many industry figures are sent to the countryside or imprisoned. Many die or commit suicide.
1968	Order is restored by the People's Liberation Army after factional fighting among Mao's Little Red Guards has reached dangerous levels. Deng Xiaoping is expelled from the Party.	
1970		Feature-length production recommences with films which record stage productions of Jiang Qing's model operas, such as *Taking Tiger Mountain by Strategy*.
1971	Lin Biao, head of the PLA, is eliminated in a plane 'accident'.	
1972	Kissinger visits China.	
1973	Zhou Enlai engineers the return of Deng Xiaoping.	Although highly controlled, regular feature film production recommences with *Bright Sunny Skies*.

1976	Zhou Enlai dies in January. Mao dies in September. The 'gang of four' (including Jiang Qing) falls in October. Hua Guofeng takes over from Mao.	Film production falls again, but rapidly returns to pre-'cultural revolution' levels.
1978	Deng Xiaoping emerges as prime leader after 3rd Plenum of 11th CPC Central Committee. Democracy Wall started up.	Cultural relaxation leads to criticism of 'cultural revolution' in many films. Beijing Film Academy reopens and takes in a new class of directors, later to be known as the 'Fifth Generation'.
1979	After the rehabilitation of various pre-'cultural revolution' figures at the beginning of the year, the Party cracks down on liberalisation, closing down Democracy Wall in December.	Films like *Xiao Hua* and *Troubled Laughter* lead the way in the filmic translation of the four modernisations, with zooms, multiple flashbacks and other techniques hitherto rare.
1980	Zhao Ziyang replaces Hua Guofeng as Premier.	*The Legend of Tianyun Mountain* extends criticism to the Anti-Rightist Campaign of 1958.
1981		*Bitter Love* banned. Film is negative not only about the past but about the present too. Film experimentation slows.
1982		The Fifth Generation graduates from the Beijing Film Academy.
1983	Anti-'spiritual pollution' campaign.	Various 'violent' or 'vulgar' films banned. Wu Tianming becomes Head of Xi'an Film Studio, and pursues a policy of subsidising experimental work with ruthlessly commercial films, which later makes the studio a haven for the Fifth Generation and a box-office challenge to Shanghai Film Studio.
1984	The 'responsibility system' devolving power and building a market economy is tried in the cities as well as the countryside.	First Fifth Generation film produced: *One and Eight*. The film is banned from export.
1985		*Yellow Earth* released. Ignored in China, it is a success on the international festival circuit.
1988	Runaway inflation promotes dissatisfaction among the urban workforce.	*Red Sorghum* wins the Golden Bear at Berlin, and is the first Fifth Generation film to be a major hit at home.

208

| 1989 | Students demanding democracy are joined by dissatisfied urban workers. The army responds with the Tiananmen Massacre. | Wu Tianming and Chen Kaige are in the United States at the time, and remain abroad. Tian Zhuangzhuang returns, and joins other colleagues still in China. Hou Hsiao-hsien's *City of Sadness* wins the Golden Lion at Venice. |

Appendix 3
Glossary of Chinese Characters

This glossary contains all the Chinese characters given in the main text of this anthology in pinyin romanisation, excluding those found in the other appendices. Phrases and names are listed according to English alphabetical order of the first character.

A JIHUA XUJI	A计划续集
AH BING	阿炳
AH CHENG	阿城
AH Q ZHENGZHUAN	阿Q正传
AI QI	爱琪
AIQING YU YICHAN	爱情与遗产
BAFANG	八方
BA HONG	巴鸿
BAQIANLILU YUNHEYUE	八千里路云和月
BASHAN YEYU	巴山夜雨
BAYI DIANYING ZHIPIANCHANG	八一电影制片厂
BAI HUA	白桦
BAI QIU'EN DAIFU	白求恩大夫
BAOLE DIANYING GONGSI	宝乐电影公司
BAO QICHENG	包起城
BEIJING DIANYING ZHIPIANCHANG	北京电影制片厂
BEIJING WANBAO	北京晚报
BI BICHENG	毕必成
BIN	宾
BINGHE SIWANGXIAN	冰河死亡线
BO JUYI	白居易
BUJU XIAOJIE DE REN	不拘小节的人
BU WANCANG	卜万苍
CAI CHUSHENG	蔡楚生
CAI E	蔡锷
CAI YANGMING	蔡扬铭
CAI ZAISHENG	蔡再生
CAO PI	曹丕
CAO YU	曹禹
CEN FAN	岑范
CHANG'AN	长安
CHANGCHUN DE DIYIGE SHENGYIN	长春的第一个声音
CHANGCHUN DIANYING ZHIPIANCHANG	长春电影制片厂
CHAOQIAN YISHI	超前意识

CHEN BAICHEN	陈白尘
CHEN BO'ER	陈波儿
CHEN FU	沉浮
CHEN HUAI'AI	陈怀皑
CHEN HUANGMEI	陈荒煤
CHEN JIANYU	陈剑雨
CHEN KAIGE	陈凯歌
CHEN KAIYAN	陈凯燕
CHEN KUNHOU	陈坤厚
CHEN RONG	谌容
CHEN SHOU	陈寿
CHEN XI	陈汐
CHEN XINJIAN	陈欣健
CHEN YI	陈沂
CHEN YING	陈颖
CHEN ZHENGHONG	陈正鸿
CHENG BUGAO	程步高
CHENG JIHUA	程季华
CHENG LONG	成龙
CHENGNAN JIUSHI	城南旧事
CHENG XIAODONG	程小东
CHONGQING	重庆
CHU-HAN	楚－韩
CHUNCAN	春蚕
CI	词
CI MINGHE	慈明和
CISHU	辞书
CONGMING DE YAZI	聪明的鸭子
CUIQIAO	翠巧
CUI WEI	崔嵬
DAJI	大己
DAMINGXING	大明星
DANAO HUASHI	大闹画室
DANAO TIANGONG	大闹天宫
DAQUANZI PIAN	大圈仔片
DARONG DIANYING GONGSI	大荣电影公司
DAXIANG WUXING, DAYIN XISHENG	大象无形，大音希声。
DAYUEBING	大阅兵
DAZHONG DIANYING	大众电影
DAI ZONG'AN	戴宗安
DAN HANZHANG	但汉章
DAOCAO REN	稻草人
DAODE JING	道德经
DAOMAZEI	盗马贼
DEBAO GONGSI	德宝公司
DENG GUANGRONG	邓光荣
DENG LIQUN	邓力群
DENG XIAOPING	邓小平
DIWUDAI	第五代
DIYI DIANYING JIGOU	第一电影机构
DIANYING	电影
DIANYINGCHANG XUYAO ZHENGCEFUCHI	电影厂需要政策扶持

213

GONGFU	功夫
GONG LI	巩俐
GONGNONGBING	工农兵
GUDU DE MOSHAZHE	孤独的谋杀者
GU HUA	古华
GU QING	顾青
GUSHU YIREN	鼓书艺人
GUYUAN WUSHENG	古原无声
GUANGONG	关公
GUAN JINPENG	关锦鹏
GUANGDONG	广东
GUANGXI	广西
GUANGZHOU	广州
GUO FANGFANG	郭方方
GUOFU ZHUAN	国父传
GUOHUN	国魂
GUO HUONIAN	国货年
GUOMINDANG	国民党
GUO PU	郭璞
GUO SHANG	国殇
GUO WEI	郭维
HAIGANG	海港
HAIYAN DIANYING ZHIPIANCHANG	海燕电影制片厂
HAIZI WANG	孩子王
HANHAN	憨憨
HAN LAN'GEN	韩兰根
HANGKONG JIUGUO	航空救国
HE CHI	何迟
HE GUOFU	贺国甫
HE JIAJU	何家驹
HE QUN	何群
HE KONGZHOU	何孔周
HEIPAO SHIJIAN	黑炮事件
HEIPI YU BAIYA	黑皮与白牙
HONG GAOLIANG	红高粱
HONG GAOLIANG: XI XING JI	红高粱：西行记
HONG JINBAO	洪金宝
HONG LEIGUANG	洪磊光
HONGSE NIANGZIJUN	红色娘子军
HONGTAI DIANYING GONGSI	鸿泰电影公司
HONG YU	红雨
HOU HAN SHU	后汉书
HOU XIAOXIAN	侯孝贤
HU BINGLIU	胡炳榴
HU JINQING	胡进庆
HU JINQUAN	胡金铨
HU MEI	胡玫
HUNAN	湖南
HU QIAOMU	胡乔木
HU SHAN	胡珊
HU YAOBANG	胡耀邦
HUA ERSHI	华而实

HUAJU	话剧
HUA JUNWU	华君武
HUASHUO «HUANG TUDI»	话说《黄土地》
HUAIHAI	淮海
HUAINAN HONGLIE	淮南鸿烈
HUAINAN ZI	淮南子
HUANXIANG RIJI	还乡日记
HUANG BAIMING	黄百鸣
HUANG BINGYAO	黄炳耀
HUANG DIMENG	黄帝梦
HUANG GANG	黄钢
HUANGHELOU SONG MENG HAORAN ZHI GUANGLING	黄鹤楼送孟浩然之广陵
HUANG JIANXIN	黄建新
HUANG JIANZHONG	黄健中
HUANG TAILAI	黄泰来
HUANG TUDI	黄土地
HUANG WEIWEN	黄蔚文
HUANG ZONGJIANG	黄宗江
HUANG ZUMO	黄祖模
JI SI	吉思
JI YUN	纪昀
JIAFENG XUHUANG	假凤虚凰
JIALE GONGSI	嘉乐公司
JIA PING'AO	贾平凹
JIAWU FENGYUN	甲午风云
JIASHI	假释
JIAYOU, ZHONGGUODUI	加油，中国队
JIANLI DIANYINGSHI CHANGXUE KEBURONGHUAN	建立中国市场学刻不容缓
JIANG HAIYANG	江海洋
JIANG HAO	江浩
JIANGHU LONGHU DOU	江湖龙虎斗
JIANGHU QING	江湖情
JIANG JUNXU	江俊绪
JIANGNAN	江南
JIANG QING	江青
JIANGSU	江苏
JIANGXI	江西
JIAO'AO DE JIANGJUN	骄傲的将军
JIAOTIAOZHUYI	教条主义
JIAO XIONGPING	焦雄屏
JIEJIE	姐姐
JIN'GE GONGSI	金格公司
JIN JIN	靳靳
JIN SHAN	金山
JINSE DE HAILUO	金色的海螺
JINSHISHANG ZHANGSHUIBU	近试上张水部
JINSHUI SAO	金水嫂
JIN XI	靳夕
JINYE XINGGUANG CANLAN	今夜星光灿烂
JING	精

216

QIU GANGJIAN	邱刚健
QIU MINGCHENG	邱铭诚
QU YUAN	屈原
REN	人
REN DAO ZHONGNIAN	人到中年
RENMIN CHUBANSHE	人民出版社
RENMIN RIBAO	人民日报
RENSHEN WAWA	人参娃娃
RENSHENG	人生
RICHU RILUO WUSHINIAN	日出日落五十年
RUXUE	儒学
RUYI	如意
RUYU DESHUI	如鱼得水
SAN CONG SI DE	三从四德
SANGUO ZHI	三国志
SAN XIAO	三笑
SANZANG	三藏
SANG HU	桑弧
SHA SENG	沙僧
SHAANBEI	陕北
SHAANXI	陕西
SHANXI	山西
SHANGHAI	上海
SHANGHAI DIANYING ZHIPIANCHANG	上海电影制片厂
SHANGHAI SHUDIAN	上海书店
SHANG SHI	伤逝
SHANGYING XINXI	上影信息
SHAOXING	绍兴
SHAOYE DE MONAN	少爷的磨难
SHEN	身
SHENBI	神笔
SHENBIAN	神鞭
SHEN FU	沈浮
SHEN GU HUI SHENG	深谷回声
SHEN XICHENG	沈西城
SHENGGANG QIBING XUJI	省港骑兵续集
SHENGHUO DE CHANYIN	生活的颤音
SHIBALI HONG	十八里红
SHIBAO CHUBAN GONGSI	时报出版公司
SHI DONGSHAN	史东山
SHI HUI	石挥
SHIKAN	诗刊
SHI MEIJUN	史美俊
SHISANHAO XIONGZHAI	十三号凶宅
SHI SHUJUN	史蜀君
SHI TIESHENG	史铁生
SHI XIAOHUA	石晓华
SHI XINSHANG	诗欣赏
SHIYUE	十月
SHIZI JIETOU	十字街头
SHIZONG DE NÜZHONGXUESHENG	失踪的女中学生

219

SHIZONG RENKOU	失踪人口
SHOU	收
SHU XIUWEN	舒绣文
SHU ZHENDONG HUAWEN DAZIJI	舒振东华文打字机
SHUIHU ZHUAN	水浒传
SHUI HUA	水华
SHUILIAN	水莲
SHUIMO DONGHUAPPIAN	水墨动画片
SONG	宋
SONG HONG	宋弘
SONGHUA JIANGSHANG	松花江上
SONG LEI	宋磊
SONG WEI	宋威
SU	俗
SU LI	苏里
SUN LONGJI	孙隆基
SUN QIAN	孙谦
SUN WUKONG	孙悟空
SUN YU	孙瑜
SUN ZHONG	孙仲
SUONA	唢呐
'T'ZHOU DE 84,85,NIAN	T州的81,85,年
TALIA HE TALIA	他俩和她俩
TAMEN QUESHAO 'QING'	他们缺少 '情'
TAIBEI	台北
TAIBEI (ZHONGHUA SHUJU)	台北（中华书局）
TAIJI	太极
TAIWAN	台湾
TAIWAN SHANGWU YINSHU GUAN	台湾商务印书馆
TAIWAN XINDIANYING	台湾新电影
TAIWAN ZHIPIAN GONGSI	台湾制片公司
TAIYANG HE REN	太阳和人
TANSUOXING	探索形
TANG CHEN	汤臣
TANG CHENG	唐澄
TANGSHI SANBAISHUO XIANGXI	唐诗三百首详析
TAO JIN	陶金
TE WEI	特伟
TENG WENJI	滕文骥
TIANANMEN	天安门
TIANGOU	天狗
TIAN HAN	田汉
TIANJING SHA	天净沙
TIANMA DIANYING ZHIPIANCHANG	天马电影制片厂
TIANYUNSHAN CHUANQI	天云山传奇
TIAN ZHUANGZHUANG	田壮壮
TIESHAN GONGZHU	铁扇公主
TIEXUE JINGQI	铁血警骑
TONGBAO SUXING	同胞速醒
TONGTIAN DADAO	通天大盗
TONG TING	童汀
TOUQIGEYUE CHENGSHIGUANZHONG DAFUDU SHANGSHENG	头七个月城市观众大幅度上升

WAWA CANTING	娃娃餐厅
WAN CHAOCHEN	万超尘
WAN DIHUAN	万涤寰
WAN GUCHAN	万古蟾
WAN LAIMING	万籁明
WANNENG GONGSI	万能公司
WAN ZHI	万之
WAN ZILIANG	万梓良
WANG ANSHI	王安石
WANG CHONGGUANG	王重光
WANGFUJING	王府井
WANG HAOWEI	王好为
WANG JICHENG	王吉成
WANG JIN	王进
WANG JING	王静
WANG LIAN	王炼
WANG QIMIN	王启民
WANG RUNSHENG	王润生
WANG TONG	王童
WANG TUO	王拓
WANG WEI	王维
WANG XIAJUN	王侠军
WANG XIAODI	王小棣
WANG XIAOHAI	王小海
WANG YIMIN	王一民
WANGYUE HUAIYUAN	望月怀远
WANG ZUXIAN	王祖贤
WEI JIAHUI	韦家辉
WEISILI CHUANQI	卫斯理传奇
WEIYOUWANCHENG DE XIJU	未有完成的喜剧
WENHUA	文华
WENHUI BAO	文汇报
WENJUN NENGYOU JIDUO CHOU,	问君能有几多愁,
QIASI YIJIANG CHUNSHUI XIANGDONG LIU	恰似一江春水向东流
WENQING MOMO	温情脉脉
WEN TIANXIANG	文天祥
WEN XIAOYU	温小钰
WENXING	文星
WENYI BAO	文艺报
WENYI GANBU	文艺干部
WENGZHONG ZHUOBIE	瓮中捉鳖
WO DE BABA BU SHI ZEI	我的爸爸不是贼
WO HE WO DE TONGXUE	我和我的同学
WOMEN DE XIAO HUAMAO	我们的小花猫
WO ZHE YI BEIZI	我这一辈子
WU'ER SHANA	乌尔莎娜
WUHAN	武汉
WU LAN	乌兰
WUMA	午马
WU NIANZHEN	吴念真
WUSI YILAI DIANYING XUAN	五四以来电影选
WU SONG	武松
WUTAI JIEMEI	舞台姐妹

WU TIANMING	吴天明
WUTU YU WUMIN	吾土与吾民
WU XIAOJIN	吴小津
WU XUN ZHUAN	武训传
WUYA YU MAQUE	乌鸦与麻雀
WUYE GUOHOU	午夜过后
WU YIGONG	吴贻弓
WU YIN	吴茵
WU YONGGANG	吴永刚
WU ZINIU	吴子牛
WU ZUGUANG	吴祖光
XI'AN DIANYING ZHIPIANCHANG	西安电影制片厂
XIBAO	喜宝
XIJU – GUOWAI ZUIMAIZUO DE YINGPIAN	喜剧－国外最卖座的影片
XI NONG	希侬
XIWANG	喜旺
XIYINGMEN	喜盈门
XI YOU JI	西游记
XIA LAN	夏兰
XIANÜ	侠女
XIA WENXI	夏文汐
XIA YAN	夏衍
XIAN SIRAN	冼祀然
XIANG KUN	项堃
XIANGCAO MEIREN	香草美人
XIANGLIN	祥林
XIANGNÜ XIAOXIAO	湘女萧萧
XIANGQING	乡情
XIANGYIN	乡音
XIAO BAOBAO	小宝宝
XIAOBI DE GUSHI	小毕的故事
XIAO HUIXIONG	萧惠雄
XIAOJIE	小街
XIAOKEDOU ZHAO MAMA	小蝌蚪找妈妈
XIAO MAO	肖矛
XIAO RUOYUAN	萧若元
XIAOSHUO YUEBAO	小说月报
XIAOXING	萧湘
XIAOXIAO YINGXIONG	小小英雄
XIAO YE	小野
XIE DIANYING JUBEN DE JIGE WENTI	写电影剧本的几个问题
XIE FEI	谢飞
XIE JIN	谢晋
XIE TIELI	谢铁骊
XIE YOUCHUN	谢友纯
XIN	心
XINHUA	新华
XIN JUZHANG DAOLAI ZHIQIAN	新局长到来之前
XINTIANYOU	信天游
XIN XIANLING	辛显令
XINYICHENG GONGSI	新艺城公司
XINGHUI GONGSI	星辉公司

225

ZHOU	周
ZHOU ENLAI	周恩来
ZHOU RUNFA	周润发
ZHOU XIAOWEN	周晓文
ZHOU YANG	周扬
ZHU	主
ZHU BAJIE	猪八戒
ZHU BAJIE CHI XIGUA	猪八戒吃西瓜
ZHU DAKE	朱大可
ZHU DAN	朱丹
ZHUFU	祝福
ZHUJIANG DIANYING ZHIPIANCHANG	珠江电影制片厂
ZHU QINGYU	朱庆余
ZHU SHOUTONG	朱寿桐
ZHU TIANWEN	朱天文
ZHU WEI	朱伟
ZHU YINGTAI	祝英台
ZHUZI	竹子
ZHUZI JICHENG	诸子集成
ZICHANJIEJI ZIYOU QINGXIANG	资产阶级自由倾向
ZONG BAIHUA	宗白华
ZONGPAIZHUYI	宗派主义
ZONGYI GONGSI	综一公司
ZUIHOU DE TAIYANG	最后的太阳
ZUIHOU YIGE DONGRI	最后一个冬日
ZUI JIA PAIDANG	最佳拍挡
ZUIWENG TINGJI	醉翁亭记
ZUO LIN	佐临

Notes on Contributors

Chris Berry is a Lecturer in Cinema Studies at La Trobe University in Melbourne. He worked in Beijing as a subtitler and translator for the China Film Export and Import Corporation between 1985 and 1987, and is currently completing a Ph.D. on Chinese film at UCLA.

Paul Clark is a Research Associate with the Institute for Culture and Communication at the East-West Center in Honolulu. Author of *Chinese Cinema: Culture and Politics Since 1949*, he has published widely on Chinese cinema and is currently completing a project on the Fifth Generation.

Chiao Hsiung-Ping is a prolific and prominent Taiwanese film critic and educator. She holds an MA in Radio-TV-Film from the University of Texas at Austin, has produced five books on the Chinese cinema, and is currently a columnist for the *China Times Express* and a lecturer at the National Institute of the Arts in Taipei.

E. Ann Kaplan is Professor of English at SUNY Stony Brook, where she directs the Humanities Institute. Dr Kaplan has written widely on feminist film theory, women in film and literature, Fritz Lang, *film noir*, and television. Her books include *Women and Film: Both Sides of the Camera*, *Regarding Television*, and *Rocking Around the Clock: Music Television, Postmodernism and Consumer Culture*. She edited *Postmodernism and Its Discontents* (1988), and her new book, *Motherhood and Representation*, is forthcoming.

Jenny Kwok Wah Lau lives in Chicago, where she has recently completed her Ph.D. on the cinemas of Hong Kong and mainland China at Northwestern University.

Leo Ou-Fan Lee is Professor of East Asian Languages and Literature at UCLA. An authority on the May Fourth Generation of Chinese writers, his latest book is *Voices from the Iron House: A Study of Lu Xun*, and he has published numerous articles on related topics in a wide array of academic journals.

Marie-Claire Quiquemelle runs the Centre de Documentation sur le Cinéma Chinois in Paris, has organised many Chinese film exhibitions in Europe, and has published extensively on Chinese animation films.

Tony Rayns is a leading freelance film critic who specialises in Asian cinema. He has published widely throughout the world, and has been heavily involved in the introduction of Asian cinema to Western audiences.

Yuejin Wang is currently a Ph.D. candidate in visual arts at Harvard. He has published on Chinese cinema in *Framework*, *Wide Angle*, *Public Culture* and the *East-West Film Journal*, and has translated Roland Barthes' *A Lover's Discourse* into Chinese.

Catherine Yi-yu Cho Woo is Professor of Chinese at San Diego State University. She has also taught at San Francisco State University, and published two books on Chinese art and poetry. An accomplished painter and poet in her own right, she has published and held exhibitions of her works in Taiwan, Korea, Japan and the United States.

Esther C. M. Yau is a Ph.D. candidate in Film and Television Studies at UCLA. She is completing her dissertation on filmic discourses on women in Chinese cinema.

Index of Names and Film Titles

232